ME
to
WE

ME to WE

Finding Meaning in a Material World

Craig Kielburger & Marc Kielburger

AVID READER PRESS
New York   London   Toronto   Sydney   New Delhi

AVID READER PRESS
An Imprint of Simon & Schuster, Inc.
1230 Avenue of the Americas
New York, NY 10020

This Avid Reader Press trade paperback edition January 2021

AVID READER PRESS and colophon are trademarks of Simon & Schuster, Inc.

For information about special discounts for bulk purchases, please contact Simon &
Schuster Special Sales at 1-866-506-1949 or business@simonandschuster.com.

The Simon & Schuster Speakers Bureau can bring authors to your live event.
For more information or to book an event contact the Simon & Schuster Speakers
Bureau at 1-866-248-3049 or visit our website at www.simonspeakers.com.

Manufactured in the United States of America

1   3   5   7   9   10   8   6   4   2

Library of Congress Cataloging-in-Publication Data has been applied for.

ISBN 978-1-9821-5457-8
ISBN 978-0-7432-9839-1 (ebook)

To our parents, for their love and support.

CONTENTS

In the early 2000s, I had the privilege of visiting East Africa and South America where I understood for the first time that I was in the minority of humans on Earth who could take food, shelter, education, health care, and safety for granted. When the magnitude of this hope gap, opportunity gap, and wealth gap sunk in, I became dedicated to learning about the importance of microfinance and its impact on the culture and livelihoods of entire villages. Essentially, microfinance allows those who typically wouldn't qualify for credit to receive a small loan, enabling them to make life-changing investments and become self-sufficient. The work particularly impacts women in developing nations. I was humbled by the opportunity offered by great organizations serving the world's most underserved population, and tried to help bring light to their impact by talking about what microfinance is and how it can change lives and empower women.

When I was introduced to the WE movement over a decade ago, I was grateful that there was a place to inspire young people in the developed world to recognize their privilege and, with it, the responsibility to be active in their communities and in other communities, to share the luck they have with others, and to improve the world. I learned that simply raising your voice can often be the catalyst to sparking real and meaningful change.

At WE Day, I was lucky enough to talk to thousands of young change-makers at stadium-sized events about some of the things I care about most. I spoke about being vegan and how it is a practice of empathy and environmental respect. I was able to discuss how my passion for women's and girls' rights led to my involvement with the Time's Up movement. And I was able to share my excitement for supporting education and opportunity-based causes for women through WE's work in Kenya.

Over several years, I've been involved with WE's initiatives for girls' education, joining the Power of a Girl campaign as an ambassador and encouraging young people in North America and the UK to raise funds for girls' education in Kenya's Maasai Mara. When the Kisaruni All-Girls Secondary School opened, I was eager to visit the school and see the impact of WE's work in the region firsthand.

Since then, I've had the pleasure of visiting WE's partner communities in Kenya on a few occasions. On my most recent visit, I shared this life-changing experience with my son. One of our most memorable moments was meeting with the girls attending Kisaruni and others at WE College, including one girl named Christine. These girls were brilliant, hardworking, and resilient. Their experiences prove that investing in women and girls can create a powerful ripple effect that transforms entire communities.

Christine explained the inequalities she faced as a girl pursuing opportunities beyond the household. She told us of her goals and ambitions, and shared how education has played a huge role in changing the trajectory of her future. It was truly inspiring to hear her stories and others, and it was even more special to see it through my son's eyes. It was remarkable for him to see the gratitude children in other places had for going to school, and to understand what a privilege and opportunity it is to have good and accessible education. As my own children grow, I find myself more motivated than ever to be part of positive change for the next generation.

What Craig and Marc have shared in these pages is a personal reflection of their growth and development in becoming responsible global citizens. In the twenty-five years since founding their movement, what started out as one twelve-year-old boy challenging the social inequalities of his time has grown into an entire generation of young people striving to work together, making a global impact that encourages kindness and emphasizes the importance of community.

The themes, lessons, and stories found within this book serve as a personal reminder of what it means to be a leader, a friend, and a changemaker at home and around the world. Me to We has taught me that we all have the power to make a difference by starting small, practicing empathy throughout our day, and finding the courage within ourselves to stand up for what we believe in.

Natalie Portman, 2020

ME to WE is a philosophy, a way of life that feeds the positive in the world—one action, one act of faith, one small step at a time. Living ME to WE has the potential to revolutionize kindness, redefine happiness and success, and rekindle community bonds powerful enough to change your life and the lives of everyone around you.

We wrote this introduction to our book more than fifteen years ago. It seems like a lifetime has passed, but we still believe every word.

Me to We: Finding Meaning in a Material World was first published in 2004, when the world was a very different place. Cell phones still had flip tops. Facebook launched and the media had just started to contend with this new thing called social media. Having your own "web log," a kind of online diary, was the latest fad. Those were simpler times. Back then, our movement was just ten years old. Already we had come a long way. What started with a group of teenagers carrying petitions in paper boxes and sending faxes from our parents' living rooms had become a global organization, empowering communities around the world to lift themselves out of poverty. But the more we worked, the more we came to realize that international development projects weren't enough. We had to shift the way people think and behave, and encourage them as citizens, students, consumers, and businesses to live with more compassion and to take action for others.

The easy part is that most people want to make this shift in their lives, from me to we. We travel all over the world, speaking to thousands of people every year from all walks of life—students, parents, educators, corporate CEOs. Despite differences, we hear a common refrain: So many people we meet are experiencing a sense of dissatisfaction. They often have difficulty explaining exactly what they're missing, but instinctively, they know it's something vital. Our belief, based on extensive personal experience, is that they're missing the feeling that comes with being part of something bigger than they are. That's why we shared our me-to-we philosophy. We believe it can provide both a starting point for change and a cure for what ails us. The challenge, especially today, is that people feel overwhelmed by the world's problems. Many folks simply don't know where to start. This book was the first step in a newfound mission to make that challenge less daunting. To make doing good, doable.

In fact, what you hold in your hands right now—or what you are reading on a screen—is not so much a book as a seed. It was the grain of an idea that has over the years sprouted in directions we could never have imagined.

When we first planted this seed, we dreamed of a world where young people were inspired and empowered to take on the world's biggest challenges. Young people are naturally more inclined to think of others when they're in need, to think of the "we" more than adults. But when we started our work, studies showed that young people were also the least likely age demographic to volunteer. At a time when adults rarely listened to youth or took them seriously, kids faced great obstacles in transforming their ideals into actions. Why wouldn't adults let kids help? Why would the world ignore its greatest resource?

So we planted seeds in classrooms across North America and the UK. WE gave youth the tools they need to make a difference, with resources we wish we'd had when we were starting out, to make it easy for them to move the needle on the causes they care about. We evolved from after-school volunteer clubs to WE Schools: a whole new way of learning that makes "we" thinking part of the core curriculum, integrating volunteer service with skills development. For example, students learn computer science through WE programs while coding apps for non-profits. Students learn about biology and biodiversity while testing water quality in their communities. Through programs like AP with WE, "service learning"—baking the ideas of "me to we" right into the DNA of education—is now a fundamental part of the learning experience for millions of students. To encourage the seed to grow in the hearts of youth, we added fertilizer. Four years after *Me to We* was first published, we brought together a few thousand students in a small Toronto stadium. The event was one part live music, one part awards show, and one part motivational speech. We called it WE Day. One event became two, two became four, four became 150+ events . . . and, well, it became a movement. You couldn't buy a ticket to WE Day, you had to earn it through local and global service—volunteering, fundraising, taking action for a cause. The harvest the world has reaped from that single seed has been bountiful. Since that first WE Day in 2008, more than 1.5 million youth have attended the celebrations live, and millions have watched via primetime TV broadcast on ABC and CTV. Over the past twenty-five years, the volunteer hours given, dollars fundraised, and food collected for community food banks, by millions of students, has delivered well in excess of a billion dollars in social value for their communities. Thousands of local and global non-profits and causes have benefited from the power of young people coming together to make change. Today, the theory behind WE Schools is built right into the education system. WE Day has taken on a life of its own, with school groups organizing their own local celebrations and events moving from auditoriums into the digital realm. A new generation of youth have the tools to continue planting and growing on their own. We can only imagine what they will create.

All along, we have never forgotten where we began. Our movement was first launched to support children who don't have the chance to go to school at all, who couldn't help others because they're stuck in a cycle of poverty or bonded labor. WE started to help create a world where every young person can go to school, and we've never forgotten that. We just started thinking bigger. We had to think beyond an end to child labor in order to create opportunities for every vulnerable child, family, and community to lift themselves out of poverty. From that kernel sprouted our holistic, five-pillar development model that provides the tools to tackle the underlying root causes of poverty. WE still partners with villages in East Africa, Asia, and South America, but we've come so far from building school rooms, digging wells, and planting community gardens. Children in our partner communities in Kenya now go from first grade all the way through high school with us, before graduating and enrolling in our WE College. Degrees in hand, these young leaders return to their communities as teachers, nurses, and entrepreneurs, taking what they've learned and using it to tackle the challenges and social issues faced close to home. These students come from places that are typically recipients of aid and now give back through their own self-empowerment. After a quarter decade, which has seen the construction of more than 1,500 schools and schoolhouses with 200,000 students, and more than 30,000 women engaged in income generation co-ops, over one million people have been empowered to lift themselves, their families, and their entire communities out of poverty.

As it has grown, the "me to we" philosophy has spread across continents and oceans, connecting people around the world as our Artisan's program did. It started in Kenya, where Maasai women were selling traditional hand-beaded jewelry, but falling short because the market was saturated and the pieces sold at a steep discount. There was no formal infrastructure. Roxanne Joyal, already a veteran at WE with a mind for business and women's empowerment, helped us realize that we could solve two problems at once. With a formal business, we could pay the artisans a fair wage and build infrastructure that would bring their beads around the world to wider markets. Artisans would get better pay to improve their households and families, and profits could be reinvested to sustainably fund our work in their communities. We could achieve twice the impact. Now the women artisans, armed with new business management and financial literacy skills, are going on to launch their own businesses. They have taken "me to we" into their own hands now, building entrepreneurship and financial security in once-vulnerable communities.

There was another byproduct of that idea: By putting traditional Maasai jewelry in Western markets, we were also sharing a story, giving North American shoppers the chance to make social change with their dollars and connect with women on the other side of the world. Roxanne's idea replaced a purely profit-driven business with a model that emphasizes social impact. And over the years, millions around the world donned Rafiki bracelets to stand in solidarity with women a world away. The Artisans program eventually grew into a plant of its own: ME to WE Social Enterprise. Over the years, five million Rafikis were produced by the mamas of Kenya. More than 30,000 travelers would come to visit, learn from, and be inspired by our partner communities around the world. The social enterprise forged hundreds of partnerships with companies looking to become better corporate citizens by donating sales proceeds or building products with social impact baked in. Our purpose in sharing these stats is to show how our dreams, the idea of "me to we," manifested to a degree greater than we could ever have imagined. And from that, our message to you is: dream big, because you too can achieve impact beyond anything you ever believed possible. In the years to come we will continue to support social entrepreneurship, and we can only imagine in what directions it will develop. But in our dreams, we see a great spreading tree—a global "WEconomy," where every company considers first what it can do for people and the planet, and then how it can profit. Imagine the whole market infused with "we" thinking.

Though we're always mindful of the future, rereading this book has been a bit of a blast from the past. So many dated references to look back on, like relics in the museum of pop culture. You'll find mentions of then-novelties *Survivor* and *American Idol*. They're both still around, but largely eclipsed by a host of new reality shows. Still, the underlying social implications of the reality TV craze are still relevant, perhaps even more due to its growth in popularity. We hope you'll consider it a chance to wax nostalgic, to look back and then consider where we might be ten years from now—culturally, socially, politically, and as individuals. For that reason, we've decided not to remove these references. Think of them as a benchmark to see how far we've progressed (or, in some cases, have not progressed enough).

Which brings us to you, dear reader. As we said earlier, this book was intended as a seed. Where you plant it and how you care for it are up to you. One thing that hasn't changed: the world still needs more kindness, more concern for our communities and less for ourselves. In fact, with more divisiveness in politics and in news media, we need people to live this philosophy, now more than ever. That's partly why we decided to rerelease this book on the twenty-fifth anniversary of the WE organization.

As you make your way through these pages, you will find that doing so involves more than just reading. At the end of each chapter, we have included three special sections filled with ideas and activities designed to help you learn about the power of "me to we." Our suggestions are grains intended to grow your imagination and to allow you to make a positive difference not only in your own life, family, and community, but around the world. You'll find the following:

Start now! These sections contain personal questions to get you thinking about the potential for ME to WE in your own life.

Take another look! These sections offer information on important social issues that challenge each of us to move from ME to WE.

Living ME to WE! These sections provide options for action to help you begin living this philosophy.

The past twenty-five years have been a remarkable journey for WE. The idea of "me to we" has grown beyond our wildest hopes, touching and empowering countless lives. There are so many to whom we are thankful for supporting us and taking into their own hands the responsibility for spreading the seeds farther than we ever could have on our own: the incredible team of passionate changemakers who have worked at WE over the years; the board members who have guided and mentored us; the donors who provided the means without which our movement could not have grown; millions of youth, and their parents and educators, who believed in our dream and made so much positive change in the world. We are especially grateful to our parents, whose patience and love taught us more about living "me to we" than anyone else. Also thanks to our life partners, Roxanne and Leysa (talk about changes, we weren't even married when all this began!), whose support and hard work have helped build the dream of WE. Finally, our thanks to all the readers who first picked up this book all those years ago, who let the seed of "me to we" take root and flourish in their minds and lives.

In a time of upheaval, change, and transition, we cannot predict how the WE Movement will look in the future. However, whatever may come, it will be the product of that first seed that started it all: the philosophy of "me to we." With this book, we pass our seed bag and tools to you.

We can't wait to see what you will grow.

Craig and Marc

CHAPTER ONE

CRAIG'S STORY:
"I'M ONLY ONE BOY!"

"Ultimately, man should not ask what the meaning of his life is, but rather he must recognize that it is he who is asked."

—Viktor E. Frankl

Some people's lives are transformed gradually. Others are changed in an instant.

My own moment of truth happened over a bowl of cereal one morning when I was twelve years old. Sitting at our kitchen table munching away, I was about to dive into the daily newspaper in search of my favorite comics—*Doonesbury, Calvin and Hobbes, Wizard of Id*. The cartoons were my morning ritual. But on this particular day, April 19, 1995, I didn't get past the front page. There was one headline that was impossible to miss: "Battled child labor, boy, 12, murdered."

I read on.

ISLAMABAD, Pakistan (AP)—When Iqbal Masih was 4 years old, his parents sold him into slavery for less than $16. For the next six years, he remained shackled to a carpet-weaving loom most of the time, tying tiny knots hour after hour. By the age of 12, he was free and traveling the world in his crusade against the horrors of child labor. On Sunday, Iqbal was shot dead while he and two friends were riding their bikes in their village of Muridke, 35 kilometres outside the eastern city of Lahore. Some believe his murder was carried out by angry members of the carpet industry who had made repeated threats to silence the young activist.

After reading this article, I was full of questions. What kind of parent sells a four-year-old child into slavery? Who would chain a child to a carpet loom? I didn't have any ready answers. What I really wanted was to talk to Marc, my older brother by six years, but he was away at college. I knew that even if Marc couldn't answer my questions, he would at least know where to start looking. But that day I was on my own.

After school, I headed to the public library and started to dig through newspapers and magazines. I read about children younger than me who spent endless hours in dimly lit rooms making carpets. I found stories about kids who slaved in underground pits to bring coal to the surface. Other reports told of underage workers killed or maimed by explosions in fireworks factories. My head was swimming. I was just a kid from the suburbs, and like most middle-class kids, my friends and I spent our time shooting hoops and playing video games. This was beyond me.

I left the library bewildered and angry at the world for allowing such things to happen to children. I simply could not understand why nothing was being done to stop the cruelty. How could I help?

I asked myself what Marc would do.

As brothers, we've never been rivals. We are too far apart in age to feel any sibling jealousy. And, as corny as it sounds, we've always been there for each other. When I was younger, I watched in awe as Marc seemed to excel effortlessly in everything—school, public speaking, rugby, and tennis. But what set Marc apart was his belief that he could make a difference.

When Marc was thirteen, he turned a passion for environmental issues into a one-boy campaign. For an eighth-grade science project, he tested the harmful effects of brand-name household cleaners on the water system. Next he used lemons, vinegar, and baking soda to create environmentally friendlier alternatives that did the job just as well, if not better.

Marc seemed to be unstoppable. He gave speeches, founded an environmental club, created petitions, and collected thousands of signatures. As a result, he became the youngest person in our province to receive the Ontario Citizenship Award.

A younger brother could have no better role model. He taught me that young people have the power to make a difference when it comes to issues they care about. Why not me?

Riding the bus to school, I would uncrumple the newspaper article and look at Iqbal's picture—he was wearing a bright red vest, his hand in the air. One day, I asked my teacher if I could speak to the class. Although

I was generally outgoing, public speaking was definitely not my favorite activity. I can still remember how nervous I felt standing up at the front of my classroom, and how quiet everyone became as I shared what I knew about Iqbal and the plight of other child laborers. I passed out copies of the newspaper article and shared the alarming statistics I had found. I wasn't sure what would happen when I asked for volunteers to help me fight for children's rights.

Eleven hands shot up, and Free The Children was born.

As I jotted down the names of volunteers, I still didn't know the next step. But, as we started to dig up information, things became a lot clearer.

We began researching the issue, and soon after we were out giving speeches. We began writing petitions and held a community garage sale fundraiser. Before long, Free The Children chapters were popping up in other schools. In a few short months, my family's home literally become a campaign headquarters. Phones rang with news of protest marches led by children. Fax machines churned out shocking statistics on child labor in Brazil, India, Nigeria. The mail brought envelopes from human rights organizations all over the world offering photographs of children released from bonded labor.

Then we learned that Kailash Satyarthi, a leader in the fight against child bonded labor, had been detained. We wrote to the prime minister of India and demanded he be set free. We collected three thousand signatures on a petition and mailed it to New Delhi in a carefully wrapped shoebox. A year later, a freed Kailash came to North America to speak. He called our shoebox "one of the most powerful actions taken on my behalf."

We were making a difference.

Then in September 1995, just as eighth grade was about to begin for me, my mother took me aside. As Free The Children continued to grow, our house had been overrun by youth volunteers, kids were sleeping on couches and floors, and the phone rang at all hours. "This can't go on," she told me. "We have to live as a family. We have to get back to having a normal life."

But how could I give up when I was only getting started?

My parents had instilled in me the belief that goals come with challenges. "Go for it!" they always told me. "The only failure in life is not trying." That's what I thought I was doing, but I guess even they were not prepared for what Marc and I would do with the lessons they had taught us.

I asked for time to think.

As I sat in my bedroom trying to figure out if I should give up or keep going, I thought about how happy I was. Working with a team toward a common goal, I felt a sense of accomplishment and joy. I was happier than I'd ever been in my life. Free The Children was also filling a gap in many kids' lives. At an age when we were constantly being told by adults what to do, this was something we took on voluntarily. I knew in my heart I could not turn back. Too much would be lost. I was no longer the person I had been five months earlier. Besides, there was so much left to do. When I emerged from my room, I told my parents I was sorry, but I could not give up. "You always tell us that we have to fight for what we believe in. Well, I believe in this."

To my surprise, they understood. I think they were even proud. Later, I would learn that the roots of their understanding stretched back generations to the teachings of *their* parents.

When he was just nineteen, our father's father arrived in Canada from Germany during the Great Depression. He earned "suicide pay," fighting boxers in Toronto. It was dangerous work, but every bruised rib or black eye was, in his mind, a small price to pay for achieving a not-so humble Depression-era dream. When he had saved enough money, he opened a small grocery store with our grandmother. They worked there day and night, closing only one day in twenty-three years to visit Niagara Falls.

That was how our father grew up: working in the store after school and on weekends. His dream, however, was different. He wanted an education. But he thought there was no chance for college. Then, in his last year of high school, his parents announced that they had saved enough over the years to make his dream possible. He was overjoyed.

Our mother, the second-youngest of four children, was born in Windsor, Ontario, just across the border from Detroit, Michigan. She was only nine when her father passed away. At ten she was working weekends in a neighborhood store. There were lots of struggles. One summer her family's only shelter was a tent. Life was hard, but my grandmother, with only an eighth-grade education, taught herself how to type and then worked her way up from cleaning other people's homes to an office job at the Chrysler Corporation. (She eventually headed her department.) Through her stoic example, she instilled in her children the belief that they could achieve anything they wanted in life.

I was unaware of this history and I was also ignorant of my parents' commitment to supporting social issues. Although they were not activists, both were dedicated teachers who believed in teaching both inside and outside of the classroom. Whenever they had the opportunity, they tried to help us learn about the world and what we could do to make it a better place. These lessons didn't involve marches or protests, they were simpler than that. When we asked a question about the environment, it would lead to an afternoon picking up garbage in the park. A comment about the Humane Society would lead to a challenge to reserve part of our allowance to help the abandoned animals we saw on TV.

Our family history of helping swayed my parents. They knew about fighting for ideals and dreams. Our house remained a zoo and Free The Children continued to grow.

Yet if they had known what was coming next, they might have had second thoughts.

Up to that point I had frequently talked with Alam Rahman, a twenty-four-year-old human rights activist and University of Toronto student. He became a mentor to me. I confided in him that I felt some of my statements on child labor lacked authority because I hadn't seen it with my own eyes. We talked frequently about whether I should make a trip to Asia to see for myself. I never really thought it would happen—I had been begging my parents for months without results.

Then one day, Alam told me that he would be going to South Asia to visit relatives. Would I like to come? My poor parents never knew what hit them. I pestered them for weeks. Fortunately, they thought very highly of Alam and eventually my mother said, "Convince me that you will be safe."

If I could somehow prove to her that I would be fine, that the trip would be well organized, that the mountain of details could be taken care of, then I could go. I began faxing organizations throughout South Asia advising them that I would be coming, applied for travel visas, and raised money through household chores and the generosity of relatives. Then, with my parents' blessing, I marked the date of my departure on my calendar.

The plan was a seven-week trip to meet children who worked in the most inhumane conditions imaginable. We met children working in metal factories, pouring metal without any protective gear. We met children as young as five years old in the brick kilns, working to pay off debts taken out by their parents or granparents and passed from generation to generation. We met a ten-year-old boy who worked in a fireworks factory, badly burned all over his body from an explosion that had killed fourteen other kids. In another encounter, we met an eight-year-old girl working in a recycling factory, taking apart used syringes and needles with her bare hands.

My first stop was Dhaka, Bangladesh, where we were taken to one of the city's largest slums, an entire valley filled with corrugated tin, woven reed, and cardboard huts. The people who lived there owned next to nothing. Their clothing was in rags. Human and animal waste filled the gutters. There was little food. When I saw the utter poverty, I wanted to stay there for the entire seven-week trip and volunteer, so I asked a human rights worker in the slum how I could help. He told me, "Continue your journey. Learn as much as you can. And then go back home and tell others what you have seen and ask them if they think it is fair that places like this exist in the world. Because it's the lack of action, the refusal from people at home to help, that allows this to continue."

Later in Delhi, India, witnessing and learning about the lives of child laborers, I learned the Canadian prime minister was also there, with eight provincial premiers and 250 business leaders to drum up trade deals. He was not raising the issue of child labor and that angered me. Free The Children's young members had repeatedly asked the prime minister to address this issue, but to no avail. We had written letters and requested a meeting, but the only response we had received was a letter informing us that the prime minister was a very busy person and would not be able to meet with our group. Now, after everything I had witnessed, I was convinced that if he knew of just one of the heart-wrenching stories, he would surely help. I gathered my courage and decided that we needed to do whatever we could to make sure these children's stories were heard. In the end, we decided to hold a press conference.

At the time I had just turned thirteen years old. In my view, the issue at stake in my struggle was one of right and wrong. I was outraged that the prime minister was signing billion-dollar trade deals without even mentioning the children who were making many of the products involved.

One of the most difficult lessons I was learning in Asia was that the fate of the children I met was shaped by the actions of people in wealthy countries like my own, especially people's tendency to consume inexpensive products without wondering how they had ended up on the shelf. I was convinced that once people were confronted with evidence of the suffering caused by child labor, they could not help but want to put a stop to it once and for all.

On the day of the press conference, all of Canada's large television and newspaper outlets were there. I tried to be as presentable as possible, despite having messy hair and wearing a dirty blue T-shirt. I spoke briefly about the horrors of child labor witnessed during my trip and then introduced Nagashir, a new friend, who told his story quietly through a translator.

I had met Nagashir a short time before at Mukti Ashram, a rehabilitation center for freed child slaves. All the children at the center had been forced into bonded labor and abused by their former masters. All had heartbreaking stories to tell, but Nagashir's was particularly horrific. Speaking with him through a translator, I soon realized he had been robbed of his childhood, his humanity violated. He couldn't tell me how old he was when he was sold into bondage; he didn't know. He simply put his hand out to show how small he was at the time. Now at about fourteen years old, he was a shell. He could barely speak and seemed numb to all around him.

Years ago, a man had come to his desperately poor village with promises of an education and a good job. Like many other children, Nagashir and his younger brother were sent with him and ended up in a factory, working at a loom, tying thousands of tiny knots to make carpets—for twelve hours a day. In exchange for his labor, Nagashir was given a small bowl of rice and watery lentils at the end of each day. When out of hunger and exhaustion he fell behind in his work, he was whipped and beaten.

It was only the hope of protecting his younger brother that gave Nagashir strength. This same feeling drew the other children together as well, and they relied on each other as a family. When the younger children cried out of homesickness, the older ones would comfort and calm them. When one child was sick, his friends would finish the work on his loom so that he wouldn't be beaten.

Sadly, I learned this wasn't always enough to protect the children. Nagashir showed us the scars that covered his body. His hands were mangled with cuts from the carpet knife. His master, unwilling to lose any productive time, would fill the cuts with gunpowder paste and light them to cauterize the wounds, then send him back to work. Most shocking were the scars on his legs and arms, and against his throat, where he had been branded with hot irons. This had been Nagashir's punishment for helping his younger brother escape from the factory. The lesson was seared into his skin and his soul. Traumatized, he lost his ability to speak; for years he didn't utter a word.

Nagashir was freed from the carpet factory in a midnight raid and brought to the rehabilitation center. At Mukti Ashram, the staff worked with him to slowly help him heal physically and emotionally. Weeks after having arrived at the center, he was found sitting in the garden, singing this song quietly to himself—his first words in years.

If you want to live, live with a smile
Live with love, don't cry
Don't shed your tears
There are storms, there are disasters
In life there are ups and downs
But don't shed your tears

Smile—pain is part of life
But finally you get job
If you want to live, live with new hopes
Live with new aspirations
Live with love
Live with a smile

Later, Nagashir was reunited with his family, including his brother. Nagashir and his brother were never again forced to work, and his brother started to attend primary school.

As Nagashir told his story at the press conference, he held out his arms and legs for the cameras to show his branding scars. The flashes of the camera bulbs were blinding, and we squinted into the large crowd of reporters. It was a frightening yet thrilling experience. But we were united, and with a small group of other children I signed a joint declaration calling on the countries' prime ministers and business leaders to remember the children as they signed their trade deals. It was all we could do.

I left India for Pakistan with no idea that the press conference was carried on networks throughout the world, including CNN. Within no time, the prime minister's handlers were looking for me. He wanted to meet. I was scared, but I also knew it was the best opportunity I'd have to date to voice my concerns.

The meeting went well and ended with the prime minister agreeing to bring up the issue of child labor with the heads of South Asian governments. It was exhilarating and strange. I was only a kid, but people were listening to me. I remember the feeling when I first realized I could actually make a change in the world. It floored me. I felt as if the laws of gravity had been broken. It left my skin tingling with excitement. It still does.

It also had the personal effect of striking down for me one of the most disturbing statements that children often hear: "Kids are to be seen and not heard."

I returned home transformed by the kids I had met. But at that point even I didn't know the extent to which my trip would subsequently shape the direction of my life. Almost as soon as I got back to Canada, life in our Thornhill house changed forever. Free The Children had initially started as a group of twelve twelve-year-olds, but now it was gaining an unstoppable momentum.

Of course, we still had a lot to learn. We had to figure out how to create an international movement and still attend high school; help educate child laborers, not just free them; and convince others to join us in our mission, not just be bystanders

At the time, I didn't think to stop and define my own personal transformation, but years later, as Marc and I reflected on the lessons we took from journeys both at home and abroad, I came to think of it as a shift from Me to We.

Having reached my own turning point almost by chance on an ordinary Wednesday, I'm now passionate about doing all I can to help others arrive at their own crossroads. I believe that every journey from Me to We is as unique as each one of us, filled with twists and turns that lead in directions we might never have expected. I know that as more and more people choose to embark upon this journey, our actions in turn encourage others to find their own routes. When I think about the future, I imagine all of our paths converging, forging a new direction for our society. As I look around today, I can see that this process has already begun.

FREE THE CHILDREN

WE is a movement that brings people together and gives them the tools to change the world.

Our unique family of organizations empowers people at home, around the world, and within our social enterprise.

WE Charity empowers change with resources that create sustainable impact. We do this through domestic programs like WE Schools and internationally through WE Villages. Our WE Schools program engages over 5.3 million students and 59,700 educators. Our WE Villages program is active in nine developing countries, creating a sustainable model of international development.

Overall, due to WE Charity:

- More than 1,500 classrooms and schools have been built around the world to date, helping 200,000 students access education
- Over $36 million worth of medical supplies has been collected and distributed
- 30,000 women have achieved economic self-sufficiency
- More than one million people have been provided with access to clean water and sanitation programs and facilities
- More than fifteen million nutritious meals have been produced to date by farmers and families with our support

WE DAY

WE Day is a powerful, life-changing experience with world-renowned speakers and performers, mixed with real inspirational stories of change. It is an opportunity for young change-makers to connect across the world and celebrate their year of action. **WE Schools** provides digital, interactive service-learning and social- and emotional-learning resources to educators and students, providing them with the opportunities and experiences to support their passion to learn through service, and to better the world in the process. In 2019:

- 12.1 million volunteer hours were logged by WE Schools participants
- $14 million+ was raised for local and global causes
- 15 million+ meals were supported through food collected by WE Schools participants
- 84 percent of students felt a stronger connection to their local community
- 81 percent of educators said they are better equipped to teach about social issues through service-based learning
- 86 percent of educators agreed that youth taking part in WE Schools demonstrated better leadership among their peers

START NOW!

Before you begin this section, find a notebook that can serve as your personal Me to We journal. As you explore the Start Now! Activities at the end of each chapter, this journal will be a place to record your thoughts, feelings, and ideas as you begin to make the shift from Me to We a reality in your life and the lives of others.

▸ Like Craig, we all have passions waiting to be discovered. Set aside some time today to make a list of the things that you feel passionately about. Ask yourself

» What do I feel most thankful for? What makes my heart overflow with gratitude? The words of a loved one? A leisurely stroll through the park?

» What kinds of things make me angry? A war being fought somewhere across the world? Negative attitudes in my community?

» What are the values I hold most dear? What five values guide me as I move through life?

▸ Once you have brainstormed answers to these questions, identify the one issue that does the most to ignite your passion.

LIVING ME TO WE

---

1. **Create a recipe for good deeds.** This Saturday, spread your morning newspaper out on your kitchen table. Read it together with your spouse, friends, or children, and discuss the articles that catch your attention. Next, choose one issue that you feel drawn to and list ways you can make a difference.

2. **Don't burn the cookies.** Firefighters play an important role in keeping our communities safe. A plate of treats is a great way to let them know that your family is grateful for all of their hard work and to make new friends at the same time.

3. **Put the world on your wall.** Hang a map of the world on a wall in your kitchen, family room, or your child's bedroom. When you discuss issues with your kids or talk about where products are made, have them find the appropriate country on the map.

My Story

KIM PHUC

I still can't look at the picture, not even today. It hurts too much.

That image of myself as a little girl in Vietnam, running with my arms hanging wide, naked, my skin on fire, my mouth open in terror and crying for help, the smoke all around me—it still is too powerful. I feel so horrible inside, like it's happening all over again. I can smell the burning, I can feel the heat, and deep in my soul, it hurts!

So I don't look. I keep the picture filed away, hidden from view.

But I don't feel hatred for that picture anymore. Instead, I feel grateful. To me, that picture is a gift.

It took a very, very long time for me to feel that way.

For many years, I was just The Girl in the Picture—and I hated it.

I had been photographed when I was nine years old and my village was hit by napalm. We were running on the highway, away from the explosions. The sky was red, as if heaven were on fire. I could not keep up with my brothers; they ran too fast. As I ran, I turned to see an airplane flying low to the ground. I had never seen one so close before. I watched it drop four bombs into the swirling smoke. I kept running.

Suddenly, a force struck me from behind. I fell forward onto the ground. I did not know what I was doing when I pulled at the neck of my shirt. I just felt so hot. My burning clothes fell away from me. I looked at my left arm. It was covered with flames and brownish-black goo. I tried to wipe it off and yelled in pain as my hand began to burn too.

I knew I should catch up with my brothers, but I felt so tired and so thirsty, like I was burning from the inside. "Oh Ma," I kept crying. "*Nong qua! Nong qua!*" Too hot! Too hot!

That's when the journalist took my picture.

I hardly remember what happened next. The journalists poured their canteens of water over my skin; it was falling off in pink and black chunks. The photographer got a poncho to cover me, then helped me into a van and drove me to the hospital in Saigon. The van swerved around refugees, and with every bump I screamed in agony. The napalm had incinerated my ponytail and left my neck, my back, and my left arm a raw, mushy, oozing mess. It had killed my two cousins. I wished it had killed me too.

It wasn't until much later that I learned that the picture, taken by AP photographer Nick Ut, had been printed on the front pages of newspapers around the world and won him the Pulitzer Prize. It made Nick famous. It made me famous too, though I wished with all my heart it had not.

For the next fourteen months I remained in an American hospital in Saigon, enduring many surgeries and painful procedures paid for by a private foundation. I had to relearn how to stand, walk, and feed and dress myself. Finally, recovered, I was sent back to my village to try to rebuild my life.

But my life would never be the same.

I could not take the hot sun on my unstable new skin nor the blowing dust in my damaged lungs. I suffered bad headaches and sudden, intense pain. My family was forced to live in a hot, airless house in the city as war raged around us. We had little money, not even for the ice I depended on for pain relief.

As the years went by, I remember as a teenager feeling so very ugly! I would look in the mirror at the scars that covered my body and ask "Why me?" I was able to hide my disfigurement by growing my hair long, wearing long sleeves, and resting my left arm on my hip so you couldn't tell it was shorter.

It was my shameful secret. Once, when I was seventeen, sitting at my desk waiting for the teacher to arrive, I heard some girls talking about a boy who had scars on his hands. "He is so handsome," one girl said. "Ooooh! Yuck!" the others chimed in. "Have you seen his scars? So ugly!"

The only thing that kept me going was my dream of becoming a doctor. I'd been so impressed with how the doctors had helped me; I wanted to help people too. I studied hard and was accepted into medical school. I was thrilled—but it was short-lived. A few months later, foreign journalists found me. They wanted to interview me ten years after the war.

At first, I was flattered—me? Famous? But then the Vietnamese communist government took over, demanding that I act as their anti-capitalist poster girl, their symbol of the war. They told me what to say and do, watching my every move. They made me abandon medical school and be available to pose for the cameras. Outside, I was smiling; inside, I felt so sad, like I was a victim all over again. I could have no friends; it was too dangerous. They warned my parents that if something happened to me, they would go to prison

In between media interviews, I went to the library, reading every book I could find on religion. I'd hoped that within those pages I would find some answers, some meaning for my life. There, I found my answer.

God, I decided, had saved me for a purpose. Through my new faith, I would find that purpose.

The Vietnamese government finally relented and allowed me to continue my education, this time in Cuba. It was there that I met my husband—and decided that I would finally escape the clutches of the communist government.

I told no one, just bided my time. And one day, I saw my chance.

It was 1992. My husband and I were returning from our honeymoon in Moscow, and the plane needed to refuel in Canada. I looked out the plane window at the wide open spaces of Gander, Newfoundland. We knew nothing of this country except that it was cold—and free. That was enough for me. I had never felt so scared in my life—or so strong. With pounding hearts, we left our bags on the plane and never turned back.

I came here to get away from Vietnam, from the war, and from my life as The Girl in the Picture. I wanted to make my life quiet. It did not work out that way, but that's okay. I have found something else— something better. I have found my purpose. I travel and speak out to tell people that war is bad, that tolerance and forgiveness are good, that our real enemy is anger and bitterness.

And I have found that people listen. I believe that's because I speak from my heart. They see me as an innocent little girl who suffered so much, who is supposed to be angry, who is supposed to be dead.

Although I did not become a doctor, I did find another way to heal. In 1997, I established the Kim Foundation, a non-profit group that provides funds for medical assistance to children who are victims of war and terrorism. In 1997, I was appointed a Goodwill Ambassador for Peace for UNESCO.

I could have stayed frozen in time, forever The Girl in the Picture, forever the victim. But I no longer run away, and I am no longer a victim. It was the photograph that saved my life, but it was my reaching out to others that finally convinced me it was a life worth saving.

CHAPTER TWO

MARC'S STORY:
"WHAT KIND OF LEGACY?"

"That which we witness, we are forever changed by, and once witnessed we can never go back."

—Angeles Arrien

When I was eighteen, I was working as a page in the Canadian House of Commons while starting my first year of college. Dressed like a penguin in a blazer and tie, I served water—with ice or without—delivered "top secret" messages, and fetched stationery for the country's most powerful leaders. It was a small job of smaller details, but just as in the U.S. Congress, it kept the country running. Except for one nervous moment when I accidentally dumped a glass of water on the prime minister, I was thrilled to be a part of history in the making. Fresh out of high school, I was accustomed to catching flak for passing notes; now it was my job. I imagined that my life in politics was off to a great start.

One day I delivered a note to a formidable and balding gentleman who stopped me with a query. "What kind of legacy do you want to leave, son?" Baffled by a question I had never been asked before, I gave a snappy answer. "Sir," I replied, "I intend to study hard and deliver water with ever greater efficiency. One day, I will become a senior page and tell all the little pages where to get the water and the stationery." He was unimpressed, but he did not let up. In his next breath, he told me about his work with an amazing charity that volunteered in the slums of Thailand. Was I interested? "No thank you, sir," I replied. I was happy where I was.

I figured that was the end of it, but this gentleman persisted. The next day *and* the next, he called me over to ask the same question.

When school ended for the year, I was on a plane to Bangkok, Thailand. The man was very persuasive.

It was a huge risk. I was turning my back on a supposed "dream job," which was writing speeches for a member of Parliament. I had to put my scholarship on hold. All my savings went to buying the plane ticket. I told my parents I was off to "change the world" and, in order to secure their permission, I had to promise I would finish school. When they asked me questions about the safety of where I was staying, I made up vague answers.

I had finally recognized that I was faced with a once-in-a-life-time opportunity to make a real difference in people's lives. I felt that if I didn't seize it right away, it would become harder and harder to do so with each passing year. I knew that if I let myself grow accustomed to life in Ottawa and its comforts, I might never again find the courage to make such a journey. And so I got on the plane.

When I arrived in Bangkok, I was startled by the airport's marble floors and beautiful architecture. Skyscrapers loomed large in plated gold. From the back of a taxi, I looked to my left and saw a BMW. A Mercedes was on my right. Why did I give up a great job to come to Thailand to help all these wealthy people? On the one hand, I was terrified—there I was, alone and far from home, unable to understand Thai and with no easy way to communicate with loved ones. On the other hand, I was angry because I felt I had been tricked into putting my life back in North America on hold just to help people who didn't really need it!

Then the cab entered Klong Toey. Forgotten by many, this slum community sits on the edge of the Thai capital surrounding the city's major port, a world away from Bangkok's wealthy neighborhoods. Stretching for miles, it is a sprawling sea of corrugated tin, mud and cement bricks, zinc roofing, open sewers, and garbage heaps. It's not on any tourist map. In fact, it isn't on *any* map. It was a world away from suburbia. My heart sank as I came face-to-face with poverty for the very first time in my life. As we headed deeper into the slum, I was stricken with self-doubt. Would I be strong enough to cope in this kind of environment? Would I really be able to make any kind of difference? Outwardly I was trying my best to remain calm, but inwardly I was quickly beginning to doubt that I would be able to stomach my new surroundings. I was certain I'd made a mistake.

Tens of thousands of people live in the Klong Toey on less than a dollar a day. In a country much loved by tourists for delicious food, beautiful beaches, and diverse culture, the people of this community are hungry, isolated, and struggling to meet their most basic needs.

I had been assigned to work at the community development center, in a part of the slum known as the "slaughterhouse." A major source of revenue for the community was slaughtering animals and preparing meat for sale.

As I drove into the slum, I considered the divide between those in Bangkok who had so much more than they required and those in Klong Toey who had little or less than nothing. I was greeted by the center's friendly volunteer coordinator and directed to my simple apartment where I dropped my belongings. From this apartment, I would hear the slaughtering of pigs every night from midnight until dawn, their shrill screams tearing through the night air.

Next I was ushered to the AIDS ward of a hospice in the slum. I would later learn that the ward did not exist, at least not officially. Not a single person in Thailand had AIDS, according to the Thai government at the time. People got "sick," of course, sometimes "very sick," but no one had AIDS. The hospice was home to an ever-growing number of "very sick" people.

I entered the ward and was greeted by two Thai nurses.

"Thank goodness you are here, Marc," said the first.

"You're a doctor, right?"

I shook my head.

"So, you are a medical student then!"

I shook my head again.

"But you know medicine, right?"

"Kinda," I offered, "I watch *E.R.* every Thursday…"

After a rapid exchange in Thai, the first one said, "No problem. Get ready for your four-hour medical school training!"

"But in my country medical school takes four years!" I protested.

"We don't have that long," she replied. "So we better get started."

During the next few hours, I learned to clean wounds, administer IVs, treat bedsores, and dispense medicine. The work was punishing, made worse by stifling heat, frequent blackouts, and an incredible stench in the air. I tried desperately to hide my weak nerves and queasy stomach, but more than once dashed for the bathroom to throw up.

Just when it seemed my training was coming to an end, the nurse took me aside. "There are only two more things you need to know," she said. "On the left-hand side of the ward, you will find what we call the

Exit Area." As it turned out, she meant "exit" in the largest sense of the word. Terminally ill patients were hidden behind a curtain and then exited out of the ward after death. "The second thing you need to know," she continued, "is that we haven't had a day off in three weeks. You'll be looking after the ward by yourself for the next shift."

My jaw dropped.

"Don't worry, Marc," said the other nurse, patting me on the shoulder before turning to leave. "Think of this as the beginning of your residency!" And with that, they walked out. Alone and petrified, I tried unsuccessfully to keep calm.

I counted to twenty-four. That's how many AIDS patients were in my charge. What am I going to do? I thought. What *can* I do? I fell back on my training with the Canadian government and put my talents to work. I served patients water—some with ice, some without. Next, I tried to cheer up everyone, myself included, giving enthusiastic high-fives to patient after patient. Soon enough, everyone was laughing. Some were laughing with me, others most definitely *at* me, but I didn't care. As long as I could keep people smiling, I was sure it would all be fine. And it was. Until a short while later, when a patient in the Exit Area began to choke. He had fluid in his lungs and could not breathe.

As I crossed the floor, I could hear the man gasping for air. Fumbling and scared, I pulled back the curtain and administered the medicine the nurses had recommended. The man didn't respond. He was still fighting for breath. I ran into the street yelling for help, my vision blurred with tears. Passersby looked on sympathetically, but no one would follow me back inside. I later learned people were afraid that by entering the ward they would catch AIDS. I ran to the choking man, whose name I didn't know and would never learn. With nothing left to offer, I sat down and held his hand, looking into his eyes as he breathed heavily for a while and then stopped. Watching him slip away, I was hit by a feeling of anguish such as I'd never felt, either before or since. It haunts me to this day.

I was crying when the nurses returned. I fought to stop, but could not. I was crushed and emotionally exhausted. "Marc, people in the ward die all the time. That's why they're there," they told me. "Now let's get back to work."

I stared in disbelief. Get back to work? As if I had no feelings? I had not signed up for this.

Fighting back the intense sorrow, I thanked the nurses for what they had taught me and told them I was going home. After one short day, I was calling it quits.

I called my parents, who arranged for my flight back to North America. It was an incredibly difficult phone call because it meant I had failed. Up until that point, I had been a cocky teenager who thought he could accomplish anything. At that moment, I knew I couldn't. I had to admit I was in over my head. I imagined people back home would ask why I was back so quickly. I was already embarrassed.

Still, I couldn't wait to leave. I ran to my tiny apartment and started to repack my bag.

I was interrupted by a knock at the door. I looked out, then down. Staring up at me was a young boy, about my brother Craig's age, in a yellow T-shirt and blue shorts. "What are you doing?" he asked. Quietly, I told him I was preparing to leave. "You can't!" he insisted. "You need to stay for our birthday party."

This boy spoke exceptional English. As part of my quick and dirty education, I had learned that if children from the Klong Toey slums speak English, it's not thanks to a private school education, or any education at all. More often than not, it's because they've worked as prostitutes for English-speaking foreigners. The boy spoke English with a European accent. I stopped, looked into his eyes, and listened.

The boy explained that as street kids, he and his friends did not know their parents, let alone their ages or birthdates. But that didn't stop them from celebrating. Each and every year, everyone would get together and pool their hard-earned pennies to hold one massive birthday party. The festivities were days away.

I was blown away.

The boy made me promise I would attend. Without thinking, I gave him my word. Of course I would be there. Or would I? I was torn. I wanted to flee, but against my better judgment I decided to stay a little longer. I postponed my return flight.

During the next few days, I met the boy's friends. They taught me very basic Thai. I watched the barefoot boys try to earn a small living by shining shoes. I learned that police would beat them up "for fun." I marveled at the way they looked after each other. It was an education unlike I had ever found in a textbook.

A few days later, I set out for the party unsure of what to expect. I heard the laughter before I saw the feast. When the children saw me, they shouted with delight, happy to have one more friend with whom to share their banquet of peanuts and watermelons.

It was one of the most meaningful moments of my life. I was humbled to be part of such a remarkable gathering. A bunch of kids, too poor to buy shoes, gave me the gift of perspective. After the food, there was singing, dancing, storytelling, and much more laughter. Unlike the birthday parties of my youth, there was no mountain of presents, yet the room was filled with joy. I was surrounded by children who were celebrating life in the middle of hardship. It was then that I began to understand the true meaning of happiness.

Though they'd never know it, it was these young boys who convinced me to stay. After the party, I extended my trip indefinitely. I lived in Klong Toey for close to a year, teaching English to schoolchildren and logging many more heart-wrenching days in the AIDS ward. I watched many people die. Yet every morning around seven o'clock, I met my young friends to play soccer.

Thailand changed my life. I arrived there with teenage baggage and left with the confidence to be myself.

As I departed from Klong Toey, I considered the question that had started my journey: What kind of legacy did I want to leave? I was now much closer to the answer.

When I returned to North America, it wasn't to the seat of Canadian government. By then, my priorities had changed. I wanted to learn from the experts about the world around me and further shape my legacy in honor of my soccer-playing friends. After a long search, I accepted a full scholarship to Harvard University to study international relations.

What a decision! The environment was fast paced, to say the least, and the workload was punishing, but I enjoyed it. I was there to learn, so I didn't argue when the library was more familiar to me than my own apartment. As time passed, I answered a lot of the questions that burned in my head. But sure enough, the minute I did, more questions took their place.

Fast forward four years and I faced my life's second big question: What would be my next step?

Here was my dilemma. For Harvard University students, the world's largest banks routinely hosted "information nights" at high-end hotels. Butlers served shrimp kebabs and oysters in the half shell while bankers led presentations to highlight company earnings and to forecast our own well-paid futures. These bankers, usually men, spoke of "private equity," "wealth management," "leverage buyouts," and "mergers and acquisitions."

Upon graduation, I was presented with a series of lucrative job offers. The funniest one came from a manufacturing icon who asked me to manage a factory in Estonia. "It's cold, but the money is good!" Mostly, though, the offers came from banks. Almost all involved going to Wall Street to become an investment banker—otherwise known as an "I-Banker" as per Harvard-speak on campus. Starting salary was approximately my parent's take-home income—combined. I would help firms become successful, restructure management, and perhaps come up with a plan on how to best lay off people so the company could become more "productive" and "cost effective." The starting salary, signing bonus, expense account, expensive suits, and fancy dinners were supposed to make me feel better about all of this.

Fortunately, I didn't have to weigh the offers too seriously because I was going to pursue a law degree at Oxford University. But there, the pressure intensified to lure me into the corporate world. As a Rhodes Scholar, I quickly found out there was an unwritten rule that I could have virtually any consulting job I wanted. Some large companies boasted publicly they had "the most Rhodes Scholars on staff." The starting salary from one job was around $160,000 with signing bonus and cost-of-living and relocation expenses. This wasn't bad for someone who had worked only as a gopher in the Canadian House of Commons making $12 an hour delivering water. No experience necessary. They would send us to "training camp," where we could learn how to speak, think, act, and make money appropriately.

I was pretty certain this was not what I wanted, although the salary was very enticing, especially for a budget-conscious student who had been living on canned spaghetti sauce for more than a few years. Judged by the standards of my middle-class upbringing, the salaries they were offering were unimaginable. But the jobs themselves were dull. Pushing paper around a desk? Nope. Not for me. When I explained to my classmates that I might just go back to North America and run a children's charity, other students actually mocked me. One classmate said he would take "pity" on me and allow me to use one of the many houses he expected to own one day, if I was ever back in London.

Deciding not to take the big job and the big salary was actually a difficult choice. I worried I was throwing away my education. After all, I probably could have returned home to run Free The Children without degrees from Harvard and Oxford. And it's also very difficult to say no when you realize that those who say yes will immediately jump to the front of the line in this world. How would I pay off my student loans, which would kick in as soon as I graduated? How would I ever begin to save for a car or a down payment on a house or condo? The financial uncertainty made me anxious, but my passion to help others won.

What did I choose?

I chose a life where I get up every day excited by new challenges. I do often work sixteen-hour days—but it is not for me that I work. Through Leaders Today, an organization I co-founded in 1999, I played a part in empowering thousands of youth across North America every year with leadership training. Leaders Today became Me to We social enterprise in 2009, continuing to provide leadership training, but expanding to provide products and experiences that help people make daily choices that change the world. With Free The Children, I work at building schools in developing countries, speaking to children, meeting fascinating people, and helping others who are far less fortunate. I'm surrounded by young people whose lives are filled with happiness and passion.

I'm humbled to be able to do this work on a daily basis. Unlike my friends on Wall Street, I don't have a $5,000 watch. My $100 model works great. I don't dine in five-star restaurants every night. And I still do make spaghetti using canned spaghetti sauce. But I can look in the mirror at the end of the day and see myself smiling back. I am simply happier helping other people.

Like Craig, I experienced my own Me to We transformation.

I got my first glimpse of the tremendous power this philosophy holds at my young Thai friends' birthday party. It was an abrupt awakening for my teenage self, yet to this day I still feel that I learned more about compassion, caring, and leadership from my street kid friends than I have from any of my tweed-clad professors with endless letters after their names. Sometimes life's most important lessons need to be literally staring us in the face before we're able to recognize their true value.

ME to WE is a social enterprise that provides socially conscious products and experiences that allow people to change the world through their everyday choices. Half of all ME to WE's profits are donated to support WE Charity, while the other half is reinvested to grow the mission of the social enterprise. As a certified B Corporation, ME to WE meets rigorous standards of social and environmental performance, transparency and accountability.

- Since 2009, ME to WE has contributed $20 million in cash and cost offsetting in-kind donations to WE Charity.

- Each ME to WE product gives back in one of five ways—helping provide education, clean water, health care, food security, and financial opportunity.

- ME to WE products give back in WE Villages communities to change lives through five pillars of impact: education, clean water, health care, healthy food, and financial opportunity, helping families and communities build a brighter future.

- The WE Social Entrepreneurship program provides mentorship, education, and business guidance to young people dedicated to launching their own social enterprise, building the future of business for good.

START NOW!

As Marc learned through volunteering, you don't need to have a degree in medicine to have talents worth sharing. Everyone has something unique to contribute. Make a list of your own talents. Ask yourself:

▸ When I have free time, what do I like to do?

▸ What would my friends say are my best qualities?

▸ What do people ask me for help with?

▸ What skills do I have that I would like to share?

LIVING ME TO WE

---

1. **Make a mentor's day.** List the mentors you've has over your lifetime. Did a teacher believe in you? Did a colleague give you good advice at a critical moment? Take the next step and thank each person on your list for the difference they've made in your life. Pick up the phone, write a handwritten thank-you note, or pay a surprise visit.

2. **Propose dress-down days.** Ask your boss or principal if he or she could offer a dress-down day in your workplace or school. Collect $2 from everyone who wears casual clothes that day. Suggest khakis instead of suits, and jeans instead of school uniforms. Each month, support a new cause with the money you raise.

3. **Wear your words.** Many of us wear T-shirts that advertise brand names. Why not try something different and war one that conveys a positive social message? Perhaps "Stop HIV/AIDS" or "We are all one human race." Wear it, live it, and speak out with style.

My Story

KEITH TAYLOR

For as long as I can remember, I had three dreams. One of them was to become a teacher. One was to live in New York City. And one was to become a philanthropist.

After fourteen years of school and about $100,000 in student loans, I had managed to fulfill one of those dreams. I had become a professor. At thirty-two, PhD. in hand, I secured the academic Holy Grail—a tenure-track job, teaching in my field, at a terrific university just outside of Nashville, Tennessee. Along the way, I had gotten married and divorced. I'd become the father of a remarkable little boy. I'd made a lot of good friends.

Still, no matter what I did, no matter how hard I worked, I couldn't make ends meet. My starting salary was barely enough to pay rent, child support, basic utilities, and my student loans. With each little increase in salary came an increase in expenses.

I still wanted very badly to be a philanthropist, but that dream seemed unattainable. To my mind, a philanthropist was someone with hundreds of millions of dollars to funnel into medical research or to build hospitals. I, on the other hand, could barely take care of myself. Just when I was ahead on my bills, something would happen—my car would break down, for example—and I'd find myself behind again.

I still wanted to help people, but I couldn't understand how. That $5 I might give to charity meant $5 worth of gas I couldn't purchase.

So this is how I lived, month after month, for two years. And every month, my dream of becoming a philanthropist seemed farther and farther out of reach until one evening in March 2002.

It occurred to me that throughout my life, there had been many times that people had pulled me through a tough time. They hadn't showered me with thousands of dollars, but rather with tens or twenties to help me with small, unexpected expenses. My father had stepped in to repair my car when he knew I couldn't afford it. My boss had helped me to buy a pair of glasses to replace the ones I had broken while working with him. My best friend in college once paid my power bill when I had been forced to choose between books for class and the light to read by.

None of these people had been rich. None of them had given me very much money and yet their small, one-time gifts had come at just the right time. And they had done this—often giving up something themselves in the process—simply because they cared.

The longer I thought about it, the more I realized that these acts were the very definition of philanthropy. Philanthropy has nothing to do with the amount of money involved. Philanthropy is simply reaching out to help, in whatever way we can, without expecting anything in return.

That's it, I told myself, no more excuses. No more waiting until I was "back on my feet." No more waiting to hit the lottery. If I was ever going to become a philanthropist, the time was now.

I began by downsizing my life. I gave up the period apartment I loved and moved into a triplex down the street—a dump at half the price. I got rid of all the "stuff" I'd accumulated over the years, whittled things down to my TV, couch, bed, and dishes. I worked out a new monthly budget. I now had $350 a month—about 10 percent of my income—that I could use to help others.

But how?

In order to find people who needed the kind of help I could offer, I put together a simple website, which I called Modest Needs. I launched that website with a pledge: I promised that every month until I died or the Internet became obsolete, I would use that site to offer 10 percent of my monthly income—$350 a month—to people who didn't qualify for conventional charity (just like me), who were working as hard as they could (just like I was), and who encountered a small, unexpected expense that threatened their financial stability (just as I had many times in the past).

The first person Modest Needs helped was a man living in the midwest United States who couldn't pay his car insurance. I asked him to send me his bill, and I wrote a personal check to the insurance company for $78. Putting that check in the mail gave me a feeling unlike anything I'd ever experienced. For the first time in years, I'd done something completely unselfish, and nothing—nothing I could buy or own or have—felt as good to me as that did.

I expected Modest Needs to sit quietly in a corner of the Internet that few people ever visited. I expected to hear from five or six people a month. It didn't matter that I couldn't help them all. I figured if I managed to help just one person a month, then that was one person whose life was a bit better off.

But things didn't go quite as I'd expected.

A few weeks later, on April 1, a friend posted a link to Modest Needs on a community blog. The next morning, I was inundated. About 10 percent of the people who e-mailed me thought Modest Needs was an April Fool's joke. Another 10 percent asked for some kind of help. The rest wanted to know how they could help.

Things snowballed after that. I was flown to New York to appear on the *Today* show and on CNN'S Morning Edition. When I returned home that evening, it took me more than three hours to download my emails.

At that moment I knew my life was never going to be the same.

People often ask me to tell them my favorite Modest Needs story. Without question, it is the mother from Kentucky who needed help for her five-year-old son. The little boy was born with Irlen's Syndrome. His eyes were unable to process shapes, so everything was a colored blur. Lenses to correct this disorder cost $500, plus the frames—which the mother couldn't afford. She told Modest Needs that her son was about to start kindergarten, and if we would send her $50 for a down payment, she'd get a second job to pay the rest.

Modest Needs was able to fund the entire cost of the special lenses. Later, I learned that when he was being fitted with these lenses, he looked in the mother's direction, pointed, and said, "Is that Mommy?"

It was the first time he had seen his mother's face.

Today, Modest Needs has become more than a non-profit organization. It is a community of philanthropists, exceptionally caring people who have chosen to give up a small indulgence—a cappuccino on their way to work, a hamburger, or a couple of movie tickets—in order to help others. They make this sacrifice not because they have to, not because they feel guilty, but because the pleasure it gives them far outweighs that small indulgence.

Today, Modest Needs helps an average of one person a day, with donations that may be as small as four quarters anonymously taped to a postcard. Since that fateful March in 2002 we've given away more than a million dollars. I don't feel like a knight in shining armor, and I sure don't look like one—more like Jerry Seinfeld, I'm told. But I do feel good. My blood pressure and cholesterol are down, I lost 50 pounds, quit smoking, and even enjoy working out. (I used to think there was no point in running unless you were being chased!) And I've met some amazing people; one even helped me find a beautiful, inexpensive period apartment in my dream town—New York City.

So, in the end, I have attained all three dreams.

Such is the power that we have when we act on the most human of desires—the desire to reach out to others.

Such is the power of philanthropy.

CHAPTER THREE

A NEW LOOK AT HOME AND HAPPINESS

*"We excel at making a living but often fail at making a life.
We celebrate our prosperity but yearn for purpose.
We cherish our freedoms but long for connection.
In an age of plenty, we feel spiritual hunger."*

—David G. Myers

We had always dreamed of meeting her. Threading our way through a labyrinth of identical dusty alleyways, we finally found the right doorstep. Expecting a guard or at least a sign, we found neither. Instead, other visitors greeted us. They smiled, their weary faces weathered by time and work. Teeth were missing; torn clothing clung to bony figures. We smiled back; their smiles were infectious. We had all managed to make our way here, and all of us were eager for what came next.

Summoning his courage, Craig knocked on the door. We were immediately welcomed and invited in. Stepping across the threshold, we found ourselves at the entrance to a large courtyard, a hive of activity. All around us were dozens of people of every imaginable nationality all dressed in white going about their tasks with an air of determination. The floor itself had been worn smooth by their footsteps, and those of visitors.

Entering a small room, our elation quickly turned to disappointment when we were told that she was not accepting visitors. Advised to return another day, we prepared to leave. But just at that moment, she entered the room.

She was much smaller than we had expected. Even in that tiny room she seemed small, frail and stooped with age. As she made her way towards us, we saw that although her features were plain, old, and wrinkled, her face shone with an intensity that we couldn't quite explain. Soon, her calloused fingers reached out to us and we were surprised to feel their strength and warmth as she took our hands in hers.

Smiling, she looked deep into our eyes, and in that instant, it felt as though she was searching our souls. There was a special kind of warmth about her that was unlike anything we had ever experienced.

We expected that this single moment would be the only one we would share with her. After all, her workload was nothing short of legendary. But this was not to be the case. In spite of her responsibilities, she was in no hurry to leave us that day. Even with her busy schedule she took the time to meet and talk with us—and to be truly present.

Our time with this remarkable woman named Agnes taught us important lessons that were destined to help shape our lives. Our visit led us to rethink our ideas about the world and our place in it, and to arrive at some important conclusions.

Humble Beginnings

Agnes was born in Skopje, Macedonia, in Eastern Europe, in what was then Yugoslavia, and from an early age, she decided to devote her life to her beliefs. Trained to teach, Agnes was soon stationed at an elite girl's school in one of the world's poorest cities.

Although Agnes enjoyed teaching, her life was far from easy. Whenever she ventured out beyond the school's high walls, she was confronted with a very different reality where order and learning were replaced with disease and misery. Upon seeing her, desperate people would call out for help. A few had simple things to sell, but most would simply raise their cupped hands to their mouths in a universal gesture of hunger. Some were barely clothed, with lengths of dirty fabric wrapped around them. Many were covered with open, festering wounds. Others could not even ask for food or money. They were too weak to move.

As Agnes lived an austere life, she had little to share with the people who approached her. It seemed there was nothing she could do to ease their burdens. She had been told that her duty was to teach. She became disheartened by the suffering that surrounded her in the same way that many of us become overwhelmed by the images of war and famine that fill our TV screens. She felt helpless.

The Turning Point

One day, Agnes became seriously ill with tuberculosis, a disease that, if not properly treated, can easily kill. Like many people facing illness and possible death, she began to reflect more deeply on the meaning of her life. After treatment, on a fateful train ride to the north of the country, where she was sent for rest and recuperation, she finally confronted some very important life questions. Who was she *really* meant to be? What was her purpose? How did she want to live the rest of her life? Her illness had jolted her away from her everyday concerns, and a more meaningful path began to reveal itself. That day, traveling on the train, watching the countryside pass by her so quickly, she vowed that never again would she close her eyes or her heart to the suffering of others. Instead, she would help.

Not long after her recovery, Agnes was forced to put her resolution to the test. While walking to school one day she came across an elderly woman who lay dying, abandoned in the street. In a flash she had made her choice—she would take her to a doctor. Hailing a taxi, she helped to pick the woman up and maneuver her inside. But hospital after hospital refused to treat the dying woman. She was bluntly told that the doctors took only paying patients; people without money could not be treated. Though Agnes had no money she was determined not to give up. She took her to the next hospital, and then the next. But no one would help.

With nowhere left to turn, Agnes brought the woman back to her own home. She gently laid her down on her bed, bundling her in her own blankets. Agnes didn't have any medical training; she wasn't a doctor or a nurse. Nor did she have any medicine to share. All that she had to offer was the comfort of her tiny room, her bed and blankets, and her own presence. So that is what she gave. Agnes sat by the dying woman's side and comforted her tenderly until a short time later when the woman closed her eyes and breathed no more.

This would become a defining moment for Agnes. It was how she first began to dedicate her life to helping the poor live and die with dignity, respect, and love. Eventually, she took a leave of absence from her teaching position in order to obtain basic medical training. When this was complete, she traded her regular clothes for a simple blue-bordered white cotton sari. Leaving behind her elite girl's school, she went out into the slums of the city determined to help the poorest of the poor.

From that day forward she was true to her word. Working tirelessly in the Calcutta slums, Agnes eventually went on to found the Missionaries of Charity, a new order of nuns whose purpose was to care for those who had no one else to care for them—the dying, the disabled, the destitute, and the orphaned. And now you may recognize her not as Agnes, but as Mother Teresa, the name she chose when she took her vows.

In 1969, a documentary focused the eyes of the world on her work, but the attention did not go to her head. Fame was never her ambition. Neither was wealth or comfort. In a profound gesture, she tore out the plush carpet donated to one of her order's homes and gave it to the poor. In 1979, when she won the Nobel Peace Prize, she rejected the elaborate banquet that is a tradition of the event, insisting that the money instead be used to feed the homeless. And despite all of its local and international fame, her convent in Calcutta was never more than a simple dwelling with only the barest of necessities, tucked away in an inconspicuous corner of a side street.

Today people often think of Mother Teresa as a kindly old nun who lived in the slums of Calcutta. While this is true, she was also a quintessential entrepreneur and leader. She had a clear aim. She developed a plan of action and worked tirelessly to achieve her goals. Her message of simple service, small actions, and deep love resonated around the world. She eventually built a huge organization in the most challenging of circumstances, formulated its constitution, and established more than 500 centers in 120 countries, including one of the first hospices for AIDS victims in New York City and others in Atlanta, and San Francisco.

We spent precious moments with Mother Teresa that day. We relished every minute. When we asked her how she managed to maintain her hope surrounded by so many sick and dying people, one humble yet profound sentence was all she offered: "They die one at a time, so I save them one at a time." With these simple words, she reminded us that the world's challenges, no matter how great, concern the welfare of individual people, individual people who we can help. It was an important lesson in the art of the possible, and one that neither of us would forget.

After a visit to North America, Mother Teresa observed that she had never seen such an abundance of material wealth. But she had also never seen "such a poverty of the spirit, of loneliness, and being unwanted." In spending time reflecting on our own experiences after returning to North America from the developing world, we couldn't help but see that there is indeed a gap between our society's soaring monetary wealth and the true wealth of happiness and well-being that all of us deserve to enjoy.

If our experiences abroad helped us to recognize our many blessings as cause for joy, they also led us to question why we saw so little joy around us here at home. If the lessons we had learned showed us that opportunities to help others can be found at every turn, they also led us to wonder why so many opportunities pass us by.

In fast-paced North America, it can often seem that helping others will slow us down, or take something away from us. Preoccupied with pressing deadlines, we rush past the homeless on our way to work. Stuck in a crowd at rush hour, we brush by the woman who struggles to lift her baby's carriage onto the bus. Overloaded with extra work of our own, we turn away from the colleague who has a problem with a project. In this sprint for material wealth and our relentless efforts to fulfill our own definition of success, we often leave others behind. But could the greatest casualty be our personal happiness?

Our search for answers eventually led us to an extraordinary study called the World Values Survey.

Arguably the most ambitious public opinion study ever undertaken, the World Values Survey is nothing less than a global investigation into the workings of society and culture. Truly a massive effort. To date, the survey has been carried out in at least 90 societies, covering all six inhabited continents and representing about 80 percent of the world's population. The survey has been carried out four times, from 1981 to 2004, measuring over 800 variables across more than 270,000 people. The data from the World Values Survey has been used in hundreds of publications in more than twenty languages.[1] Conducted by an international network of more than 100 social scientists, it is a goldmine of information for anyone interested in learning about the values and beliefs of people around the world.

Although the survey has obtained interesting findings on everything from peoples' ideas about democracy to who they would most like to have as their next-door neighbors, what was most interesting to us was that it also measured how happy and satisfied with life people reported being. Here the results are particularly intriguing. Do you know what country has the happiest people? Would you care to guess?

If your choice for first place lies somewhere in North America or Western Europe, you're in good company. When we first put this question to friends and family members, nearly all their first choices were from these continents—but they were wrong.

The winner? Nigeria. The researchers found that Nigeria has the highest percentage of self-identified happy people, followed by Mexico, Venezuela and El Salvador. That's right: not one of the World's wealthiest countries managed to crack the top four. And what about the United States? It came in at number sixteen.[2]

For a lot of us, the idea that people with a relatively low standard of living can be happier than those with life's luxuries at their finger tips doesn't make a lot of sense. What's more, how is it that those of us who enjoy a standard of living unequalled anywhere else are not bursting with joy? Searching for answers, we now found ourselves faced with difficult questions.

HAPPINESS IN AMERICA

On the face of things, it seems that Americans should now be happier than ever. After all, according to the goals of previous generations, millions of us should now have it made—with a car in (almost) every driveway and a chicken in (almost) every pot. Since World War Two, the inflation-adjusted income per citizen has almost tripled[3] and the luxuries now available to us appear (almost) endless.

However, despite this newfound wealth, levels of personal happiness in the United States have remained virtually unchanged since the 1950s. Despite the huge increase in personal spending power, and the sheer numbers of resources (fancier toys, faster cars, new technological gadgets), the fact is that our happiness levels have not budged. Maybe the age-old saying is true: "money doesn't buy happiness."

Rethinking the Cash Connection

All it takes is a quick look around to realize that many of us try to buy our way to bliss. Hence the rise of "retail therapy" as the cure for feeling unfulfilled. But as we began to dig a little deeper into what money can buy and what it can't, more often than not, the answers to our questions surprised us.

In 2003, Jean Chatzky, a financial editor for the *Today* show and a columnist for *Money Magazine*, commissioned a fifteen hundred person poll by the Roper Organization to study how money affected the happiness of Americans lives. For anyone clinging to the idea that wealth brings happiness, the results of Chatzky's poll strike a resounding blow. It was found that 84 percent of those with a combined household income of $50,000 a year reported overall they were either "somewhat" or "very happy" with their lives. Even when income increased to $100,000, there was "no discernible difference in overall happiness with friendships, standard of living, marriage, children, and appearance."[4] For us, this study was a wake-up call, a lesson that happiness truly doesn't depend on how much money you have to spend.

To understand why this might be the case, take a moment to think about the role of money in your own life. Would having a bit more money in your pocket make you happier? What about an extra $500? An extra $5,000? An extra $5 million? Initially, your answer might well be an enthusiastic "yes." Ours certainly was—in the nonprofit world money can be tight, and any amount can make a huge difference! As we later learned, however, the answer isn't as obvious as it might seem.

The problem is that when it comes to money, the more you have the more you want. In a famous psychological study, researchers interviewed people who had won between $50,000 and $1 million in the lottery within the past year, and compared them to a sample of people who had not won the lottery. Within only one year of their win, people's happiness returned to what it was before they had won.[5] The issue at stake is a simple one: as your wealth increases, so do your "needs." Soon, things that were once luxuries become run of the mill, and before too long the excitement fades.

Psychologists such as Nobel Laureate Dr. Daniel Kahneman of Princeton University call this experience "the hedonic treadmill." The thrill it brings is a short-term boost. Before long it wears off, leaving us feeling no happier than before. So we buy more stuff. We may shop till we drop, but we don't get any happier.

To complicate matters, there's the issue of "keeping up with the Joneses," the urge not be outdone by those annoying neighbors who always seem to be doing just a little better than you are. This phenomenon was recently confirmed by researchers at the University of Pennsylvania and at Harvard, who studied a representative sample of nearly 20,000 Americans from 1972 to 2002. They discovered that when people are evaluating their satisfaction with life, they tend to compare themselves to others, specifically to their peers who are doing a bit better than they are.[6] Because there is always someone who has more than we have, the constant shuffle to "keep up with the Joneses" becomes a source of pressure that leads not to happiness, but to envy, anxiety and stress. In our own lives, this is a phenomenon we've had ample opportunity to witness.

MARC'S REFLECTIONS

Since finishing my studies at Harvard and Oxford, I've watched one friend after another land high-ranking, high-paying Wall Street jobs. As executives at investment banks, consulting firms, established law firms, and major corporations, many are now well on their way to impressive careers. By society's standards, they seem to have it made.

On the surface these people seem to lead "charmed lives." As they left student life behind, many had a last drink at their cheap-but-friendly local watering hole, shook hands with longtime roommates, and moved out of small and cozy apartments into swanky condos decked out with expensive gadgets. They made reservations at restaurants where the cost of a bottle of wine equaled a month of rent at college. They replaced their beloved old jalopies with sleek new sport cars.

The thing is, a number of them have admitted that despite their apparent success, they aren't happy. Some complain of back-biting co-workers and lament 80-hour workweeks devoted to tasks they hate. Some do not respect the companies they work for, and talk of feeling exploited, exhausted and empty. However, instead of devoting themselves to work they feel committed to, they find themselves working to support the lifestyle to which they have so quickly become accustomed.

One friend, now an ad executive at an important firm, always speaks wistfully about her dream of becoming an elementary school teacher. She loves kids and considers this the ideal job—except for the fact that it can't offer the status and salary that comes along with her current position. She complains bitterly about the demands of her work and talks about leaving to go into teaching, but somehow it never seems to happen.

People often speak of trying a more fulfilling path, and yet in the end the idea of leaving their jobs to work for something they believe in or finding a position that would give them more time with their families almost always leads them to the same conclusion: it's impossible. They have loans, bills, a mortgage to pay off, retirement to save for. They recognize there's something missing in their lives, but it's hard to step off the treadmill.

When I traded my comfortable job in Ottawa for a ticket to Thailand, I learned firsthand just how difficult it can be to begin making new decisions when the results diverge from society's traditional notions of "success." Some of my friends and family members thought I was being irrational, and even I had my doubts. Was it right to leave a good job in order to pursue something as seemingly nebulous as a legacy?

We all know that any decision involves making certain trade offs, but it's how we weigh these trade offs that counts. In a society that tends to measure everything in terms of dollars and cents, we learn from a young age to consider the costs of our decisions in financial terms. But what about the personal and social costs involved in pursuing money over meaning? These are exactly the kinds of costs many of us tend to gloss over—and the very ones we need to consider most.

The Rich-But-Poor Phenomenon

If money itself doesn't necessarily lead to happiness, neither does what it often takes to obtain it: time. The fact is, we only have so much time, and once it's gone we never get it back. When we get caught up in the race to get ahead, taking time away from our loved ones and our children, we risk falling victim to an overwhelming emptiness we have come to call the rich-but-poor phenomenon.

We coined this term a few years ago at the World Economic Forum, an elite gathering of world leaders that is held high in the mountains of Davos, Switzerland. Every year, 1,000 of the world's wealthiest CEOs come together to hob-knob with kings and queens, presidents, prime ministers and movie stars. Admittedly, it was an unlikely place for two youngsters from the charitable world, but we were invited as "Global Leaders of Tomorrow" because of our work with Free The Children. We were the odd ones out, in more ways than one.

One night at dinner, a guest joked that if an avalanche ever hit the conference center, a third of the world's wealth would be wiped out. Everyone had a good laugh, except us. We thought it was a rather frightening statement. There they were, just a few hundred people, and a third of the world's wealth was in their control!

During the course of our stay in Davos, we had a chance to talk informally to a number of other participants. When we spoke about Free The Children and Leaders Today (now Me to We social enterprise), CEOs would confide to us about the challenges they faced with their own children and families. One man, the head of an internationally renowned company, told us that he had two sons about our age. He explained that for years he had worked hard to give them the best of everything: the best private school education, the best trips around the world, the best tutors, the best cars. But while he was always working to give them the best of everything there was one thing he couldn't give them: the best dad. The demands of his job meant that he was almost never home, and was often working in foreign cities and moving between condos. Now, a few divorces later, he usually saw his kids only on the holidays. Even then, they were barely on speaking terms. He sounded like a very loving father with the best of intentions, but it was clear that in trying to provide his children with "only the best," he wasn't able to give them the best of himself.

Listening to such stories, it didn't take long to realize that wealth and power don't always ensure a happy ending. Witnessing the unhappiness of those thought to be the most successful was enough to shatter all the traditional stereotypes about success.

On the final day of the conference, the organizers urged guests to relax and enjoy some of the town's world-class skiing. For days, conference-goers had been tied up in meetings, attending to the business of signing contracts and generating wealth. At last, we thought, here was a chance to have some fun!

When the two of us hit the slopes, however, they were almost totally empty. There was hardly a soul in sight! In answer to our puzzled questions, the resort's staff told us that the lifts were almost always idle during the forum because the power brokers rarely take the time to ski or explore the town—they are all too busy. Despite their immense wealth, they cannot afford to spend even a day enjoying one of the most magnificent winter resorts in the world. This is how we discovered the rich-but-poor phenomenon, the tendency to live to work, rather than work to live.

Difficult Choices

In the struggle to meet deadlines, impress clients and advance through the ranks, it's easy to become so focused on accomplishing specific tasks that we lose sight of how our actions impact our personal well-being, not to mention that of those around us. Many of us fall into a trap and work the long hours because of a sense of responsibility to others, not being able to say no at work, or trying to provide only the best for our family, or ourselves.

We want to play with our kids, get a good night's sleep, spend some quality time with our loved ones or get together with friends, but then we realize that we have that project to finish, those emails to reply to, that deadline looming. We try to get away for the weekend, but we take work with us, and find our relaxation interrupted by cell phone calls, a ringing smart phone, and the constant urge to check our email. Americans are now amongst the most over-worked people in the industrial world, putting in, on average, 350 hours (nine work weeks) more on the job each year than their European counterparts.[7]

The effects of our choices extend far beyond family life. Across North America, the value of community has come under attack. Meanwhile, actual communities are struggling to survive as people race after material success and turn their backs on familiar forms of community involvement in order to embrace the idea that if we do not look after ourselves, who will? In his critically acclaimed book, *Bowling Alone: The Collapse and Revival of American Community*, Harvard professor Robert Putnam helps to explain the phenomenon of withdrawal from community as both the cause and result of a larger societal change. Americans, he argues, have become much more isolated. Civic engagement, group activities and volunteerism are on the decline. As more and more people chase after the ideal of the huge suburban dream home and America sprawls out into suburbs, we are losing our familiar community meeting grounds and increasing the amount of time we spend commuting, by ourselves, in our cars. It's estimated that every ten minutes of commuting time cuts all forms of civic engagement by 10 percent.[8] In an age of gated communities, the very idea of becoming involved in social life beyond the reach of security guards is becoming less and less attractive.

Our point is not that a fast-paced life is necessarily a bad thing. Indeed, it's a necessity for many people who have a lot they would like to accomplish. Positions of influence in our society often demand heavy commitments of time and energy, and the desire to make a contribution leads busy people to lead busy lives. In this regard the two us are no exception—between running three international organizations, managing hectic speaking schedules and participating in fact-finding missions abroad, our agendas are often extremely full. Being busy can be as invigorating as it is rewarding—when you are doing something that is intrinsically fulfilling.

But when the choices we make in our lives leave us with no time, energy or incentive to focus on anyone but ourselves, there's a problem.

Me, Myself and I

Caught up in the daily grind, many of us are often just too busy for anything, or anyone else. The result is something that we have come to call the "Me" mentality, a way of thinking that focuses on self-interest above all else, and leads us to act accordingly. Some people now proudly espouse this idea, and can't imagine a life not devoted to "looking out for Number One." But even those of us who are skeptical of this approach to living can find it creeping into our high pressure world. Surprisingly, even those whom we often look up to as models of good behavior are not immune. In one study, a group of Christian theology students found themselves running late for a lecture they were told they had to give. Trying to arrive on time, the students were faced with the need to make it from one side of the campus to the other as quickly as possible. On the way, they passed a shabbily dressed man who lay moaning in a doorway and some even had to step over him. Only 10 percent of the class stopped to help. Ironically, the students were on their way to give a lecture on the biblical parable of the Good Samaritan.[9]

As people of faith, this study hit particularly close to home for us. The gap between the principle and the practice is impossible to miss, and it raises important questions about what it really means to live one's faith in today's world, where "success" usually refers to money and power. It doesn't seem as if any of the students necessarily had bad intentions, but most were so caught up in being on time that they missed an opportunity to live the message they were supposed to share that day. For us, this is a powerful example of just how easy it can be to slip into the Me mentality as we race through our daily lives. However, one thing is clear: the 10 percent who stopped were able to do more than just talk about their beliefs—they were able to act on them. Despite the pressures they were facing, they made a decision to reach out to someone in need. With one simple act of kindness, they took a stand for their ideals. This study could encourage many conclusions, but we believe the most important one is this: the Me mentality may be far reaching, but there are those who are following a different path.

IT'S TIME FOR A CHANGE

It's tempting to believe that the way that we're currently living is the only way to live. It's also misleading. We all make choices every day, and by making different ones we can change the path we are on.

We believe that the stirrings of change are already underway. With the changing environment brought by 9/11, the tech boom and bust, corporate scandals, and the changing role of faith in our lives, people are reevaluating their approach to life and making new decisions about their priorities.

Moving from thought to action, many people are challenging the assumption that the person with the most toys wins. More and more, people are choosing to downsize, trading long hours and high pay for the chance to spend time with family and friends and do work they find inherently rewarding.

A study by the Merck Family Fund found that 28 percent of a national sample of Americans, and 10 percent of the executives and professionals sampled, reported having "downshifted" or voluntarily made life changes resulting in a lower income to reflect a change in their priorities in the preceding five years. [10] Recently, we've begun to witness this trend in our own lives, as friends start to make new choices, whether leaving behind hectic schedules, finding time to volunteer, or turning to careers in the non-profit world. As each person makes a new decision to stand up for what's most important to him or her, this trend gains strength.

The questions we began asking a decade ago would eventually lead us to seek solutions. Was there a better way to live life? Were we too young to find out, as some adults seemed to be suggesting? In our search for answers we began to look beyond our own backyard, and learn from the insights of people and cultures around the world. Our journey wasn't always straight forward, but it certainly never ceased to be interesting. Little did we know just how many surprises were in store for us.

START NOW!

- Open your Me to We journal, close your eyes, and think about the major sources of stress in your life.

- Ask yourself:

  - » What worries flash through my mind while I'm trying to fall asleep at night?

  - » What do I tend to complain about the most? Do I worry about the state of our world, how to pay this month's bills, or what people at work or school think of me?

- The things you worry about can be a good indication of where your priorities lay. What do your worries tell you about what you attach importance to? Are you focusing on your family? Fashion? Community? The global community?

TAKE ANOTHER LOOK!

By connecting with our global family we learn that there is an untold story uniting all of us. At times that story is tragic, and it seems easier to disengage ourselves from the world. At other times the story is a joyous one and we are both proud and humble to be part of something larger. Me to We is about acknowledging the global story and writing our own chapter within it.

- The 2006 *American Idol* finale drew in more votes than have ever been cast for a president in a U.S. election.[11]

- About 61.2 million people in the United States volunteered between September 2005 and September 2006.[12]

- On July 2, 2005, about 3 billion people around the world watched the Live 8 concerts drawing attention to the issue of poverty.[13]

LIVING ME TO WE

1. **Provide a "time out" for new parents.** Around the world, many family homes contain multiple generations living together. This means a lot of babysitters! But in North America, smaller families are the norm. Volunteer to babysit for some new parents and send them out for a night on the town.

2. **Plan a reunion. Do you find it difficult to keep in touch with people?** Organize a reunion for family friends, or those with whom you have a special connection. Not only is this a great opportunity to spend time together, it can give you a chance to share your ideas about the social issues you care about and learn more about those that are closes to others' hearts.

3. **Celebrate motherhood around the world.** Next Mother's Day, surprise your mom with a fair-trade gift. Many typical gifts including chocolate, coffee, and flowers come from regions where women are exploited in the fields or factories. When you buy fair trade your mom will know you care—not only about her, but about mothers around the world.

My Story

TIM LEFENS

I was never a "kind" person. It wasn't in my nature. Back then I was anything but. Wildly self-centered, I didn't give presents or flatter people, stuff like that, no tenderness. My friends referred to me as ruthless and I guess I was.

I ran around, did all kinds of stuff whether anyone liked it or not, was King of the World.

My abstract paintings were being shown in New York, in solo exhibitions, getting kudos from the critics. I was swaggering with my buddies through lower Manhattan and across northern Italy, climbing trees, surfing monster waves—artists' loft parties, great women, fast motorcycles. Total freedom. Total celebration.

Total self-absorption.

One day a friend asked if I'd show some slides of my artwork at a school for the severely disabled—people who couldn't walk or even talk. What the hell, I thought. Why not?

I had no idea what I was getting into.

It turned out to be more a hospital than a school. And like you, I'm not eager to go into a hospital, no matter what the reason. So when I strode through the automatic doors, down the shiny linoleum halls in my ratty jeans and T-shirt, I was totally blown away. There were all these contorted bodies, arms strapped to wheelchairs or poking out at weird angles, limbs flailing, mouths drooling. Pretty radical stuff.

This was definitely not a world I wanted anything to do with, such suffocating limits, no freedom. In the room where I was to show the slides of my paintings there was a guy sitting in his wheelchair, his brittle underdeveloped body strapped in, head held aloft by a network of stainless steel wires, hands dangling off the end of the armrests, fingers twisted, bent backwards, welded into knots. I didn't know where to look, but before I averted my eyes from fear, the guy caught me with his eyes, and held me with them. "I'm in here," they said without words, steely gray, intense, not weak. "Do you see me?"

I felt a bolt of energy pass from him to me, the charge blowing through my body. There was a person in there! I took a closer look at the other patients who'd been wheeled in to see my art. The woman I'd seen in the hall, appearing brain-dead, staring at the floor, met my gaze with warm brown smiling eyes. They had given up looking at the staff, but a new person, they'd give a shot to see if there would be any recognition. She threw her head back with laughter, seeing both my fear and the fact that I had indeed seen her, seen the light of her life inside. Next to her, a boy with red hair glared at me. His little arms strapped to his chair, the anger sparked from his eyes to the closed windows, to the lap tray in front of him, back to me again, then back out the sealed window to the outdoors. A worshipper of freedom, this tore me up. This little kid was as fierce as a wolf I'd seen held in a dog's pen, no thought of surrender.

I see them! I thought. And they see I see them! Getting past their outer appearance, they suddenly appeared as people full of energy.

The hospital staff bustled about, distant and distracted. I was supposed to talk about my work, so when the first slide went up, I spoke of the power and freedom of pure abstraction, speaking as I would to colleagues, not as to what some would think of as broken kids incapable of sophisticated thought or feeling.

Pushing the shock of the experience even further it was clear they were linking with the images, no doubt about it. My life of total physical freedom, their lives of total physical limitation, maybe, maybe, painting could be a world we could enter together. But how, with no use of their hands, could this ever be?

Back home, I lay my forehead on the kitchen table, my mind lashed by unfamiliar emotions. I was being disassembled, my old arrogance shattered. All my life I'd been seeking a kind of keen energy in other people, most times to be sorely disappointed, and now here it was, in the most unexpected place, in the least likely people. It was too brutal, them trapped not just by their bodies but by the people around them, paid to aid them toward freedom.

I became obsessed, thought about it 24/7, stopped working on my own stuff, dropped everything. Finally, after a bunch of sleepless nights, I knew what I had to do. I had to go back, to get that energy out somehow. Maybe they could paint—not with their bodies—but with their minds.

In a first, somewhat primitive technique, they directed their wheelchairs over paint-covered canvas, their wheel-tracks speaking for them as drawing. It was like unleashing a bunch of maniacs—very raw. One of the first artists, one of the rare ones who could speak, shouted "Wow!" as each new painting was revealed. "Wow!"

Her turn. She attacked her canvas, which was taped to the studio floor, jacking hard on the joystick of her electric wheelchair, jetting forward, then back, her head snapping back, then forward. Then, her wheelchair still, she began to revolve in place on the center of her painting, slowly at first, then faster and faster, round and round, faster, faster, faster. "Take me away!" she cried. "Take me away!"

After that, I was hooked. I thought of a better way for them to paint, with a laser attached to a headband. The students simply looked at where they wanted the paint to be placed and a trained studio assistant applied the paint. Every choice was now theirs—every detail, of color blending, application tool, size, and orientation of their canvas. The results were awesome. In no time the art world took notice. They had sellout shows in important galleries in New York City, their work selling for thousands of dollars. We expanded to include other schools. But for me, the best part was still the "outing": the moment when a quadriplegic snapped free of his limits and lost himself in the paint. Sometimes it happened immediately; sometimes I needed to goad him on, whisper a little in his ear: "Come on, get it going. Do it!" Suddenly that trapped spirit was free, expressing itself through the paint in a way that was absolutely coherent, absolutely magical.

And that's how it happened, how a group of "ultimate underdogs" tenderized my heart, how my casual what-the-hell stroll into a strange institution changed my life and led me into one of the most beautiful and profound things in the world—the liberation of people who never thought they'd be free.

I have my own physical challenge now. Got diagnosed with something called RP, retinitis pigmentosa. Doctors said I had two to five years of useful vision left. Don't get weepy for me; it's been scary but I can still paint. The thing I want to tell you is how, when I was lowest, way down there, pretty close to giving up, it was the kids and young adults I worked with who lifted me up. As my sight got worse, they managed to ask about it without me having to say a word. When I fessed up, they gathered around, a close little circle, one of them saying quietly, "Maybe we don't have that much time." Then to break the spell of sadness they jumped back into their painting with added gusto, abandon, showing that when things go black you have only two choices: sit back or push on.

I helped them, then they helped me. It was rich, rich, good stuff. Proves it for real, that it's what's inside that counts and that anything is possible, the spirit indestructible. Thanks to this new world I entered and the vital power I'm touched by, it's a much deeper, more enthusiastic life than I could ever have dreamed.

CHAPTER FOUR

SEARCHING FOR ANSWERS

*"Travel has a way of stretching the mind. The stretch comes
not from travel's immediate rewards, the inevitable myriad
new sights, smells and sounds, but with experiencing
firsthand how others do differently what we believed to be the
right and only way."*

—Ralph Crawshaw

As we began our search for a different way to live, we became students of
the global community, and experts at asking questions. Important lessons
emerged from the ideas and traditions that we were exposed to during our
work and travels. The many different people we met and the customs we
learned about opened our eyes to a host of new possibilities.

We learned one of our most important lessons in the company of a
remote and welcoming Maasai village community in Kenya. We arrived
eager to help build a school, but the knowledge we received from our
hosts went far beyond anything taught in a classroom.

Of all Africa's people, the colorful Maasai are among the best known
to Westerners. They share their land with some of the most spectacular
wildlife on earth, and their tall, graceful figures and brilliant red cloaks
are a familiar sight to adventure-seeking tourists. Historically, the Maasai
lived as nomads, grazing their cattle, sheep, and goats on the once ex-
pansive African savannah. Today, however, much of their land has been
taken for private ranches and reserves, forcing many to eke out a living
through subsistence farming.

The village we visited that day was a dusty collection of low,
thatched- roof mud huts. Visible from miles off, their conical roofs stood

out like beacons against the parched land, the only sign of community for as far as the eye could see. In the heat of midday, the place was alive with activity, as children in ragged clothes played amongst small clouds of dry red dust and women wearing colorful beaded necklaces went about their daily tasks, preparing food, collecting firewood, and fetching water. Before long, children were crowding around excitedly, eager to discover how two strangers had arrived in their midst. Wide-eyed and laughing, some reached out to touch us as if on a dare. They were as curious about our lives as we were about theirs.

This was to be our first of many meetings as we worked to help the close-knit community realize its dream of building a primary school. Seated outside on the dry earth, we spent much of the day immersed in conversation with village elders. We learned that the people desperately wanted education for their children, but with their meager resources could not afford the costs of sending them away to study in town. Their goal was to build a school in the village, one that could be open to everyone. So focused were we on the rich melody of voices around us that we barely noticed as the sky began to grow darker and darker. As clouds hovered threateningly over our heads, we were all but oblivious.

Then the sky burst. As the first rain drops pelted down our faces, they took us completely by surprise. Our first thought was a resounding "Take shelter!" We quickly got up and ran for cover.

And that's when it happened. Jumping, running, crying out, the community was going the wrong way—into the rain, not out! In a rush of excitement and jubilation, men, women, and children began to pour out of their huts and into the downpour. Then, to our disbelief, they began to dance, with as much energy as the falling raindrops! We stood stock still for a moment watching the scene unfolding around us, unable to comprehend what was happening. In the middle of the torrent, people were smiling and laughing.

Almost before we knew it, youngsters were grabbing our arms and dragging us over to join in the fun. We soon found ourselves dancing to the upbeat rhythm in the air, totally caught up in the exhilaration of the moment. The rain poured down, hitting so hard it was all we could do to keep our eyes open. But on and on we danced, losing ourselves in the energy of the crowd and the force of the rain. To our surprise we soon found the village chief beside us, taking our hands. Looking up to the sky, he repeated these joyful Swahili words, "It's a miracle, it's a miracle."

We learned that for the Maasai, rain means life. It means the crops will grow, and that families will have food to feed their children. Rain is something to be celebrated. Rain is a blessing. Celebrating with the rest of the community, we felt lucky to share in their jubilation. True, we were soaked and cold, but we were happy. The joy around us was infectious, an elixir for the spirit as well as the senses. As we danced, we too felt ourselves in the presence of the miraculous.

In North America, we seek shelter when it rains. A storm is often considered an annoyance, an affront to our efforts to keep everything under control. Our first instinct is to open an umbrella or rush indoors, and we complain bitterly about the rain-filled streets. It's hard to imagine exactly what it would take to get us outside dancing in the rain. A winning lottery ticket? A Superbowl victory for our favorite team? A sudden rise to stardom? Can it be that we who have so many blessings can no longer recognize a true miracle when we see one?

What initially surprised us most in our travels to many poor countries of the developing world was not the misery or the extensive poverty, but the happiness and the hope that survived despite it. We saw not only scenes of hunger and suffering, but also moments of community, compassion, trust, and laughter. We saw people coming together to protect one another, sharing what little they had, celebrating with a smile, music, or dance the small pleasures of the world.

We don't mean to glorify poverty. We know from working alongside people in countries like India, Brazil, Ghana, and Nicaragua that poverty is bitter, destructive, crippling, and brutal. But in rural areas, urban slums, and shantytowns, the poor reach out and help one another, and this spirit of generosity is the difference between life and death. These people have something valuable to teach us. When we stop competing against one another and choose instead to cooperate, we strengthen the community to which each one of us belongs.

We soon found that our observations were not unique, but shared by many human rights workers who had also spent time overseas. They too had gone for work, to help lay the foundations for a brighter future, and they too found inspiration and happiness unlike anything they had ever known at home. Like us, they discovered they had a lot to learn from different cultures, important lessons about what it means to live a fulfilling life, and how to do it.

Looking back, we know we were in search of an elusive idea we call the Me to We philosophy. Truthfully, there was never a single instant when everything magically became clear. Instead there was an evolution in understanding, an accumulation of small instances. Witnessing moments of joy as we interacted with people around the world we were inspired to ask ourselves what it was that brought happiness. As reaching out to others began to transform our lives in positive ways, we began to understand how the decision to lend a hand to someone in need leaves everyone better off. As we began to see it transform the lives of others in the same way, we came to see that we were discovering a way of life more powerful than we had ever imagined.

In this chapter we would like to share with you the defining moments in our journey towards a different way of life, moments in which we glimpsed a powerful alternative in action. Coming face-to-face with the unfamiliar can sometimes help to put things in perspective, and this was certainly the case for us. Volunteering in far corners of the world, spending time far away from cars, one-bedroom condos, and the glare of television screens helped us like nothing else to understand the power of community, and appreciate the true value of gratitude, empathy, and happiness. Our classroom would stretch from the African plains to the slums of India to the mountains of Ecuador, where a group of serendipitous events forever changed our views about life, setting us on the path from Me to We.

BACK TO THE FUTURE

In 1998, we returned to India with a ragtag group of kids, aged twelve to seventeen from across North America, so they could see firsthand the horrors of child labor. They saw child slaves making flip flops—a staple of any kids' outfits back home—by dipping their bare hands into highly toxic glue and smearing it on the rubber sole to attach it to the shoe. Our group helped build a school on the outskirts of Calcutta, working side by side with Indian children. And they opened their eyes to a world outside the comforts of North America.

For us, this trip was an experiment of sorts. We wanted to see if we could duplicate our first response in others. Could exposing North American children to the horrors and wonders of this part of the world create a spark that would send them home to empower others? Would it transform their perspective on their own lives, and lead them to look at happiness in a different way? Would they empathize with these children just as we had, and feel moved to action? We were also answering a challenge, first issued to Craig by that human rights worker in Dhaka two years earlier, to go back and tell others that it wasn't fair that children lived in these conditions. We didn't just want to tell others that volunteering could change their lives; we wanted to show them how.

This time around we had chaperones. We had cases of water and first-aid kits that rivalled the ones our mother made when we first went to South Asia and Thailand. But even though we were well stocked, we weren't prepared for the level of emotional support we would need to provide. Seeing child slaves is very disturbing and harrowing. Many in our group were devastated.

The trip was eye-opening for everyone and near its end, all the young people had a chance to reflect on what it had meant. We recalled the first night we had arrived. We had all gone into the markets of Delhi, so those who had not been to Asia before could experience its energy, and also see its hardship and poverty. They were simply overwhelmed by it all—the surging bodies, the people begging for money, the smell of sewage. Walking home, passing under a low bridge, we came across entire families of homeless people, seeking a bit of concrete to sleep on for the night. We literally had to step over bodies as we found our way through the darkness.

The poverty was worse than anything our young companions had ever imagined. Back in the hotel room, a deep gloom settled over the group, and those who had not been to Asia before broke down crying. Spending time in this environment moves a person to care about humanity. We had to be very strong for this group. We had seen all this before, but the others had not. Our job was to make the group understand and help them figure out what to do next.

That evening, our group spent hours talking about what we had all witnessed. Gently, we encouraged everyone to talk about the difficult feelings that day's discoveries had inspired. Sitting together in a circle as everyone had a chance to speak, we all began to realize that none of us was alone in our struggle to cope with our reactions.

Drawing on our experiences in the developing world, we suggested that while the emotions we were all confronting were incredibly painful, they could also be important in helping us to move forward. We could all agree that we had seen things that should never be allowed to happen. Now, what could we do about it? Together, we began to brainstorm ways we could all help to alleviate the suffering we had seen. As we encouraged group members to focus on what they could do instead of what they couldn't, a sense of determination replaced the previous gloom. Instead of despair, these young people began to feel a call to action.

Amid all of the challenges we witnessed during that trip, there were moments of hope and inspiration. In Delhi, we returned to Mukti Ashram, the rehabilitation center for child slaves. We were warmly embraced by the volunteers there, who were grateful that Free The Children had raised funds to build another similar center. We were hoping to see Nagashir, but were told he had left that day to share his story throughout the villages around Delhi. Disappointed that we wouldn't get to meet, the members of our group heard firsthand the stories of other children who had been bonded laborers in the carpet industry. The tales were very hard for some of the young people to hear. Many cried throughout the presentations. As we were standing there, we heard someone say, "Nagashir."

There, standing in the distance, was the child laborer who had courageously told his story at the press conference during Craig's last visit. The two embraced. Nagashir now worked full-time traveling through the rural areas near his village, visiting families, showing his scars, and telling his story. He did it to warn others of the false promises of the middlemen who frequent the villages and try to entice parents into letting their young children work in carpet factories. Nagashir had discovered that his calling was to do all he could to save other children from the abuse and exploitation that he himself had been forced to endure. In sharing his story he helped to prevent other such tragedies and also to continue his own healing process. Through his work, he could ensure that some good would come out of his own horrific experiences. Hearing his story, our group excitedly began to discuss what we too could do to help.

This first group trip marked a crucial stage in our lives and work. Returning to Asia with other young people, we saw that just like us, our young companions were moved by what they were witnessing. We saw that we weren't alone in being affected by this kind of experience, and we watched firsthand as other young people's lives changed for the better as they became committed to making a difference. We watched despair turn to determination, and looked on as they too found a new sense of purpose and direction, and took action to help others. We came to see that the experience of helping others could have a powerful impact on the lives of anyone ready to reach out.

This one trip became the first of many. That first group of young people returned home with their lives transformed. Almost twenty years later, some of them are still involved in human rights work. We accomplished what we had hoped: these young people had come to see their lives and happiness in a new way. They were enlightened ambassadors who would take these stories back to North America and educate others.

It was the beginning of overseas trips for thousands of young people that we would lead in the ensuing years. Although all of them would be eye-opening, few had more of an impact on our own thinking than one special trip to build schools in South America.

VOTING YOURSELF OFF THE CONTINENT

High in the mountains of Ecuador, far from the shopping malls and the showbiz of North America, we were participants in a bizarre series of events that opened our eyes to some interesting new ideas. Against all expectations, these came about by means of an elderly woman with a strong set of lungs, a past participant on a hit TV show, and a unique challenge that ultimately turned out to be a blessing in disguise.

We had been to Ecuador before with an Oprah Winfrey film crew to document the building of schools she had helped fund for the Puruhae people, who like many indigenous groups around the world were subjected to slave-like serfdom on their own land. On this trip, we were bringing sixteen young people, almost all from across North America, to help build a school. Free The Children builds schools in the most marginalized regions of the world, and this community, like that of the Maasai, is locked in a daily uphill struggle for survival. In the 1960s, the Puruhae people won their freedom, but not before the best farm land had been claimed by their previous masters, the *hacienda* owners. The only farms left to them were located in Ecuador's rugged highlands.

It's a rough life. At such a high altitude, the climate is extreme and unforgiving: the howling winds scratch the skin, the heavy winter snows sap strength from the strongest legs, and the scorching summer heat pounds the earth with cruel intent. It's amazing anything manages to survive at all. Locals seeking protection from the harsh elements bury their homes five to ten feet underground, with just enough room to squeeze in and out, leaving a patchwork landscape of rooftops.

This was the scene that greeted us as we headed up the mountains to build our school. It made for a difficult journey, to say the least. After many days filled with gruelling treks, and the unfamiliar sounds of Spanish and Quechua, the local languages, we were amazed to encounter a fellow *gringo*, another foreigner. When we saw him, our curiosity was immediately aroused. We went over to strike up a conversation, asking the obvious question: "What are you doing here?"

Not inclined to give us an answer, he instead asked us what *we* were doing there. When we explained that we had come to build a school, he relaxed. "Well" he said, "at least you're not here looking for me." Seeing our confusion, he continued, "For a second there, I thought you were journalists." After pausing for a moment, he continued, "I was a participant in the first-ever season of *Survivor*, one of the last people to get voted off the island. It was the beginning of the reality-television craze, and for a while the paparazzi wouldn't leave me alone."

Surviving *Survivor*

Later that evening, warmed by a blazing campfire, our new friend explained how he had been chosen to participate in what is now an infamous TV show, but was then unknown. He was dropped off on a tropical Malaysian island and left to compete against fifteen others for a million-dollar prize. The winner would be the one who could last the longest in the wild. At the start of the show, the contestants were divided into two tribes, who competed against each other in a series of gruelling challenges. Each week, island residents gathered together to oust one of their own. Suddenly, personal failure meant being "voted off the island." Team success wasn't applauded; it was attacked. Just as the teams learned to work well together toward a goal, they were broken apart, and teammates were realigned to compete against each other. People schemed to remain on the island, and lying, broken promises, and scandalous betrayals replaced cooperation and civility.

Far from being repulsed, the public devoured *Survivor*. Ratings went through the roof, and it spawned all kinds of copycats. People loved it because it was "reality" television—they identified with the ruthless competition they witnessed.

At the end of the show, our companion had returned to the United States and to fame and fortune. A modeling agency quickly signed him and he received offers to appear in well-paying commercials. He even dated another *Survivor* participant. Everywhere he went he came to be known as "the guy from *Survivor*."

Gradually, though, a new reality dawned on him. He had become trapped in *Survivor*—not the role, but the constant rivalry it stood for. He felt that life in the Western world was just as competitive and brutal as the television series. All of the opportunities that came his way had hidden costs. Instead of feeling worry-free, he felt like he was back on the island. Relationships were treated like commodities—opportunities to get ahead. He could never let down his guard and be himself.

In the end he did what no one expected. He voted himself "off the island"—of North America. Without telling a soul, he visited his travel agent. He was searching for a place with no TV and no crazy journalists. On his agent's advice, he bought a one-way ticket to South America, and then flew to Quito, Ecuador. He then took a bus into the mountains as far as it would take him, and then he bought a donkey—yes, a donkey— and rode it even higher into the mountains. Finally, he began to walk. For most of a year, he traveled from one small village to another. All his possessions were in one backpack. He carried no money and, most of the time, no food. He ate and slept only when strangers opened their doors and shared their homes. Although he had never before had so few material possessions, he began to experience a happiness greater than any he had ever known.

Just like we had, many people asked him what a *gringo* was doing so far from home. What answer could he give? Even *he* didn't fully understand why he was on the move. And he couldn't possibly explain *Survivor* to people living in the mountains of Ecuador. All he could tell them was that he had learned a great deal from his journey, that he was thankful for their kindness.

Truthfully, he had learned much since leaving North America. As he accepted food and shelter from some of the most marginalized people on earth, he was amazed at how different the local culture was from his own. It seemed to him that the fewer possessions people owned, the more they shared. Instead of the win-at-all costs competition he had left behind, he found that all he really wanted or needed was a caring community to which he could belong. He wanted to be a part of a culture where people didn't plot to edge him out, but instead valued and respected each other's natural gifts. As he traveled about the Ecuadorian countryside, witnessing the desperate, he found purpose and meaning in his own life. In remote areas, he began to encounter those who were working in partnership with villagers to bring clean water and schools to poor communities. He wanted to help, and he began to lend a hand whenever he could.

Sitting around that fire and listening to his story, we wondered if we weren't ignoring the lessons learned by other societies. As much as we loved North America, perhaps it was time to open our eyes a little wider to other ways of life. During the next few weeks, we saw many examples of what our *Survivor* friend had described to us, enlightening lessons in community support and cooperation. As we set to work, there was one crucial lesson ahead, one that would help us appreciate just how important our fellow gringo's insights were.

What's a *Minga*?

In Ecuador, the mountain passes are treacherous. The roads wind down from high peaks to the valleys far below in an infinite maze. They are a lifeline to the outside world, the sole means of communication. In harvest season, which this was, these roads are the only way the harvest gets to market. And this was our challenge. Mules with the harvest were going down, our supplies were coming up. We needed lumber and cement mix if we were to finish on time, yet we were facing a traffic jam of sorts. A traffic jam of mules, to be precise. As our group of young people set to work, it became obvious that construction was running far behind schedule and time was running out. Our return tickets were booked, and we were afraid we would have to leave without finishing the school.

Unsure what to do, we went to speak with the village chief, the oldest woman in the community. We found her at home in her simple hut. With the help of a translator, we explained our problem. To our surprise, she told us in Quechua, "No problem, I'll just call a *minga*." Oblivious to our puzzled looks, she headed for the door. More confused than ever, we just watched her leave. We exchanged worried glances, hoping we hadn't offended her. After taking only a few steps out from her low door, she stopped suddenly. Although we couldn't see her face, we heard her voice as she shouted at the top of her lungs, "Tomorrow... there will be a... *minga*."

And that was it. Neither of us had any idea what had just happened. Her words had had no apparent effect that we could see. People working close by had barely looked up and no one had stopped what he or she was doing.

Masking our disappointment, we thanked the chief and went back to tell our eager team of volunteers we probably wouldn't finish our school after all. Understandably, everyone was upset. We all went to sleep that night dejected, feeling sorry for both ourselves and our team. We had failed.

When we awoke the next day we couldn't believe our eyes. Hundreds of people milled about in the village square. Where had they come from? Men had left their fields in peak harvest, women carried babies on their backs, children stared up at us with bright eyes and rosy cheeks. They had come to build the school! This huge crowd had come from miles around. Many of the children lived too far from the school to attend class, but they had come just the same. They asked for nothing in return, and even brought food to share with the rest of us. In a matter of hours, they did what would have taken us days, if not weeks, to accomplish. After taking part in a lively celebration to inaugurate the completion of the new school, as quietly as they came, the community departed. That was a *minga*. Of course, our group of young volunteers was ecstatic. One North American youth after another began telling us that this was the most special event they had ever been a part of! Amazed how everyone had pitched in to help at exactly the right moment, our group was incredibly excited and eager to know what had just happened. So were we. Though we were thankful beyond imagination, we still didn't get it. And so once again, we sought out the village elder.

We found her in her hut, as before, and she explained that a *minga* was basically a call to action. Roughly translated it means, 'a community coming together to work for the benefit of all.' Upon hearing the word, people stop everything for individual gain, no matter how important, to come together for the collective good. Our translator struggled to explain this concept, and finally asked us whether we knew of an English word for *minga*. We were dumbfounded. But the English language has hundreds of thousands of words, there had to be a word. It couldn't be volunteer work, you can do that alone. Mission work, perhaps? No, that didn't fit either. The closest we got was to compare a *minga* to a barn-raising, but how many barns do you see going up in downtown New York? Again, we were at a loss. Stretching our brains, we came up with something we thought might fit. A *minga* is like a riot, but for good. It is a quiet riot where a community comes together in a collective effort. That's the closest we could get.

Linguists tell us that language reflects culture. The more words you have for something, the more important it is. Hence the old joke about why the Inuit have so many words for snow—there's a lot of snow! Take a moment to think about North American society. How many words do we have that revolve around money? Seriously—stop reading and count the number of words that come to mind: cash, credit, dollars, cents, checks, paychecks, down payments, banks, mortgages, the list goes on. What does that reflect about our society and its priorities? Why should it be so easy to talk about money, yet so hard for us to define something as beneficial as a *minga*?

Survivor and the *Minga*

One of the reasons why this one trip to Ecuador would eventually become such an important turning point in our lives was that it forced us to confront two radically different mentalities: the one that inspires *Survivor* and the one that creates the *minga*. These mentalities are polar opposites, miles apart.

On the one hand, the *Survivor* approach epitomizes the now rampant Me-mentality. A cut-throat competition, the show had one clearly defined goal, to single out one winner and many losers. The winner was the one who fought the meanest and deceived the best. A master manipulator, the winner's actions were driven by greed and a coveted million-dollar prize. Money was the bait. Lost friendships, a lack of community spirit, and an individualistic single-mindedness were the consequences, but that was considered acceptable.

While sociologists tell us that this me-focus has long been a concern in our individualistic culture, many people agree that it reached epic proportions in the 1980s, when excessive consumerism took on a whole new meaning. Think of the hit movie *Wall Street*, and Gordon Gekko's slogan "Greed is good!" As a culture, we have latched onto this motto and run with it, without looking either forward or back.

And we still haven't stopped running. The result is that we are rapidly losing touch with what defines us as a community, breaking our connection to something larger than ourselves. And children, not having grown up with anything different, don't feel the loss. In our singular pursuit of wealth and success, we ignore what we are letting go. We often take for granted our family and friends. It is becoming ever more difficult to recognize the rallying call that brings us together for the collective good.

As we learned, the *minga* is based on a very different set of values, grounded in the conviction that success is never a solitary pursuit. Unlike *Survivor*, it operates on an "all for one, one for all" basis. Caring, not competition, is the order of the day. The "We" is as important as the "Me."

MAKING CONNECTIONS, ASKING QUESTIONS

Experiencing a string of seemingly unconnected events in different parts of the world, we began to see a pattern emerging. In our exposure to diverse cultures and customs, we came to discern common themes that seemed to stretch across continents, connecting very different communities. Gratitude for simple blessings. Empathy for others, a willingness to feel for the less fortunate and reach out to help. Happiness and joy in small things. Strength in community.

Time and time again, many of the people with whom we worked had very little in the way of material possessions, yet expressed a sense of happiness more powerful than anything we had experienced. As we worked together, we began to share in their joy, and we learned that this wasn't just true of us personally, but of the many who accompanied us on our trips.

Helping others was enriching our lives in ways we never would have imagined, yet it was also challenging us to reexamine our assumptions about the ingredients of a fulfilling life. Our experiences among the Puruhea people of Ecuador, the Maasai of Africa, and the peoples of South Asia and many other places around the world brought home the truth that we had a lot to learn about life and how to live it.

START NOW!

- Open your journal and describe the times when you have felt truly fulfilled and happy. These magical moments may have happened years ago, days ago, or just five minutes ago.

- Ask yourself:

  - » When was the last time I was able to forget my worries?

  - » When was the last time I laughed so hard it hurt?

  - » What is the most thoughtful gift anyone has ever given me?

- Why are these some of your best memories? Did they make you feel grateful? Did they connect you to something bigger? Did they teach you new lessons?

- Use your answers to create your very own recipe for moving closer to your happiest state!

TAKE ANOTHER LOOK!

How many kids in North America grumble about having to go to school? How many parents worry about helping their children with last-minute assignments? Whether our school days begin tomorrow or are long behind us, we need to remember that millions of children in developing countries will never see the inside of a classroom. In North America many of us are fortunate to have the opportunity to learn, but the quality of education that students receive can greatly vary between schools. Quality education is a right, both for students here and in the rest of our global community—it's time to make it a priority.

- There are 45,024 shopping centers in the United States and 37,100 secondary schools.[1]

- Almost 80 percent of undergraduate students in the U.S. work 30 hours a week while attending school, yet the average student who borrowed money to finance state or private college will have a median debt of 17,400 (public school, $15,500; private, 19,400).[2]

▸ Almost one in five of the world's children is not attending school.[3]

LIVING ME TO WE

1. **Learn with youth.** Children typically spend six to eight hours in the classroom each day. Do you know what they're learning? Join a parent-teacher association or meet with the principal. Does your school have a community-based service program? Does the curriculum include character education and global citizenship learning?

2. **Create a new family tradition.** As you raise your own family, carry on old traditions and create new ones. Challenge yourself to cultivate a family tradition that will provide learning and laughter for years to come. What about an annual camping trip, a road trip, or a weekend spent volunteering together?

3. **Adopt a village.** Come together with others in your workplace, faith group, or school to support a community and build a school overseas. You can build a classroom and transform the lives of children for generations to come. Through Me to We's international volunteer trips, you can even help in the construction process.

My Story

ARCHBISHOP DESMOND TUTU

When I was just a small boy, I was sitting in a South African ghetto township, maybe thinking that I didn't count for too much. But I soon learned that each one of us is a glorious original and has the capacity to be God's special partner. At a tender age I discovered that it isn't doing spectacular things that makes you remarkable in the eyes of God, but instead, it is when you light just one candle to dispel a little bit of darkness that you are doing something tremendous. And if, as a global people, we put all the little bits of good together, we will overwhelm the world. In my young life, there were many key individuals and moments that embodied this spirit for me, but three stand out most of all in my mind and I want to share them with you.

As a child I had tuberculosis and went to hospital for nearly two years. During that time, about once a week, Trevor Huddleston, a priest who became a renowned anti-apartheid activist, came to see me. He lived in Sophiatown, as a member of a religious community, and he shared the life of the poor and deprived people. I wasn't aware of it then, but his actions made a strong impression on me. In South Africa it was unusual to see a white person caring for a black township urchin like myself, and his example contributed to a lack of bitterness I felt against whites. Trevor touched my life and I'm so very grateful, because he was just a tremendous champion of goodness and the dispossessed. Through small examples of his humanity he cared for others and for me; he was one of the first strong examples for me of someone working those little bits of goodness.

Now, the next experience was one I shared with many black South African kids. Because of the turbulence in my own country, I was greatly influenced by the heroic struggles of African-American sportspeople, Jackie Robinson especially. I think that I was about nine years of age when I picked up a tattered copy of *Ebony* magazine that happened to describe how Jackie broke into Major League Baseball to play with the Brooklyn Dodgers. I didn't know baseball from ping-pong, but I could read, and here was the story of a man who had overcome enormous adversity and suffered tremendous abuse for simply following his dreams. His example, the way he had made it against all those odds, made me feel several inches taller. He convinced me early on, though he never knew it, that we mustn't aim to do spectacular things—but maybe we *will* do spectacular things. Instead, Jackie Robinson left the impression that we should do what we can, because in the end, by standing up to that bully, you win a little victory for righteousness and you give just one other person the example to stand up for truth. It may not get a banner headline, but it makes a difference. It made a difference to me.

Above all, however, my greatest mentor through everyday examples of goodness was my mother. And while I have said to many, many people that I resemble her physically (she, too, was stumpy and had a large nose you see), it has been one of my missions in life also to resemble her in her spirit, in her generosity and in her concern for others. Our family was of modest means, but my mother was a wonderful cook and she never cooked just enough for our hungry family. She always imagined that there might be somebody who would come to our house and who would need to be fed. This was her way of showing her great heart and empathy for other human beings, through her wonderful cooking! And her generosity extended to far more than food. She almost instinctively had a way of comforting whoever was getting the worst side of an argument, and with good intention my wife aptly called her the Comforter of the Afflicted.

Unlike Trevor Huddleston and Jackie Robinson, my mother was a quiet hero whose greatest achievements were never obvious to the outside world. But through each of them, I have learned to trust in the love and the example of others; that we are made for interdependence. I have also learned that we are made different, capable of our own special miracles, not in order to be separated, but to know of our need for each other. True happiness is not when you are there only for "number one," but when you are there for others. It is a very simple but powerful truth that leadership and greatness emerge when one is able to follow the Lord's words and to, figuratively perhaps, wash the feet of others. Since that day when I was sitting in a South African ghetto township feeling sorry for myself, I have been blessed more each day with the happiness that springs from this truth.

CHAPTER FIVE

THE ME TO WE
PHILOSOPHY TAKES SHAPE

---

*"The voyage of discovery is not in seeking new landscapes
but in having new eyes."*

—Marcel Proust

Our search for the best way to live would eventually take us not only out into the world, but also deep inside our own hearts, leading us to reexamine our own innermost beliefs and convictions. We knew that the questions we were struggling with were far from new, and we were eager to learn all we could from the collective wisdom passed down through the ages. We hoped the world's greatest texts could shed some light on what we were witnessing and experiencing in our lives and work: a movement away from a mentality of Me toward a community of We.

Having grown up attending church, the Bible was one of the first books we picked up. We soon found that when you turn to almost any page, story after story, parable after parable, and the teachings in psalms, prayers and songs all carry the same central message of service, community, and humankind's highest calling.

The biblical stories of Jesus' service to others are almost endless. He performed powerful miracles, brought acceptance and hope to the poor and disenfranchised, and provided guidance and inspiration to countless others. As word about His healing power spread, people who were ill, lame, and blind began to seek Him out in huge numbers, and He treated all with kindness. Reading Luke 10:25-37, we lingered over the story of the Good Samaritan. We read Jesus' words on the importance of neighborly love, and of his praise for the selfless compassion shown to a traveler attacked by robbers. Such teachings and actions were obviously guided by love, kindness, and compassion.

We discovered that this same message of service to others was apparent among the many different faiths we encountered during our travels. We spent time in temples, mosques, and monasteries around the world, sitting with religious leaders for long hours asking question after question. In Stockholm, Sweden we had the privilege of spending five days with the Dalai Lama, who advised us all to "practice compassion in every day life." As he has written, "though we may find differences in philosophical views and rites, the essential message of all religions is very much the same. They all advocate love, compassion, and forgiveness."[1]

When, through our work with Free The Children, we traveled to the Middle East, we discovered that a tradition of service to others is central to the Islamic faith. Sitting on the intricately woven carpets sharing meals with Bedouin elders, or entering great mosques as guests, we learned about Islamic traditions. We learned that one of the pillars of Islam is charity, or *zakat*, which requires Muslims to give away a certain percentage of their belongings to the poor as well as make regular donations to those in need. This act of charity and helping others is a means of purifying one's soul of selfishness. We also found that the Qur'an contains many passages that encourage social service: "Have you ever seen a human being who contradicts the essence of faith? That is the person who pushes the orphan aside and does not promote feeding the needy."[2] Helping others is believed to yield rewards—for example, the love and care of other people—and Allah's blessing on the Day of Judgment.

In Israel, we engaged in a religious pilgrimage, making our way to the holy Christian sites but also visiting the Wailing Wall, and praying with Jewish elders. We watched as slips of paper were inserted into the cracks of this famous wall in the hope that the prayers they contained would be carried to God above. We learned that the Mishna, which contains the compilation of Jewish Oral Law along with the commentaries of philosophers and rabbis, clearly outlines the importance of helping others. On one hand faith says, "If I am not for myself, who will be for me?" The next line follows, "If I am only for myself, what am I?"[3] The Torah, which reveals God's instructions to the Jewish people, clearly mandates responding to the needs of the poor and the infirm, be they Jews, strangers, or even enemies. Doing *tzedakah*, or righteous deeds, is part of one's obligation to help repair the world.[4]

As we explored the religions of the world during our travels, we found that every faith we encountered shares the basic tenets of service, compassion, and love for others. Whether learning about Hinduism and making a pilgrimage to the holy city of Varanasi, or learning about First Nations spirituality in sweat lodges and sacred ceremonies, or learning about Sikhism or Jainism, we came to recognize these common elements. The basic idea can be summed up in a simple phrase: "Do unto others as you wish them to do unto you." The following is a list of world religions and their interpretations:[5]

WORLD RELIGIONS AND THE ETHICS OF RECIPROCITY

- **Hinduism:** "This is the sum of duty: do not to others what would cause pain if done to you." (Mahabaratha 5:1517)

- **Taoism:** "Regard your neighbor's gain as your own gain, and your neighbor's loss as your own loss." (T'ai Shang Kan Ying P'ien, 213–218)

- **Indigenous spirituality:** "We are as much alive as we keep the earth alive." (Chief Dan George)

- **Buddhism:** "Treat not others in ways that you yourself would find hurtful." (Udana-Varga 5.18)

- **Islam:** "Not one of you truly believes until you wish for others what you wish for yourself." (The Prophet Muhammad, Hadith)

- **Judaism:** "What is hateful to you, do not do to your neighbor. This is the whole Torah; all the rest is commentary." (Hillel, Talmud, Shabbat 31a)

- **Christianity:** "In everything, do to others as you would have them do to you; for this is the law and the prophets." (Jesus, Matthew 7:12)

- **Sikhism:** "I am a stranger to no one; and no one is a stranger to me. Indeed, I am a friend to all." (Guru Granth Sahib, p. 1299)

- **Baha'i Faith:** "Lay not on any soul a load that you would not wish to be laid upon you, and desire not for anyone the things you would not desire for yourself." (Baha'u'liah, Gleanings)

- **Jainism:** "One should treat all creatures in the world as one would like to be treated." (Mahavira, Sutravitanga)

- **Unitarianism:** "We affirm and promote respect for the interdependence of all existence of which we are a part." (Unitarian principle)

- **Zoroastrianism:** "Do not unto others what is injurious to yourself." (Shayast-na-Shayast 13.29)

MARC'S REFLECTIONS

While studying at Harvard, I discovered that an emphasis on service to others is found not only in the religious texts and oral teachings of faith groups, but also in the works of the great philosophers who have contemplated the meaning of life, happiness, and the importance of community.

Founded three hundred and seventy years ago, Harvard is the oldest university in the United States and has the largest academic library in the world. Early mornings I would enter the colossal Widener Library through the main hallways, past the circulation desk, to where the great minds of the past rested on dusty beds. Heading to a solitary desk with armful after armful of books, I would carefully leaf through the pages. Reading the thoughts of history's great thinkers, I began to see that their ancient ideas had not lost their relevance with the passing of time. Their ideas would prove to be important in laying the philosophical background of our emerging ideas.

Plato and Aristotle

Immersed in the wisdom of ancient Greece, I learned from Plato that life is best lived in the pursuit of knowledge. In his view, such knowledge is best gained not in isolation, but instead through simple dialogue, in exchanging opinions with others. In essence, he argued that we are all able to find some share of happiness so long as we are willing to listen to others and to consider their ideas carefully. He believed that open dialogue is what allows us to work with others and to think up new and better ideas for pursuing and understanding meaning in life. Similarly, Aristotle argued in his book titled *Politics* that human beings develop virtue (that is, develop their excellence as human beings) through social interaction. I came to see this as a call to exchange ideas, and to remember the value of asking questions. These ideas highlight the importance of respecting others and creating social connections.

Lao Tzu

Reading on, I discovered that a life of service is not just a Western idea. Among the earliest philosophies to emphasize the importance of helping others is that of the sixth century B.C. philosopher Lao Tzu, reputed author of the *Tao Te Ching* (the way and its power). The Tao, in its wisdom, teaches that we should be humble and peaceful in our dealings with others. It teaches that we learn best when we listen to and respect the wisdom of others, and that we contribute to individual and community harmony when we avoid contention by striving to resolve issues through peaceful means. One cannot, therefore, strictly distinguish between what is good for oneself and what is good for one's community—these "goods" are one and the same.

Al-Farabi

Immersed in the wisdom of the ancient Islamic world, I read of the great philosopher Al-Farabi, who explained that the best citizens actively seek to develop the best virtues of others, and in so doing become more virtuous themselves. He argued that in helping others, people become the best that they can be, and suggested that the community as a whole benefits.

Adam Smith

Imagine my surprise when I found that even capitalism, one of the world's most Me-centered philosophies, is not bereft of notions of community. At first, I found it hard to believe that these ideas could be shared by Adam Smith, the Scottish economist touted as the father of the free market. In his famous work, *An Inquiry into the Nature and Causes of the Wealth of Nations*, Smith encourages people to follow their individual self-interest. But what is less well known about Smith is that he wrote his economic work as part of a larger work on moral philosophy. In *Theory of Moral Sentiments*, he suggested that although human beings tend to be self-interested, they benefit from cooperative interaction to secure their individual and collective well-being. These two seeming extremes—free market competition and moral cooperation—actually go together.[6] Basically, Smith argued that if we hope to enrich ourselves (both economically and morally) we must constantly be aware that we are rooted in communities.

FROM THEORY TO PRACTICE

We soon found that it wasn't just the great thinkers that provided inspiration. As we explored the realm of ideas, we began to see them coming to life all around us. If we had initially recognized these ideas in our travels, as we continued our journey we began to see that the spirit of We is alive in the hearts and minds of people everywhere.

While we continued to learn from other cultures, we also began to recognize new aspects of life at home. We began to pay attention to the small acts of kindness we witnessed and experienced every day, and to learn about the efforts of others to reach out with new appreciation. We became interested in studying caring and kindness, and the more we looked for it, the more we found.

Gradually, we began to understand that what we were dealing with stretched far beyond any single culture or tradition. We began to see that it wasn't about any one particular practice, but more about a mindset. Most importantly, we began to realize that some of the answers we sought had been right under our noses all along.

A Grandmother's Wisdom

As we struggled to make sense of our newfound ideas and experiences, we eventually found ourselves seeking advice from none other than our grandmother. At ninety years of age, our grandmother is truly a remarkable woman, with a small frame and a big loving smile.

To this day, she is loved by everyone who knows her. She is a vibrant woman with a sparkle in her eyes; she still reads the newspaper every morning to keep up with current events. She lives alone in her home of many years, taking care of not only herself, but also everyone else in the neighborhood. When someone is sick, she is the first to visit with a friendly word or a pot of soup. They, in turn, all keep a watchful eye on her. Sitting in her kitchen, we asked her the same questions we asked many others. We wanted to hear her reflections on happiness and the meaning of life. "I think that we are all born for a purpose," she said. "We have a job to do in our own place and time in history."

She told us that one of the most important lessons she learned in her many years is "being rich is a state of mind." She has seen countless people go through life "obsessed about collecting things that eventually sit in a closet or collect dust in a garage." She explained that if she had done this, no one would care about her today. She would be alone, with only a house full of trinkets to keep her company. She told us, "Measure your success by the number of hugs you give and smiles you bring to people's faces." Our grandmother has never had a lot of money, but in that moment we came to realize that she is the richest person we know.

Speaking with our grandmother opened our eyes to the reality that We is a way of life, one as central to our well-being at home as abroad. We finally began to understand that all of the instances of caring, kindness, and community we had seen and experienced added up to more than a string of random, isolated cases. We began to see the pattern, to recognize the common element underlying all of these diverse ideas and practices we had been exposed to. Eventually, we came to call it the Me to We philosophy.

Moving from Me to We

It's easy to get into the habit of Me thinking. In our current culture, we constantly receive messages that success is about the things we have. At practically every turn we're bombarded with advertising that links our self-worth to our net worth and before we know it, it sinks in. It's easy to get caught up in the materialism that we're surrounded by, and to devote the lion's share of our attention and energy to surrounding ourselves with the best, latest, most expensive stuff.

From an early age, youth face intense pressure to be "cool," and fitting in often means having the latest designer clothes, music, and sports equipment. Popularity often goes hand in hand with being able to follow the latest trends. Not being able to keep up seems like the end of the world, a worst-case scenario for any young person's social life at an age when friends have incredible influence.

As parents, we're eager to ensure that our children enjoy high self-esteem; we want them to fit in and get a good start on getting ahead in life. We yearn to provide them with the things they want. We encourage them to pursue sports, drama, music, or anything that helps them develop their talents. We're proud when they do well. We feel the pressure to provide them with all of the opportunities we can, and we soon find that many of them cost money. It's all too easy to begin to equate caring for our children with what we can spend on them.

Meanwhile, even school breeds competition. Students often talk about the "Bell Curve," which suggests teachers should only hand out only a certain number of A's, B's and C's. Instead of being encouraged to work together to make sure everyone learns, students are encouraged to compete against each other for the best marks. And the best marks guarantee entrance to the most prestigious school. We're taught that getting ahead means looking out for ourselves.

In an increasingly competitive work environment, this same mentality dominates. We face off for jobs, promotions, and those stunning corner offices with the windows overlooking the park. Many of us have struggled to survive eras of downsizing and cutbacks, and at a time in which "job security" sometimes seems laughable, the pressure to "look out for number one" is often intense. Keeping up doesn't even seem to be good enough; we must constantly strive to keep ahead. Our primary preoccupation becomes Me.

Creating an Awareness of We

To move beyond the mentality of Me, we first need to become aware of We—the world outside of ourselves and everyone in it. In making this transition we can draw on four important skills, innate abilities that we all possess and can develop with practice. We all have the power to begin seeing the world differently, we just need to get used to using it!

The first of these skills is gratitude. Through gratitude we can shift from a mindset of scarcity, in which nothing we have or do is ever enough, to a perspective of abundance, in which we can appreciate all of the blessings we have in our lives and gain an awareness of what we have to share.

Empathy is a second skill that we can develop in order to expand our awareness of We. A way of building upon our emotional connection with others at the deepest level, empathy is what allows us to look into the eyes of another—a family member, friend, neighbor, colleague or a complete stranger—and see ourselves. It is what allows us to understand how much we share with those around us, no matter how large the differences may be in our circumstances, lifestyle and outlook. When we develop our ability to empathize with others and apply it as broadly as possible, this becomes one of the most profound ways to connect us to our common humanity.

A redefinition of happiness is a third way that we can begin to develop our awareness of We. This is what can help us to understand that happiness is not about having the most toys—whether teddy bears, smartphones or summer homes—but about what we choose to do in our lives. In reconsidering the meaning of this concept, we can begin to make a distinction between two very different experiences—the short-lived thrill that our possessions can bring, and the deep, profound sense of contentment to be found in living a life of meaning and purpose, aligning our goals with our values, and leaving a legacy we can be proud of.

The fourth way we can further develop our awareness of We is through redefining our notion of community. In our current culture, our ideas of community are often extraordinarily narrow, and our compassion reserved for a select few with whom we believe we have much in common. In redefining community, we can begin to create a more useful, meaningful, and inclusive vision. We can begin to expand our spheres of compassion, and recognize the unifying goals that benefit us all, those basic things we all desire no matter who we are. Best of all, we can work toward these goals, and achieve them.

Reaching Out

As we develop our awareness of We in all of its different manifestations, we begin to recognize opportunities to live Me to We in daily life. Hurrying to work, we spot the child who is wandering around lost. Caught in rush hour, we see the motorist struggling with a flat tire. Instead of remaining oblivious to those in need, we recognize these situations as opportunities to help. Instead of turning away, we take action. We may start with simple things. Words of encouragement for someone who is feeling down. Help with yard work for an elderly neighbor. A hot meal for a person who can not afford one. A few hours a week at a local shelter. Instead of complaining that the park is dirty, we spend a few hours cleaning it up. Instead of bemoaning an issue, we write a letter to our congressperson. We may start out slowly, but gradually helping becomes a habit.

As our commitment grows, living Me to We impacts the way we make decisions, and affects the decisions we make. It becomes a litmus test that we can use when confronted with life's choices. Instead of asking, "How will my choices affect me?" we begin to ask ourselves, "How will the choice I am making in my life affect our family? Our community? Our nation? Our world?" As we gain confidence, the choices we make may become larger, affecting more and more of our most important decisions.

The best part is that as we begin to make Me to We choices and transform our lives as well as the lives of those around us for the better, we have even more incentive to expand our efforts. As individuals, we can begin to enjoy improvements in our physical and emotional health as well as our spiritual well-being, and we can watch our overall quality of life soar. Meanwhile, the choices we make strengthen our families, neighborhoods, and workplaces, as well as our country and the global community as a whole. Instead of facing a situation where our gain is someone else's loss and vice versa, we can reap the rewards of a win-win scenario where we all end up better off. In living Me to We, we can create a better life and a better world, all at the same time.

Creating a Connection

As we live Me to We, we create a sense of connection that helps to not only sustain this transformation, but also to amplify it. Often when people choose to reach out to others, they may attend a fundraiser or become involved in a charity. A good deed is done, but without the profound, life-changing shift in perspective that will propel everyone forward in a deeper way on a larger scale. The true power of the Me to We philosophy lies not only in the kinds of activities we undertake and the fact that we undertake them, but also in the sense of connection with others that it enables us to create.

This sense of connection is what truly makes the spirit of Me to We come alive, allowing us to connect with the people we are serving and working with side by side. It is what allows us to rejoice in our collective experiences and accomplishments, and to share in the progress we make with each step we take. It is powerful enough to span continents, uniting all of us in North America with people around the world. It can span countries, cities, neighborhoods, workplaces and families. It can be experienced in remote locations and amid unfamiliar cultures, and it can be experienced here at home wherever we spend time in our everyday lives. Ultimately, it is this sense of connection that allows us to experience our own transformation from Me to We, and to share our inspiration with others so that they can begin their own journey. It is this sense of connection that enables Me to We to thrive and grow, allowing personal decisions to create a world of change.

No one is ever too old or too young to begin the move from Me to We.

Consider Kim, Mike and Brenda. On the surface, they seem to have little in common with each other. Kim was just eleven years old, starting out in life; Mike was a middle-aged cab driver; and Brenda was a hairdresser who never finished high school. They all live in communities in different parts of North America and in many respects, all three lead very ordinary lives. Despite their differences, all three live the Me to We philosophy in their own unique ways.

Kim's Story: Doing the "Write" Thing

For eleven-year-old Kim, home was a spacious house in an affluent suburb. Life revolved around sports, school activities, and friends. This was her world. She had never really thought about what life was like for kids outside her neighborhood, much less in other countries.

Then, one day in class, her teacher started talking about children's rights. She explained how many children around the world don't have access to basic necessities like food, clean water, shelter and education, and are forced to work in horrible conditions. Kim was shocked. A short time later, at recess, she was hit by a chilling thought. "I realized that the clothes I was wearing might have been made by a girl my age. It totally burst my bubble," she explained.

Kim made up her mind to start a petition in support of children's rights. In large bold letters she wrote: "Please sign below if you would like to stop child labor." Fighting back her fears, she began approaching everyone she knew—and a lot of people she didn't—telling them about the horrible reality of child labor and asking them to sign on the dotted line. With each person who signed her petition, Kim felt more hopeful. She wasn't the only person who wanted to protect children's rights.

Day after day, Kim's petition grew longer. She did more research on petition-writing and refined her approach, including more information on the impact of child labor for prospective supporters to read. It might have been a short-lived project, but she was determined. Whenever she considered giving up, she remembered her outrage and the thought of a girl like herself, working day and night at a sewing machine to make clothes for other kids living far away across the oceans. Months passed, then years, and Kim was even more committed to her goal than ever. Everyone kept expecting that she would give up. But she didn't.

Four years later, at fifteen years of age, Kim had collected an astounding six thousand signatures!

Her petition was presented to the government. It was a powerful learning process. Kim learned a lot about children's rights, especially the rights of girls around the world, and her petition helped to educate and inspire others to take action on child labor. The media attention her petition received helped to alert many people to an important issue.

In the years to come, Kim would become an active speaker, fundraiser, and volunteer, raising awareness about the issues facing children around the world. Today, her goal is to inspire others as she was inspired that day in sixth grade when she first felt the pull to reach out and help others.

Mike's Story: Hacking Emissions

For most of us, a taxicab seems like an unlikely place for an epiphany. A few minutes before his fateful moment, Mike Kehoe would have agreed. But now he might not. Unloading a family's luggage from the back of his cab one day, Mike was standing in the thick fog of his car's exhaust when an outspoken eight-year-old passenger piped up, "What are you taxi-drivers doing to my environment?" He stood there at a loss for words. He didn't have an answer for the youngster, at least not a good one.

It was just a one-second comment in a long and hectic shift, but this child's question lodged in Mike's brain. Thinking about it, he knew the answer to this question only too well. What were taxi drivers doing? Not much. The environment was not something he spent a lot of time thinking about.

At first, Mike told himself that pollution was simply too big for someone like him to tackle. After all, he needed to make a living, right? He wasn't about to trade his cab for a bicycle. But over the next few weeks he started thinking about what he could do rather than what he couldn't. And when he shared his ideas with a few other drivers, he found that they were as interested as he now was in working toward a cleaner environment.

It wasn't long before Mike decided to learn more about what drivers, personally, could do to become more environmentally friendly. When he felt he had learned enough, he offered seminars to cabdrivers around his city on how to cut emissions and reduce idling. He didn't know how people would react, but he decided to try his best. To his amazement, the local government, environmental groups, and other drivers were all interested in coming on board.

Today, Mike is still driving his cab and leading educational seminars. Although he never planned on becoming an "activist," he is amazed by what he has managed to do. When we talked to him recently, he was smiling from ear to ear when he said, "Now I know people like me can be ambassadors for the environment." The huge smile on his face made it clear that he was not only happy, but positively ecstatic about being able to educate other drivers and to help to reduce his industry's environmental impact.

Brenda's Story: She's A "Do" Gooder

Brenda Wittle is another person with a smile bright enough to light up a room. A hairdresser by trade, and a people expert by nature, she quickly makes you feel like you have known her forever. Always ready to lend an ear if you want to talk, Brenda's also the first to be there with a shoulder to cry on when you need support.

When we met Brenda she was very busy working two jobs, but until a few years ago she had spent all of her time working as a hairdresser. All that changed, though, when several of her clients quietly confided they had been diagnosed with cancer. Although she wanted to help, Brenda wasn't sure how. But like most good entrepreneurs, she thought she should use what she already had: people skills and hands that could fix even the worst bed head. Like Mike and Kim, she trained herself for the next steps she would take. She learned how to fit wigs and spent long hours researching post-chemotherapy skin care. As she started to help her clients, she realized she had found her calling.

As Brenda's expertise grew, so did her reputation. Cancer survivors sought her out, and soon she was spending as much time counseling as cutting hair. Brenda felt she needed more know-how, so she went back to school to study community service work. This was a huge step for someone who hadn't finished high school, and who had a family and a job. But she got her diploma.

Today, Brenda works part-time cutting hair to pay the bills, and then spends the rest of her time teaching other hairdressers and aestheticians how to care for people with cancer. Although her days are long, she told us she sleeps better at night knowing she is helping those around her. "Being able to bring a smile to someone's face when she is in a time of trouble is my satisfaction," she says.

Reading about Kim, Mike and Brenda, you may be thinking "That's nice, but what's the big deal?" After all, they've all done a few good deeds, but not the kind that make the evening news. But that's exactly our point. The only real similarity between them is that they are all pretty normal people. Their stories are not filled with massive relief operations, huge fundraising campaigns, or examples of super-human bravery; they simply recognized a problem and did something to help. For Kim, that problem was child labor; for Brenda, it was the impact of a cruel disease; for Mike it was pollution. The fact is, it could have been any number of issues that got them moving and it could have been any one of us who took action. They all found themselves confronted with a challenge, and used this opportunity to make the shift from Me to We.

What people like Kim, Mike, and Brenda have in common is they have listened to the voice inside them when it spoke. They asked the questions that some people are afraid to. They took actions even though they were worried they wouldn't succeed. They tried. Our experiences over the past decade have convinced us that they are not alone.

We have come understand that these three people and the thousands of others like them are all part of a larger shift from Me to We, one that is transforming our world in profound ways, even as you read this. Although this shift unites people from all walks of life all around globe, there's nothing exotic about it. It can start wherever you are, because ultimately it's about how you decide to live your everyday life. Many of those who are creating this shift have families, most have day-jobs, and almost all make time for pesky chores like weeding the garden, taking out the recycling, and cleaning the house. Chances are, you might even know one of these people yourself: it could be a person in your community, a member of your family, or, perhaps, even yourself.

I AM ONLY ONE PERSON. WHAT DIFFERENCE CAN I MAKE?

Several years ago, we attended an international conference with thousands of other young people to learn about the challenges facing our world and to brainstorm possible solutions. By the last day, we were feeling inspired, but we were also secretly worried that we wouldn't really be able to have an impact.

During the closing ceremonies, the auditorium was plunged into darkness, as one young person stood in the center holding a lit candle. Quietly at first she called out the one question that was on everyone's mind:

"I am only one person. What difference can I make?"

She then turned to the four people closest to her and lit the candles they held. Those four then walked out to the corners of the auditorium, repeated the question, and each lit the candles of four people they met there. This same question echoed from person to person, from group to group, and on each occasion the flame was passed forward. In this way, the light spread, until every candle was lit, and the vast room was aglow in a sea of light.

This simple yet powerful exercise helped us understand that all personal and social change comes about in this way, through simple questions and humble beginnings. It helped us to see that even the smallest actions can have powerful impacts. Such is the power of Me to We.

START NOW!

- If someone asked you to describe your life philosophy in just a few sentences, could you do it? Take out your Me to We journal and give it a try. Ask yourself:

    » What is it in life that means the most to me? My family? My job? The environment?

    » What do I give priority to in my week?

    » Who has played an important role in shaping my life? A parent? A spiritual leader? A teacher?

    » What experiences have helped me to decide which things are most important to me? A trip abroad? A compelling book?

- Now think about the Me to We philosophy and list the way it is similar to ideas that have guided you in the past.

TAKE ANOTHER LOOK!

Every choice we make affects the environment. We have an impact whether driving to school or work, brushing our teeth, or cleaning the house. It's up to us to decide whether our impact will be big or small, positive or negative. Are we going to let the car idle? Are we going to let the water run? The choice is ours—and the world is waiting.

- In 2000, 9,500 hybrid cars were sold in the U.S.; in 2006 this rose to 254,545.[7]

- In 2005, Americans produced approximately 4.5 pounds of waste per person each day.[8]

- Every year in the U.S., more than 28 million gallons of oil from things like driving cars or heating homes run off streets and driveways into our lakes and rivers. This is more than double the amount of the Exxon Valdez oil spill.[9]

LIVING ME TO WE

1. **Make the switch.** Compact fluorescent bulbs use half as much energy as incandescent bulbs. By switching your home and office lighting, you'll save money, reduce pollution, and help the environment. It's not every day we face a win-win-win situation!

2. **Buy fresh.** In a globalizing world, many of us now enjoy access to food that is better traveled than we are. But when our fruits and vegetables log miles to get to our table, the environment pays a hefty price. Save energy and savor the flavor by buying locally—and support farmers in your community at the same time.

3. **Use a cup that shows you care.** Purchase an environmentally friendly, reusable coffee mug. Sure it's a small action, but your love affair with fair-trade organic Arabica could save 365 disposable cups a year from being thrown in the garbage.

My Story

RICHARD GERE

Besides His Holiness the Dalai Lama, my father is the most spontaneously generous, responsible, and committed person I've known. I didn't quite understand what that meant when I was a kid, and I certainly didn't understand the special quality of spontaneity that my father embodied. I found it a bit confusing that he would respond to anyone who would call the house with a problem. He was gone a lot doing that. I probably was a bit jealous that he was off helping almost anyone who would call. Later in life I've come to value and understand it more.

When I met His Holiness the Dalai Lama, I had been practicing Buddhism for some time. The wisdom aspect of it attracted me enormously: the exploration of the nature of the mind and the evaluation of reality, what we take to be reality. But the compassion side of it was something I hadn't worked on very much, although I think I had an instinctive feeling of empathy for other people's suffering and my own. Meeting the Dalai Lama and the Tibetan community and feeling this incredibly textured and deep exploration of the mind, along with their extraordinary ability to explain, communicate, and activate compassion—a deep, emotional, and unmistakable connection with all beings—had an enormous impact on me. It still does.

Very quickly when I began to be a student of His Holiness and other fine Tibetan teachers, I realized that true spiritual work is much more all-inclusive than I had originally thought. It rejects nothing of life. It is beyond any idea of religion, beyond any concepts. It really is universal in the sense of heart and mind encompassing universal connections, universal responsibility—beginning to have an actual taste of what is called relative *bodhicitta*, which we would probably call genuine compassion. I began to see that nothing I can do will bring me happiness unless it includes happiness for others. Whenever I suffer, it's really because I have discounted the other. The flip side of that is being genuinely concerned for the other. When this happens, we have a true spontaneous moment of satisfaction, happiness, and joy. There is no question in my mind that everything of value that I have done in my life since then has been informed by at least trying to engage that deep sense of open-hearted commitment to relieving the suffering of others that I witnessed in my father and His Holiness the Dalai Lama.

I am continually amazed that the simplest thought, the simplest action has waves that, when motivated properly, resonate with joy and creativity throughout the universe. I see this when I get a card or a letter or meet someone on the street who was deeply moved by something that I had been involved in. We have a photograph here by Nicky Vreeland of a monk from Rato Monastery. I knew we were helping a lot of people by starting a health insurance plan in the Tibetan refugee community, but for some reason I never personalized it. Then Nicky gave me this photograph of this young monk who had not been able to walk properly his whole life. He was able to have an operation through the insurance plan that we put together and now he's walking and able to sit properly in meditation without pain. We now have this photograph of this wonderfully happy, joyous, young monk. I didn't do it specifically for him, but these are the waves that go out. As soon as any well-motivated thought or action begins, those waves do have a positive effect on the world.

I think that prayer is a really important part of any worthwhile activity—spending quiet time with oneself, literally praying, whatever your idea of praying is, but talking to your purest heart. Life for us is a given and we very much exaggerate our place in it, but I think the universe is more or less indifferent as to what our lives mean. It is our job to make life meaningful; no one can do that for us. We start by looking at our own hearts and by sympathetically realizing that all beings are just like us. We all want to experience happiness and avoid suffering. That is true of animals, insects, those we take to be our enemies, and all beings in all universes. From this point of view there's no enemy, there are only brothers and sisters. We also need to realize how a simple thing like walking in a room and thinking, genuinely from the heart, "I wish you happiness" to everyone in a room, how transformative and healing that is, not only for them, but also for ourselves

There are a lot of good people doing wonderful things in the world and as soon as you talk to your own heart and genuinely wish to do good, the opportunities arise almost immediately. They don't have to be big. These waves can start quite small but as they go through the universe, they can have an enormous effect. Even stopping ourselves from getting angry in a moment when we normally would have gotten angry without thinking—that moment of catching ourselves and perhaps even turning that into love and patience and compassion—that has an enormous effect on us and everything around us.

In dealing with difficult people, you have to start from a place where you don't have the answers. I think we genuinely have to listen and to see that everyone has a story and a point of view. There are no true monsters; we're all redeemable and we're all in this together. I'm constantly amazed by the number of times that the people I may be diametrically opposed to politically, who seem to have a totally different world view from mine, someone I may even take to be an enemy, how often we end up doing extraordinary things together to help the world. You have to be able to quiet yourself a little bit to be able to listen. Then something effective and positive can happen.

CHAPTER SIX

BENEFITS FOR ME

"It is one of the beautiful compensations of this life that no one can sincerely try to help another without helping himself."

—Ralph Waldo Emerson

If Me to We is so wonderful, why hasn't everyone already embraced this new approach to life? Research tells us that the answer is both incredibly complex and astonishingly simple: fear. The fact is we're afraid. A lot of us have grown up with the belief that if we don't look out for ourselves, no one else will. We worry that notions of community are idealistic tales from the past, irrelevant in our cut-throat, mile-a-minute world. We're concerned that if we think in terms of We, then Me will suffer. The good news is that nothing could be farther from the truth.

If you consider yourself a hard nut to crack, we'll help change your mind. As we walk you through our collected research, sharing our stories and armchair conversations with eminent psychologists, we hope to get your feet moving on the journey from Me to We. Your first steps will be both surprising and enlightening as you discover that in living Me to We you stand to improve your emotional and physical health, strengthen your faith, and access a higher quality of life.

For many people, moments of enlightenment come in unexpected forms. On our continuing journey to understand the value and importance of the Me to We philosophy, one such moment arrived courtesy of an unlikely teacher. During our first trip to Kenya, the trip of our rainstorm dance, we leapt at the chance to explore one of the most beautiful ecosystems on our planet, the savannah plains of the Maasai Mara.

We encountered many kinds of wildlife on this trip, but it was the zebra that helped us to see life in a different way.

Huddled around the campfire one crisp morning, still brushing the sleep from our eyes, we both found ourselves scanning the horizon. As suburban boys unused to being preyed upon, a few weeks in Kenya had done nothing to ease fears that, while we were watching our breakfast on the fire, something else was watching us in exactly the same way. Even under the safe watch of the local *askari* (Swahili for guard), we were nervous about lions and leopards.

As we scrutinized the skyline, we saw a herd of zebra grazing off in the distance. On the open savannah zebra are among the easiest animals to spot, because their bold black and white suits stand out against the muted browns, greens, and deep reds of the Kenyan landscape. We wondered if evolution had played a cruel joke on this creature by making it an easy fast-food lunch for sharp-eyed lions and leopards able to spot them miles off.

When we asked an *askari* about this, he just laughed. "The zebra can tell you the answer," he said with a smile. We had grown accustomed to indirect answers, parables and riddles from our wise Maasai friends, but this response had us more confused than usual. Evidently deciding that we weren't as smart as he had guessed, the *askari* chose to give us a clue to his cryptic comment. "Look!" he said, as he pointed to the zebra-filled horizon, "Now imagine that you are a lion, which zebra would you want to eat?"

We looked over the herd, trying to pick out just one. But all we saw was a swirling mass of black and white—it was impossible to see where one zebra ended and the next began. This was like trying to pick one snowflake out in a snowstorm! After a few frustrating minutes we admitted defeat. "Right!" said the triumphant *askari*. "When there are many zebras, one zebra is not so easy to see." Smiling, we began to understand the lesson. Far from being a curse, a zebra's stripes are excellent camouflage—but only when surrounded by other zebras. Talk about safety in numbers!

Apparently, we were not the only Westerners slow to understand the ways of the zebra. Several years before our visit, a group of European scientists had arrived in the area eager to study these fascinating creatures. Enlisting the help of local trackers they set off into the Mara, determined to start their research. However, like us, the scientists found it difficult to tell one zebra from the next. After a while, they devised a simple solution: a blot of red paint on the rump of each zebra under study would ease identification. As in life, in science you often learn more from your mistakes than from your successes—and this was no exception. All the zebra they marked were quickly singled out by their predators and killed. For weeks the "experts" were mystified, until finally they did what they should have done first: they asked their guides. The *askaris* promptly told the "wise" scientists that by adding that touch of red paint, they had foiled the herd's collective camouflage and made it much easier for the predators to distinguish one zebra from the other. No longer able to blend in, the marked zebra never stood a chance.

As our guide stirred the coffee pot, he concluded his story, "The zebra belong together. One zebra is weak, many are powerful. That is their strength. It is our strength too. Like the zebra, the Maasai people act together. No person can live alone; it is not possible. We need each other. When we come together we are powerful. We too belong together."

It isn't only the Maasai who find strength in numbers. This wisdom is as old as humanity. Aesop, the Greek storyteller who lived many moons ago, put this wisdom to words when he wrote in the *Four Oxen and the Lion*, "united we stand, divided we fall." It is as simple as that; community is in our bones. Human beings are not particularly strong, stealthy or fast, but our ability to cooperate with others—to think, communicate and work together—makes us powerful. America's own early history is full of examples that illustrate this point. In 1621, the Mayflower II landed at Plymouth Rock. Coming ashore, the Pilgrims had high hopes but little real idea of what to expect. All they knew was that the first years would be the hardest. Winters were harsh, illness was a constant threat, and environmental conditions were unfamiliar. All that was certain was uncertainty. It would take all of their collective faith, ingenuity and strength to persevere. Time would tell if they would survive the challenge.

People had good reason to pull together. Settlements were tight-knit communities of mutual support. Without the collective strength of the community, individual settlers would have had difficulty providing for their families. The community shared knowledge, responsibilities, and leadership. Cooperation was the keystone in their system of community-based labor that built houses, raised barns for livestock, and laid the foundations of America's first villages. This in turn laid the foundations for the communities, the cities and the country that exists today. Community spirit started it all. Cooperation was the foundation of society—it was our *minga*. Though our communities have changed since then, we cannot afford to forget the lessons of the past.

> *One of the signs of passing youth is the birth of a sense of*
> *fellowship with other human beings as we take our place*
> *among them.*
>
> —Virginia Woolf

Our research has convinced us that we need each other—not only to survive, but to thrive. Human beings are social creatures. Relationships with others are important not only when it comes to getting things done; they are essential for living a life that has meaning and value. No two individuals have done more to persuade us of this fact than Dr. Dan Dolderman and Dr. Dorothea Gaither, two psychologists who work in very different spheres. Dr. Dolderman is a professor of social psychology at the University of Toronto. He works in the field of positive psychology, exploring how to cultivate strengths that help individuals to realize their full potential and live fulfilling lives. Dr. Gaither is a clinical psychologist who has spent years in private practice, guiding deeply depressed and often suicidal patients through their long healing process. As we sat with them, in Dr. Dolderman's case in the rare moments between classes, and in Dr. Gaither's case after long days spent seeing patients, we did our best to soak up their experience and wisdom. We were to learn that helping others has important benefits for all of us as individuals, and to become convinced that the Me to We philosophy can help all of us to flourish.

In the Halls of Academia

Tucked away in the halls of academia, Dr. Dolderman's office is as warm and welcoming as his personality. Sitting in on his classes and meeting in his office, his affable nature and quick sense of humor guided our discussion toward a number of important points.

Dr. Dolderman's first lesson to us was that belonging is a fundamental human need. This sounds obvious, but it goes deeper than you might think. Research has shown that feeling like we belong, and that we are accepted and valued by other people, is essential to our well-being.[1] Satisfying this need takes more than just frequent contact with other people: it involves creating a sense of connection through deep, meaningful relationships. As Dr. Dolderman pointed out, our need to belong plays itself out at three important levels, each serving a somewhat different function. First, we need to feel a sense of self-worth and to not feel lonely, which we achieve primarily through our most intimate relationships. Second, we need to feel a deep sense of interconnectedness with others, which we achieve through our network of friendships and family relationships. And finally, we need to identify with important social groups. This group-level belonging underlies our identification with teams, clubs, and other organizations; it manifests itself as pride in one's community or nation; and it may even be met through a more universal sense of being part of the human race, or for some people, by being part of the living world. These three levels of belonging reflect three ways we think about ourselves, from the private, to the interpersonal to the collective, and each is essential to our emotional health and well-being.

An impressive body of research suggests that it is the love and care we receive in our earliest years that gives us our basic sense of emotional security. This follows us throughout the rest of our lives, influencing our personalities, self-esteem, and confidence, and affecting how we behave in friendships and relationships. In short, it is through the love of others that we learn whether the world is a good, safe place, or an uncertain and scary one; whether we are worthwhile, valuable people, or incompetent and worthless. To illustrate, studies of children who have grown up in extraordinarily challenging circumstances show that the rare children who are able to thrive in these environments are those who have strong and supportive social connections. It has been shown that even one helping hand can make a difference. Support can come from a parent, a coach, a mentor, a friend or even an older sibling; the important thing is that someone else cares. A single person can be the deciding factor in a child's future.

As Dr. Dolderman spoke to us, it seemed foolish that we were asking questions that for many of us seem so apparent. But, as he pointed out, it is often life's simple truths that go unnoticed and it is up to science to point out the obvious: we need to receive love early and in abundance in order to develop into functioning adults. At any age, social acceptance is necessary and crucial.

Sitting in Dr. Gaither's office, we felt like telling her about our worries and concerns, much as her patients do every day. We were looking to her for guidance, and we were not disappointed. She explained that in her many years of work, she has witnessed the benefits of reaching out time and time again. Smiling, she told us that she has yet to meet a suicidal volunteer. "They don't kill themselves on Monday when they know they will be needed at their volunteer placement on Tuesday," she explained. Feeling needed by others gives meaning to the life of people who are deeply depressed. They feel a community connection, an obligation to others, and a reason to continue living. Helping others, it would seem, can literally be a lifesaver.

There is perhaps no better way to feel socially useful than to make a positive difference in another person's life. Elation and accomplishment, feelings we experience when we reach out to others, are powerful positive antidotes to negative feelings of inadequacy, incompetence and helplessness. In our discussion, Dr. Gaither referred to an interview with Yale professor Lowell Lewin, quoting his words: "When you're a helper, your self-concept improves. You are somebody. You are worthwhile. And there's nothing more exhilarating than that."[2]

Whether we're depressed or not, reaching out to others who face difficult circumstances can help us keep our own difficulties in perspective. Through this experience, we may even come to see our problems in a new light, as we realize that some of our own day-to-day dramas aren't really so dramatic after all. If all of us spent time with someone who lacked food and shelter, or who suffered from spousal abuse or a serious illness, we would be less likely to get upset about the long line at the grocery store, the rude driver that just passed us, or our inability to make it to the gym every day. When we reach out, we begin to understand just how trivial so many everyday problems really are.

When we asked Dr. Gaither about happiness, she encouraged us to take a look at a *Time* magazine poll conducted by SRBI Public Affairs in 2004, which explored what brings Americans the most happiness in life. Tellingly, an overwhelming majority placed their loved ones right at the top of the list. When it came to "major sources of happiness" the top nine answers were similar: relationship with children 77 percent, friends and friendships 76 percent, contributing to the lives of others 75 percent, relationship with spouse/partner or love life 73 percent, degree of control over one's life and destiny 66 percent, leisure activities 64 percent, relationship with parents 63 percent, religious or spiritual life and worship 62 percent, holiday periods such as Christmas and New Year's 50 percent.[3]

While psychologists like Dr. Dolderman and Dr. Gaither could no doubt cite many more interesting studies to prove that humans are by nature social beings, does it really matter what such studies say? All of us have learned at some point in our lives that reaching out to others, being socially active and experiencing satisfying personal relationships *feels* good. When we reach out to others, we laugh, learn, and grow together and in innumerable ways we share positive emotional experiences.

The power of the Me to We philosophy resides in the way it strengthens our relationships not only with those closest to us, but also with the larger communities of which we are a part. In living this philosophy in our daily lives, we can satisfy our innate need for belonging, and improve not only our emotional health but also our physical and spiritual well-being.

PHYSICAL WELL-BEING

We all know what it takes to keep our hearts healthy. Outside of our emotional needs, we need to exercise, eat right, moderate our alcohol consumption, and replenish our bodies' batteries with plenty of sleep—easy as low-fat pie, right? Although these things are essential for overall health and longevity, there is an interesting story out of a little town called Roseto, in Pennsylvania, that caused medical researchers to realize that there's more to the issue then meets the eye. Researchers examining heart-attack rates looked at the town's mortality records beginning in 1955, and noted that the people of the community broke virtually every healthy living rule that exists. Compared to other Americans, they reflected a relatively high incidence of alcohol, red meat, and fatty food consumption, as well as an overall lack of exercise and dieting. However, despite all these risk factors, the residents of Roseto had a lower incidence of heart attacks than residents of comparable neighboring communities.

This doesn't mean that we should start throwing booze and T-bones into our morning health shake. Any of us who have seen the fast-food documentary *Super Size Me*, the story of Morgan Spurlock who ate only fast-food for a month, knows the consequences of eating such foods for any length of time. It can quite literally kill you. As it turns out, Roseto residents were healthy not *because* of their eating habits, but *despite* them.

After a little digging, the researchers began to suspect that the distinguishing factor was social support, noting that "the town was known for its close family and community ties and its low levels of social competitiveness." Sadly, over many years the "closely-knit mutually supportive social structure" started to fall apart, and, correspondingly, the good health enjoyed by the majority of its residents began to decline. When community cohesiveness fell apart, the prevalence of heart attacks neared the national average.[4] In other words, as the community bonds in Roseto disintegrated, the residents became more like the rest of America: isolated from one another and increasingly unhealthy. The bottom line? In an age when heart disease continues to be the number one killer in the United States, and 71.3 million Americans suffer from this ailment,[5] being part of a healthy vibrant community can give you not only a better quality of life—but also a longer one.

A wave of very interesting research that began in the mid-1970s solidifies this argument. Study after study has revealed a "dramatic decrease in health problems and death rates for people who are socially involved, compared to those who are isolated."[6] It has been found that social support networks protect against a range of illnesses from arthritis and tuberculosis to psychiatric illnesses, and that "people with few social ties had mortality rates two to five times higher than those with more ties."[7]

Meanwhile, it has also been found that volunteering provides people with increased "social contacts and stronger support networks," which make for "lower premature death rates, less heart disease, and fewer health risk factors."[8] In fact, a Government of Canada study argues that "the health benefits of social relationships may be as important as health risks such as smoking, physical inactivity, and high blood pressure."[9]

Recently, Dr. Allan Luks, a researcher at the U.S.-based Institute for the Advancement of Health, concluded that "helping others can truly be one of our most self-serving acts."[10] Luks has made a career out of examining the health benefits of helping others. He popularized the terms "Healthy Helping Phenomenon" (HHP) and "Helper's High" to represent the physical health effects of helping others.

The first stage of HHP is a physical high—a rush of good feeling caused by the sudden, powerful release of the body's natural painkillers, the endorphins. It is similar to the high that running and other high-intensity exercise can cause.[11] Phase two of the HHP is an equally beneficial sustained calmness, which relieves the distressed body from the cycle of tension, leading to a less taxing use of the body's function and allowing the immune system to restore itself and make the body healthy again.[12]

Interestingly, Luks found that it is the "process of helping, without regard to its outcome, that is the healing factor." Any type of good work will bring benefits! Positive emotions and attitudes of "trust, optimism, and happiness… are available through the act of helping… reinforcing feelings of commitment to something worthwhile, thus producing moments of joy and a lasting sense of optimism."[13]

Even *thinking* about helping others boosts our health. Psychologist Dr. David McClelland of Harvard University had a group of students watch a film about Mother Teresa's work in the slums of Calcutta. Sit and watch was all they did, but later tests revealed that students responded to the film physically, with an increase in immunoglobulin A, an antibody that defends against certain diseases.[14] If social involvement and volunteering were a drug, we'd be popping pills like there was no tomorrow.

A MESSAGE TO OUR ELDERS

As a senior in your community, you not only have a wealth of knowledge to share with others, but also stand to gain special benefits through social involvement. According to psychologists, "Although few studies have explicitly examined whether helping others increases longevity, sociologists note the ubiquity of giving to others, and studies show that individuals derive benefits from helping others, such as reduced distress and improved health. Moreover, volunteering has beneficial effects for volunteers, including improved physical and mental health. Even perceptions that are likely to be associated with giving, such as a sense of meaning, purpose, belonging, and mattering, have been shown to increase happiness and decrease depression".[15]

Not only has volunteering been linked to improved quality of life, stronger social networks, and a decrease in symptoms of depression among the elderly, it has even been linked to longevity itself.[16]

A 2003 study by researchers at the University of Michigan followed 423 older married adults for five years to see how giving versus receiving practical and emotional support affected longevity. And, you guessed it, those who helped others—providing support to friends, relatives, neighbors, and spouses—lived longer. Over the five-year period in which the study was conducted, people who helped others were significantly less likely to die than people who did not. Even after researchers took into account other variables, such as the age and health status of the adults, those who helped were more likely to stay alive. This was an important finding because it showed that people live longer because they give practical and emotional support, not that people offer support to others because they are healthier and as a result are more likely to live longer.[17] It was clearly the giving, not the receiving, of support that affected longevity.

FAITH/SPIRITUALITY

One of the greatest rewards of helping others is finding purpose and meaning in life, something integral to our personal understanding of faith and spirituality. Helping others leads us to rediscover our connection to the world, and in an age when many people are questioning their faith, charitable work provides renewed hope and belief. Although each of us interprets the meaning of faith in different ways, we have seen that no matter what faith you ascribe to, all of the world's major faiths emphasize the importance of helping others.

One often reads stories of people whose charitable deeds are motivated by their religious beliefs, and both the Aga Khan and former U.S. president Jimmy Carter immediately spring to mind. The Aga Khan Foundation organizes annual Partnership Walks, international walks for global solidarity that raise millions of dollars for poverty reduction around the world. Jimmy Carter lives his faith through his work with Habitat for Humanity. When homes are built through group service work, the new owners are handed the keys and a bible.

For the two of us, our awakening came in reverse order. Yes, we grew up attending church and learning the parables, but we never felt *really* connected to our faith. In wasn't until we began helping others that we unlocked the true meaning of what we had always been taught. Putting our passion into practice, we found our faith.

It was during our experiences volunteering that the familiar teachings came to life. During our visits to countries such as the Philippines and Nicaragua, we were amazed by actions taken by faith-based organizations to assist local populations. From the slums of Manila, to the mountains of Waslala, we found religious groups running soup kitchens, establishing shelters for street children, and running support groups for battered women. In these countries, practicing one's faith involves much more than simply attending a religious service. It means actively living the message to create community and networks of mutual support.

People ask us how we maintain hope when confronted with overwhelming human deprivation, the scourge of HIV/AIDS, and the devastation of war. We respond by saying that in doing the work we do, we can't help but have our faith renewed. It is often in the midst of suffering that we find the greatest virtue and human potential. We have seen teachers spending their own money to help at-risk students in America's urban centers, aid workers toiling to the point of exhaustion to care for desperate people in refugee camps, and mediators risking their lives to secure peace in the middle of war zones. Witnessing extraordinary acts of passion and courage stirs the deepest faith within one's soul—even those not motivated by religious beliefs can be filled with a renewed faith in humanity, a conviction that the world can be a better place, and the knowledge that peace and cooperation are worthy ideals.

One of our most memorable encounters with the power of faith occurred during an unforgettable school-building trip to Nicaragua. As we set to work in a remote region of this small Central American country, we began to hear whispered stories from locals of a benevolent secret society. We learned that its members were tireless advocates of the poor and disenfranchised, dedicated to working on their behalf. While their exploits were the stuff of legend, their identities were shrouded in mystery: the word was that they could be recognized only by a plain black ring worn on the left forefinger.

Was this a troop of modern-day Robin Hoods? Of course, we were intrigued. Try as we might, we never saw that tell-tale ring, so we spoke with someone who knew where to locate one of the members of this secret society and we set up a meeting. Our high expectations weren't disappointed.

An eloquent speaker of at least five languages, Father Carlos, a Catholic priest, remains to this day one of the most interesting individuals we have ever had the pleasure to meet. Originally from Brazil, he was groomed for leadership in the Church at a very young age. After completing his education at the Vatican, he returned to his native country to assume an important role in the church hierarchy. However, when he saw that the church's extensive land holdings could be better used to help the poor, he rallied supporters and organized a group to take possession of the unused lands in accordance with Brazilian law.

Instead of elevating their native son to the position of power for which he had been groomed, his superiors promptly shipped him and his group of renegade priests to Nicaragua, then the site of a fierce civil war between the Sandinistas and the contras.

It would have been difficult to find a more violent place. Although this posting had been intended as a punishment, it was, in fact, a blessing for Father Carlos and his followers. It gave them the opportunity to do what their faith had compelled them to do in Brazil: serve the poor.

The priests soon entered communities to offer medical training, education and religious support. They declared that their side was with the poor, no matter who controlled their village. Unfortunately, this position was highly unpopular with both warring factions. As Father Carlos explained it, the contras believed his group supported the Sandinistas, and the Sandinistas believed they supported the contras. The priests quickly became targets of violence.

With the traditional black robe and simple white collar now the subject of unwelcome attention, Father Carlos decided that he and his followers would need to adopt a new habit. They shed their usual clothing and began to dress as peasants. Now their only distinguishing feature was a simple ring carved from a black Brazilian rainforest nut, worn as a symbol of their marriage to the poor. Today, anyone wearing this ring is said to continue their mission of service to the poor. According to tradition, the rings can not be bought, only given.

Our initial meeting with Father Carlos was to be the beginning of a deep and lasting friendship. With his extensive knowledge of the area, he and a number of other priests guided us throughout our work in Nicaragua. Spending time with this extraordinary man, we gained tremendous respect for his work, as well as for his faith. He and his followers found themselves at odds with their church, yet they remained committed to their religious beliefs, expressing their devotion by serving the poor.

When it finally came time for us to leave the country, we were treated to a humbling surprise. Taking a small wooden box out of the drawer of his desk, Father Carlos opened it to reveal a bundle of purple cloth. Slowly and carefully, he removed two black rings and placed them in our hands. Honored and somewhat embarrassed, we tried them on; they fit perfectly. We hoped that we would be able to prove ourselves worthy of such a generous gift.

START NOW!

———

Living the Me to We philosophy doesn't just help everyone around you—reaching out to others can hold tremendous personal rewards.

▸ Take out your Me to We journal and jot down a few times you've set out to help others and have personally benefitted in the process.

▸ Now think to the future. What would you like to change in your own life? Are you interested in becoming healthier? Or finding that special someone? Ask yourself:

    » How can I achieve my goals in ways that benefit others? Could I become healthier by running a marathon for a cause? Could I find that special someone through volunteering?

    » How can I develop new skills while helping others at the same time? If you yearn to paint or draw, you could teach these skills to kids. If you are determined to become a good cook, you could make a meal for a sick neighbor—you'll nurture a new skill while nurturing someone else.

TAKE ANOTHER LOOK!

———

There are a lot of lonely people in our world today. Loneliness can strike anyone, from a new coworker to an immigrant who has just moved to the neighborhood to the woman on the street corner. Take the time to reach out. Chat with a new neighbor or say hi to someone who is homeless—a little effort can make all the difference.

▸ The U.S. National Runaway Safeline has reunited more than 10,000 runaways with their families.[18]

▸ In 2003, more than 10.5 million people in the Unites States aged sixty-five and older were living alone.[19]

▸ By 2010, an estimated 25 million children around the world will be orphaned by HIV/AIDS.[20]

LIVING ME TO WE

1. **Fill a pocket full of love.** If you are a poet, a teller of jokes, or simply a kind-hearted soul, sneak a note into the pocket of a loved one who hasn't been feeling well lately. It is guaranteed to bring a smile to his or her face... especially if it doesn't go through the wash!

2. **Pay a friendly visit.** Stop by a nursing home and spend time with someone who has no family nearby. Listen closely—storytelling is therapy for the loneliest soul.

3. **Step up against AIDS.** Put on your running shoes and get moving! Participating in a charity marathon or walkathon is a great way to meet new people, get involved in the fight against HIV/AIDS and other causes, and improve your health all at the same time!

My Story

JANE GOODALL

Sometimes I think, How did the little girl who was born in England to a family with very little money come to be traveling around the world doing such fulfilling work? When I do, it makes me think of a fable my mother used to read to me and my sister when we were little, about the birds coming together to have a competition to see who could fly the highest. The eagle is sure he will win and majestically, with those great, strong wings he flies higher and higher, and gradually the other birds get tired and start drifting back to the ground. Finally, even the eagle can go no higher, but that's all right, because he looks down and sees all the other birds below him. At least that's what he thinks, but hiding in the feathers on his back is a little wren, and she takes off and flies highest of all.

I love this story because it is very symbolic for me. If we think of our life as an effort to fly always just a little bit higher and reach a goal that's just a little bit beyond our reach, we are faced with a question: How high can any of us go by ourselves? We all need our own eagle, a special life mentor, and when I look back and think of all the people who have helped me on my wren's flight, I think of my mother most of all. My whole life history is punctuated by fond recollections of her guiding hand.

As a child, I grew up in a family of women (my father was off fighting in World War II), with my mother and her two sisters, my grandmother, and my sister. My bold passion for animals was supported by my mother. It was a testament to her gentle and accepting character that she didn't freak out even when I took a whole handful of earthworms to bed with me. She just gently said, "Jane, if you leave them here, they'll die. They need the earth." So, only one and a half, I toddled back with them into the garden.

She supported so many childhood escapades to do with animals. So it was natural that when I read Edgar Rice Burroughs's *Tarzan of the Apes*, fell in love with Tarzan, and then was extremely jealous of Tarzan's Jane, my mother was one of the few people to encourage me to follow my ridiculous dream of going to Africa to live with animals. Everyone else laughed at me, but she said, "Jane, if you really want something and work hard and you take advantage of opportunity and you never,

ever give up, you will find a way." And when I left school—I didn't go to university because we couldn't afford it—I did her bidding, which was to become a secretary so I could get a job in Africa.

Almost by miracle, my mother's wisdom proved true. Through a series of serendipitous events, I met Louis Leakey, the renowned archeologist, and was offered an amazing opportunity to go to Tanzania's Gombe National Park on the romantic-sounding shores of Lake Tanganyika. My mission was to try to learn about chimpanzees, but there were problems, most of all that I was a female. Back then, in 1957, a female going to live on her own in the African bush was unthinkable. The British government, which ruled Tanzania at the time, proved obstinate. It denied permission for two to three months, but finally it said, "Well, all right, but she must have a companion." So who volunteered to come? My mother, of course.

So when I started my work in Tanzania, my remarkable mother was there for me when I got done in the evening. Although I loved it, those early days in the forest, when the chimpanzees would run away from me, were frustrating beyond belief. If I failed, I knew that everyone would say, "We told you so!" So I was becoming increasingly agitated, and having my mother there to give me support and reassure me was great. But even more than that, my mother, by simply being herself, established a wonderful relationship with all the local people. She started a little clinic, handed out aspirins, band-aids, and things of that sort, like a nurse or doctor, though she wasn't one. The same kindness that she showed to me when I was a little girl, she showed to others. And in the months, years, and decades to follow, even after my mother passed away, I formed many trusting friendships because of her gentle and generous ways. Even today, I still feel her very much around me, and throughout my entire life she was my greatest inspiration and support.

CHAPTER SEVEN

BENEFITS FOR WE

"No man is an island, entire of itself; every man is a piece of the continent, a part of the main."

—John Donne

Have you ever seen a thousand dollars in pennies? Two thousand?

It's enough to make most accountants weep, but not Victor Li. The arrival of $1,000 in pennies makes our accountant break out into a huge smile. He knows this is the currency we deal in. Every jar of pennies represents a community of young people coming together for a cause. Jars and jars of pennies arrive at our headquarters more than twenty years after Free The Children launched its first penny drive.

Yet we were surprised when we started to receive penny jars from Monarch Park Collegiate, a school that most in Toronto thought of as needing, rather than giving, help. It certainly wasn't the type of school that would raise money for poor kids halfway around the world. At least that's what everyone said.

At Monarch Park, more than seventy languages are spoken among students from one hundred different countries, including Sudan, Somalia, China, Vietnam, India, Mexico, and Guatemala. It is perhaps the most racially diverse school in the world. And with so much diversity, it was difficult to unite students.

Sally Hakim was terrified to start ninth grade at Monarch Park. She knew it by reputation and had heard that gangs roamed the halls and violence was a daily occurrence. True or not true, Sally resolved to make the best of a bad situation and got involved at the school. By eleventh grade, she'd been elected student council president. One of her first acts was to invite a volunteer from Free The Children to speak to the students.

Free The Children has a team of gifted speakers who make presentations throughout North America and the world. These young people share stories about their own experiences traveling overseas, talk about the situation of young people in developing countries, and discuss how North American students can make a difference.

So when Cheryl Perera picked up the microphone at Monarch Park, the crowd wasn't sure what to expect. Neither was Sally Hakim.

Cheryl, eighteen, didn't look much older than the students, but since joining Free The Children in 2002, she had traveled to Nicaragua, Ecuador, and Macedonia. During more than five thousand hours of volunteer work, she had spoken to more than twenty thousand young people.

Cheryl mesmerized the students with stories about the conditions in which children throughout the world must live. The audience was stunned silent; some were moved to tears and others were angered. Many more wanted to know what they could do to make real change. Instead of returning to class work, teachers led discussions and asked the students if an inner-city school could really make a difference in the world. Some students thought no. Many said yes.

"Cheryl from Free The Children made a snowball and left us to begin to roll it," Sally Hakim says. "It was the little snowball that couldn't be stopped. Staff and students became one, together working towards the goal of building a school. Weekly coin collections were started. Food sales were held; clubs began fundraising; classes took on activities." The students formed a "global committee" and decided Monarch Park Collegiate would become a global school and focus on global issues.

On December 26, 2004, a tsunami struck Southeast Asia and Africa. The Monarch Park students flew into action. In just one week, they had raised enough money to cover $32,000 worth of medical supplies for the tsunami zone. Television cameras arrived at the school to record the students' generosity, which continued to swell. On top of that, before school let out for summer, they'd also raised $7,000 to build a classroom in Kenya.

Monarch Park is now working to sent twenty students to Kenya to build that school. As Sally Hakim says, rather than being "needy," the school has developed a spirit of giving. "Students have begun to realize that the ability to make a positive change is within each of us regardless of where we come from, what we did in the past, where we live, our race or nationality. None of this really matters. What does matter is that we act… not to help ourselves but to understand that the greatest joy comes from making a difference in the lives of others."

What happened at Monarch Park is the tip of the iceberg, as thousands of students around the world have adopted villages or committed themselves to building a school. It starts with pennies. The pennies fill a jar, then the jars fill our office. Our accountant smiles as the jars are dumped and the coins are counted.

When the counting is done, we contact one of our overseas coordinators. Peter Ruhiu is our project director in Kenya. After he gets the call, he can usually be found sitting under a tree with a group of women discussing the possibility of building a school for their children. Peter knows the outback of Kenya because his father was one of the first workers for the Kenya Wildlife Service. Although he jokes around and says he doesn't know anything about it, he actually knows how to read footprints and track animals. He also knows how to find a good place to build a school. Peter speaks with the women to learn their community needs. Next he meets with the men in the community. He ensures they know that girls must attend whatever schools Free The Children builds. That it has to be built near a water source, and that it must have a garden to provide food for lunch for the students. Peter walks over every inch of the community's land until they find the perfect plot. Once the school is built, then comes the time to hire a teacher and purchase resources and supplies. When the new school opens, students come from miles around, often walking long distances in order to attend class. It all starts with a few pennies.

Years and years of penny drives have taught us that our communities are stronger and more prosperous when we work for the greater good.

A COW BY ANY OTHER NAME

When Marc arrived to study at Oxford University, suitcases in hand and still a bit bewildered, he was handed three items. The keys to his college room. To be expected. A course list from which to choose his classes. Also to be expected. And what looked like a parking space for his cow. Not what he expected.

Marc was more than a bit confused; a devoted pedestrian who cared for the environment, he didn't require a parking space—least of all for a *cow*.

Finally, he asked his college porter what it meant. It really was a space for his cow. Not exactly a parking space, but a plot for pasturing.

The porter told him that many of the Oxford colleges have meadows or common spaces where, through an age-old tradition, students can graze their cows while they study. When Marc did some digging he found that common lands, like the famous Boston Common, now one of the oldest city parks in America, have played important roles in the history of Oxford as well as in the greater history of Western civilization. So what is so interesting and important about a few grazing cows? Why were these lands so important? Because their history is tied up in the shift from Me to We. At one extreme the commons symbolize anarchy, and at the other they serve as a shining example of community cohesiveness and collective responsibility. Here's how.

The We-Thinking Farmer

Hungry cows need to eat. And when you put them out to pasture they'll do just that. Eat. They won't stop, even if you ask them nicely. In a famous article called "The Tragedy of the Commons," published in the *Science* journal in 1968 this problem was dramatically illustrated by a man named Garrett Hardin. He asked that we "picture a pasture open to all," where local people are free to graze their animals as much as they wish. In this scenario, as long as there aren't too many hungry cows, and the farmers are mindful of one another's four-stomach beasts, then the land can support them virtually forever. No problems. If, however, each farmer acts out of short-sighted self-interest and continues to increase the number of pastured cows, the collective group will suffer as, mouthful by mouthful, the land is degraded to the point of collapse. The end result is that the system falls apart, *all* of the cows go hungry and *nobody* benefits but the vultures. This is Hardin's Tragedy of the Commons.

What does this mean for community? Simply, that while we don't have four stomachs or four legs, we all live in our own commons every day. The commons, of course, is a metaphor for our communities. Just as commons provide pastures from which cattle gain sustenance, our communities provide us with sustenance in other ways. If we take from our communities more than we give—overgrazing in ways that only humans can—we all stand to lose. If, however, we help our communities to flourish through proper care, we all gain together. The shift from Me to We lies at the heart of this second scenario.

At times, all it takes is a single person to determine which of these paths a community chooses. In *Better Together: Restoring the American Community* by Robert Putnam and Lewis M. Feldstein, there is a unique story that serves as a good introduction to the power of one We-thinking person to make a difference. In the early 1940s, Tupelo, Lee County, Mississippi, was one of the poorest communities in all America. The population was predominantly rural and involved in agriculture, and times were desperate.

One day, George Mclean, a newcomer to the community, had an idea. He calculated that by using the new technology of artificial insemination a single prize bull could quickly expand the county's population of milk-producing cows. This, he projected, would directly increase the farmers' income.

There was one very large catch: this bull cost a whopping $50,000, today's equivalent of about $600,000—a small fortune. Individually, there was no one in the town with this kind of capital. Nevertheless, he approached several local business owners and encouraged them to invest in a bull together, arguing that if farmers had more money in their pockets they would have more to spend in local shops.

In the initial year alone, it was estimated that the milk produced from cows sired by the wonder bull we call Don Juan, brought in around $1 million dollars (approximately $12 million in today's dollars). Within only ten years, Lee County, Mississippi, had become one the nation's greatest milk producing counties.[1] Tupelo's story, the story of the prize bull Don Juan, has become a model example of leadership, technological innovation, and above all community spirit. All because of one We-thinking farmer.

This is just one small example of how the Me to We philosophy can build community. It can work miracles, almost literally, but it works best if you already have a solid base to work from. And what is the basis for any strong community? You guessed it, family. When family life is vibrant and full, the Me to We philosophy has rich soil in which to take root.

THE FAMILY THAT EATS TOGETHER

Research shows that low family cohesion is associated with a range of problems, including greater depression in adolescents, increased attempted suicides and suicidal thoughts, substance abuse, and violent behavior.[2] While this is worrisome, it is far from inevitable, because family unity, harmony and cohesion can be built. As with so much in our lives, this begins when we commit to finding the time for each other.

As youngsters, we were told that breakfast was the most important meal of the day. For us, this was true in more ways than one. Growing up, both of our parents were teachers, and with the two of us in school, each morning meant a struggle to stay on schedule. Yet as busy as we were, we always found time to sit down together for a bite to eat. Spread out on the table, the morning newspaper was part of our family's breakfast routine, and we ate up the morning news along with our toast. It was a learning free-for-all, a breakfast classroom. We commented on pictures, new words, and interesting news stories. We read clips and quotes aloud. We laughed at the editorial cartoons. Mornings were great, plain and simple. They made our family strong. Years later, we still fondly remember those weekday mornings, both for the time we spent together and for what we learned.

Many of our best memories seem to revolve around the times we spent as a family engaged with our larger community, either volunteering or going on family trips. One of our favorite events was an annual father-and-sons camping trip, which was arranged through a local service organization. During the day, Dad cooked in the camp with the other fathers, while we scampered off into the bush for fun-filled summer adventuring. In the evenings, tired and exhausted, we'd huddle around the campfire frightened to death by ghost stories, and roasting marshmallows. Several times, when the others had left, we stuck around for a few extra days and went fishing, just the two of us and Dad. These are some of the fondest memories we have of our father.

Research over the last fifty years has validated what we experienced during those early years.[3] Shared moments around the kitchen table, fun games in the summer evenings, quiet chats with our parents after school, camping, picnics, sports events, family volunteering—all these rituals add up to one simple equation: quality time equals strong families. Together, a collection of strong families makes for stronger and more vibrant communities. It's a natural progression.

A CHIP OFF THE OLD BLOCK

When we conduct workshops with parents, we start by asking participants a simple question: "What qualities and virtues would you like to encourage in your children?" The answers usually come easily: compassion, empathy, confidence, courage, and responsibility.

Next, we ask parents what kinds of activities they encourage their children to participate in. Answers usually have something to do with academics, music, and sports. Pretty normal, right? Maybe. But when we look at how our society tends to measure success in these activities, the phrases that leap to mind have little in common with the qualities discussed above. Instead, they include things like "winning," "placing first," and "ranking highly." In practice, personal growth often takes a backseat to competition. Nevertheless, parents willing to sign their kids up for Sunday music lessons balk at arranging for them to volunteer at a food bank every Saturday. Money can be found for a summer sports camp but not for a volunteer trip. Private math classes win out over joining a social issues club.

All parents want what's best for their children, but many have yet to appreciate the benefits of social involvement for young people. We hope the following real-life stories will encourage you to think twice. The first involves an at-risk youth, a young boy from an underprivileged background. The second tells of a boy who grew up wanting for nothing, except the motivation to use his gifts. The third explores the path of a young woman, privileged and motivated, but unsure about what direction to take in life.

Overcoming Hardship

Growing up in South Central Los Angeles, Luis J. Rodriguez faced many difficulties. His family had come to America seeking opportunities for their children, a better life than they had known back home. But the poverty they experienced was overwhelming and their son, Luis, rebelled.

At the age of seven, he began to steal from local shops, at eleven he joined a gang, at twelve he was using drugs, and at fifteen he dropped out of school. "From ages thirteen to eighteen, he was arrested for numerous crimes, including stealing, fighting, rioting, attempted murder, and assaulting police officers." At eighteen, he faced a six-year prison sentence. He was addicted to heroin and his trial was set. Many gave up hope, but others did not. There were those who had seen his potential for good. They had witnessed his community involvement as a muralist and as a student leader. They remembered his return to high school, and how he finally earned his diploma. Recognizing this, they rallied around him. People wrote many letters of support, and as a result his sentence was reduced. This was all the help he needed.

Wanting to show others that the faith they placed in him meant something, Luis turned his life around. He kicked his drug habit cold turkey, did his time, got himself a job, and worked his way to stability. It was a long journey, and it was never easy, but through the support of others and his own determination, he progressed from street thug, to high school graduate, to college journalism student, to beat reporter, to radio broadcaster. Eventually, he became the nationally acclaimed writer, journalist, and community activist that he is today. [4]

Affluence and Apathy

When we first met Alex, we could have called him "Alex the Apathetic." Unlike Luis, Alex grew up in comfort, but far from lessening his uncaring attitude toward the world, all his privilege seemed to feed it. In 1998, a brazen 14-year-old, Alex defiantly walked out of his first day of leadership training at one of our summer camps. We were sure we wouldn't see him again.

To our surprise, his parents dragged him back the next day. He was visibly annoyed, and he didn't waste any opportunity to challenge his facilitator's patience. Brooding, he sat at the back of the room staring out the window. When it came time to practice public speaking, he used his speech to mock his facilitator.

Smiling good-naturedly, this facilitator suggested Alex had a talent for public speaking. Why not use his talent to talk to young people about something important? This praise flattered Alex, and the challenge it implied was enough to make him stop and think. He began to see his time at the camp as an opportunity rather than a punishment.

Since that defining moment, Alex has led volunteer trips to Kenya, India, and Mexico; coordinated and led training in high schools; delivered speeches to tens of thousands of young people; and facilitated leadership training in North America, Europe, Africa, and Latin America. Simply put, Alex discovered his potential. And all it took was a gentle but firm nudge from his parents.

A Lack of Direction

It isn't only young people from challenging environments who benefit from making the shift from Me to We through social involvement. Allison Sander is a prime example. A student at Lewis and Clark College in Portland, Oregon, she was a shy and confused teenager, unsure of her life goals. For her, it wasn't so much a question of overcoming adversity or banishing apathy, but of trying to make up her mind about what to do with her life. A trip to Africa was *her* moment of truth. She returned to her family transformed. Her shyness had melted away, replaced by confidence and the firm conviction that she would be part of the solution to the problems she had witnessed overseas. Allison had learned that finding happiness in day-to-day life starts from within, through converting the quiet compassion she felt for others into real action. She needed the support of her parents to get her there, but her decision to join her community was her own. She too had moved from Me to We.

LESSONS LEARNED

In our years of working with young people, we have witnessed how reaching out to others helps youth develop self-esteem, gain leaderships skills, and acquire a sense of purpose and direction. As with other positive extracurricular activities like sports, music, or the debating society, volunteering allows young people to develop important skills such as leadership, teamwork, and communication. Unlike popular pastimes such as television and video games, it allows youth to learn respect for themselves and others while fulfilling their true potential. In case after case, we have seen self-doubt replaced with self-respect, and watched apathy give way to action. These are not isolated cases but the expression of a greater and growing phenomenon. It isn't hard to come across stories like these, whether by reading the newspaper, talking with friends, or perhaps turning to your own family. It lends credibility to the idea that a little love can go a long way.

A SPECIAL MESSAGE TO YOUTH

If you're thinking about becoming socially involved, these seven steps are guaranteed to help you take action.

1. **Choose Your Issue**
   What social issue are you concerned about? Is it climate change, homelessness, illiteracy, child labor, or something else?

2. **Do Your Research**
   Knowledge is power. If you know your issue inside and out, when it comes time to communicate your ideas, your knowledge will provide both answers and opportunities.

3. **Build Your Team**
   Talk to friends, family and mentors. Get them energized and excited. With a solid team of dedicated leaders, no problem is too challenging; you will succeed together.

4. **Call the First Meeting**
   Get together with friends to share ideas and skills. Make sure everyone has a chance to have a say and help make decisions.

5. **Make a Plan of Action**
   This is where you put your heads together. Brainstorm fun and creative ways to motivate people in your community that will appeal to your team as well as your target audience.

6. **Take Action...and Reflect on What You Learned**
   Now go for it with all you heart! Afterward, your team should reflect on successes and challenges so you can learn from your mistakes and do even better next time.

7. **Have Fun!**
   A sure sign of a successful project is that it's enjoyable. So make it fun and celebrate, celebrate, celebrate your achievements. Did we mention celebrate?

WHAT MR. ROGERS KNEW ABOUT NEIGHBORHOODS

If you're wondering how to reap the benefits of Me to We in you neighborhood, you can begin by asking yourself the simple question, one not spoken but rather sung by American icon, Mr. Rogers. What was his enlightening query? "Who are the people in your neighborhood?" Sometimes, it really is as simple as this.

About forty years ago, Jane Jacobs revolutionized the world of urban planning with her book, *The Death and Life of Great American Cities*. In exploring Mr. Rogers' insights in a scholarly way, she saw that healthy communities exist when people know and have a basic sense of trust toward one another, and that this in turn comes from social interactions, the innumerable little social conversations and interactions that occur when we go about our daily lives. In better words than we could ever write, she said:

> *"The trust of a city street is formed over time from many, many little public sidewalk contacts. It grows out of people stopping by at the bar for a beer, getting advice from the grocer and giving advice to the newsstand man, comparing opinions with other customers at the bakery and nodding hello to the two boys drinking pop on the stoop...hearing about a job from the hardware man and borrowing a dollar from the druggist, admiring the new babies and sympathizing over the way a coat faded... The sum of such casual, public contact at a local level... is a feeling for the public identity of people, a web of public respect and trust, and a resource in time of personal or neighborhood need."[5]*

For us, these words ring true. But we also realize that the trust she is talking about does not grow when we live as isolated individuals, when we see others as competitors in a dog-eat-dog world, when we fail to put down roots in the areas where we live, and when we spend our days in a swirling mass of disconnected strangers.

Psychologist Philip Zimbardo conducted an interesting experiment that supports Jacobs' insights. In 1969, Zimbardo and his team bought two used cars, both in good condition, and left them in two different locations: one in the Bronx, New York, and the other in Palo Alto, California. Both vehicles were made to look as if they had broken down and been abandoned—their license plates were removed and their hoods were left open. The team then sat back with the cameras running to watch what would happen.

In the Bronx, as you can imagine, it didn't take long for the action to start. Within ten minutes, the car had been vandalized, and this was just the beginning. Over the next forty-eight hours, the researchers recorded twenty-three separate destructive acts as passersby attempted either to take something from the car or to simply destroy it. At the end of two days, the car was no longer recognizable: it had been completely stripped, and vandals had set to work demolishing what was left.

The car in Palo Alto fared much differently. After two days it had only been touched once—when a passerby closed the hood when it rained. What's more, when the researchers finally went back to remove the car themselves, three local residents promptly called the police to report that an abandoned car was being stolen. Luckily, the police had been notified about the study in advance![6]

Many of you are probably thinking what we first did, that geography tells the whole story. While this may be partly true, something larger is at play here. This study was carried out in Palo Alto before the 1980s tech boom, and East Palo Alto, notorious for its poverty and crime, was at one time the country's murder capital. Like the Bronx, it was a challenging area.

In the Bronx, the buzz of activity around the abandoned car told an interesting story. In all of the attacks on the car, only one was made by an adolescent. The others were carried out by adults, a number of whom were well-dressed and already drove cars of their own. In other words, many of the perpetrators were not people motivated by desperate need. Nevertheless, the lightning speed with which the destruction took place was astonishing. "Within ten minutes the 1959 Oldsmobile received its first auto strippers—a father, mother, and eight-year-old son. The mother appeared to be a lookout, while the son aided the father's search of the trunk, glove compartment and motor. He handed his father the tools necessary to remove the battery and radiator. Total time of destructive contact: seven minutes."[7]

In concluding his study, Zimbardo contrasted the sense of anonymity that prevailed in the Bronx, where people were not likely to know, or be known by, anyone, with the strong community ties in Palo Alto, in which people were more likely to "care about what happens on their turf even to the person or property of strangers, with the reciprocal assumption that they would also care about them."[8] His study offers a powerful message not only on the dangers of anonymity, but also on the virtues of community.

Ultimately a great neighborhood depends on more than just avoiding problems—it's about creating a lively, vibrant community. Overall, it's about being part of the glue that first binds and then heals fractured communities. We all stand to gain: the kind of social cohesion that results is powerful protection against the community decay that happens when people avoid dealing with social problems or refuse to take responsibility for their actions. This means safer streets, cleaner parks, and better schools, to name just a few things that all of us deserve to enjoy. In the end, when the effort is made, the community web we create will be strong enough to support us as we strive to build the kind of neighborhood we all yearn for. Stronger than the steel frame of a used but solid, 1959 Oldsmobile.

VALUE AND PURPOSE IN THE WORKPLACE

Since the Industrial Revolution, many attempts have been made at implementing Me to We in the workplace, but early efforts were few and far between. It wasn't until 1924 that the ball really got rolling. Peter Koppel, an eminent business professor at a leading Canadian university, told us one of our favorite stories on the subject. It is a story he likes too, because in management circles it is one of the few that have stood the test of time. In his best storytelling voice, he told about the Hawthorne study.

In 1924, Elton Mayo, a Harvard professor, approached the owner of Western Electric Company's Hawthorne plant. In a bold statement to the plant's managers, Professor Mayo claimed that for minimal input he could increase the productivity of the plant's workers. His idea was simple. Mayo felt that for too long business management had emphasized productivity over the happiness of workers. He believed that if the working conditions within a business were improved, the employees would react in a positive way, increasing productivity in a more socially productive but roundabout way. To test his hypothesis, he told the managers all he would need was a handful of workers and some space to observe them.

With nothing to lose, the Hawthorne management agreed to his test. Mayo proceeded to remove a group of employees from the general assembly line and place them in a separate room where they could be monitored. His specific plan was to test the influence of lighting on the workers' productivity levels, with the idea that the better the lighting was, the greater the workers' productivity would be. All that the workers were told was that they had been specially chosen to play a part in a productivity test.

And so it went. Guinea pigs under bright lights, the workers went about their jobs and the test began. From the start, it worked brilliantly. As the lighting increased, so did productivity. Mayo was ecstatic. He was proving exactly what he had felt would happen. To verify his findings, he brought in a separate group of participants. This time, he decreased the lighting levels. And he was stunned. Productivity actually *increased*. So, he decreased the lighting again, but still, productivity increased. He tried this again and again and each time productivity increased until the lights got so low that employees complained that they couldn't see their work.

After some head scratching and further tests, Mayo determined that yes, working conditions affect productivity. There is no question about that. But, the real reason for the increase in productivity was that the group of employees felt special. They were a part of a "special test." They had been made to feel part of something larger than themselves, a part of a unique community.[9]

Since this landmark study, there has been an evolution towards employee empowerment that seems more important now than ever before in our age of globalization.

Today, employees want more than a paycheck—they're looking for meaning. Many successful companies are empowering their employees to reach out to others and supporting their efforts in a host of different ways. Direct Energy bases its charitable giving on the number of volunteer hours put in by its employees. Xerox allows social service sabbaticals. Wells Fargo gives personal growth leaves. LensCrafters empowers its employees with challenging service projects all over the world. The list goes on. From Ben and Jerry's ice cream, to Paul Newman's salad dressings, to The Body Shop, businesses and social entrepreneurs are hearing the call of Me to We and are revolutionizing business practices in a colossal way.

Increasingly, companies are finding that corporate social responsibility has rewards that extend beyond employee morale. In recent studies, socially responsible and community-oriented companies have been shown to do better than their competitors. In 2001, *Business Ethics Best Citizen* companies did significantly better than the remaining companies in the S&P 500. The ranking was based on eight statistical criteria, including total return, sales growth, and profit growth over one-year and three-year periods, as well as net profit margins and return on equity.[10]

ME TO WE ON A LARGER SCALE

In every strong community, at whatever level, there are challenges. Moving from Me to We means we all do what we can to help. Our contribution is not measured by the amount given but by the sacrifice it represents. There are innumerable national and international examples of how Americans have both come together in a show of support and been helped by others. We will look back into U.S. history and then forward into present day international cooperation, ending this chapter as it began, with a story about cows.

The Efforts of Citizens

As we discussed in the last chapter, community cohesiveness has traditionally been central to the American way of life. As historians Susan Ellis and Kathrine Moyes remind us, from the beginning "just about every public organization or service group in America, whether schools, libraries, churches, hospitals, police forces, fire departments, or newspapers began when people came together to overcome or solve a problem. Committees formed around issues and people gave their time in compensation for the betterment of the community."[11] In this spirit, Benjamin Franklin, one of America's first great social architects, did more than help to draft the Declaration of Independence. He also worked to establish and refine institutions such as circulating libraries, public hospitals, mutual insurance companies, agricultural colleges, and intellectual societies. In a time when a single fire could consume a whole city, he established the first volunteer fire department. Only three buckets were required for membership.

Americans' willingness to help has not diminished over time. During the hardship of the Great Depression, when millions were unemployed, volunteers created and managed employment networks and bureaus, ran soup kitchens for the hungry, and established shelters for those in need.12 In World War II, America's brave men and women volunteered to help the war effort both at home and abroad, in many cases sacrificing their very lives to the cause.

Over the past decades, America's volunteers have stepped up to tackle some of the country's biggest problems: hunger, illiteracy, poverty, racism, and disease. One example was after Hurricane Katrina, where Americans from all walks of life reached out to those in devastated areas of the Gulf Coast, donating money and supplies to aid survivors, and sometimes even welcoming them into their own homes.

Global Cooperation

In times of need, we act globally. In the wake of the tsunami that hit Southeast Asia in December 2004, it was America that pledged the most in aid, with the government promising $857 million, and private donations reaching an astounding $1.78 billion.[13] Such generosity after one of the worst humanitarian tragedies in recent years reveals the power of Me to We to strengthen not only the groups that form a part of our immediate lives but also the largest group to which we belong: humanity itself. The challenge before us lies in ensuring that this kind of We-thinking becomes the norm. At present, the United States devotes only 0.22 percent of its gross national income to official development assistance,[14] a long way from the 0.7 percent target that the world's developed countries have repeatedly committed to delivering.

In our new global village, America is both giving and receiving. On June 3, 2002, *The New York Times* ran a curious story that caught our attention. Our friends the Maasai had made the news. Kimeli Naiyomah, a twenty-five-year-old Maasai who was studying in United States, was in Manhattan, on September 11, 2001. When he spoke to his tribe back in Kenya about the devastation, they responded in the only way they knew how: with cows. Fourteen fat and healthy cows were offered to the deputy chief of the United States Embassy in Nairobi. In relative terms, this gift was a large and generous one, because, in the Maasai culture, cows are as valuable as rain; they are sacred. They are named, talked to, given as bridal gifts. For the Maasai, cows hold great spiritual power, and such a gift is an extremely significant gesture of solidarity.

If we have learned anything in our journey, it is that Me to We is the glue that holds communities together. Whether the community in question is a small family or a huge nation, its strength depends on the choices made by its members. When our choices support the welfare of the community as a whole, the We, everyone benefits both as individuals and members of something larger than themselves.

START NOW!

In your last Me to We journal entry, you explored some of the ways you benefit by helping others. Now take time to consider the ways that the wider community benefits when you set out to help just one or two people.

▸ Jot down a few times you've done something to help out a few specific people and in the process have ended up helping a larger group or community.

▸ Now think about the future. Make a list of five things you would like to change for one or two people, and explore how this could benefit everyone else. Ask yourself:

» What do I want to change for specific people around me? Does violence mean that my elderly neighbors feel unsafe? Are outdoor play areas too dirty for my kids?

» How can I help to change these things in ways that will ensure that everyone benefits? Could I join the neighborhood watch so my whole community feels safe? Or clean up a playground and help everyone in my community to enjoy spending time there?

TAKE ANOTHER LOOK!

▸ Most North Americans have more than enough food to eat. In fact, we spend billions of dollars every year just trying to lose weight. But did you know that in North America many adults struggle to afford nutritious meals and many children are forced to rely on free school lunches? It's not just people in other countries who are going to bed hungry—there are also those closer to home. Lend a hand at a neighborhood soup kitchen or a community breakfast program—people in need will leave with full stomachs, and you'll leave with a full heart.

» During the 2004-2005 school year, the National School Lunch program provided free or reduced-priced meals to 17.5 million children.[15]

» It is estimated that the U.S. spends up to $100 billion every year on the diet industry—more than what the government spends on health, education, and welfare combined.[16]

» There is more than enough food in the world to feed every person,[17] yet a child dies from hunger-related illness every five seconds.[18]

LIVING ME TO WE

1. **Plan a café surprise.** Surprise the person behind you in line at the coffee shop with a fresh coffee. But wait, first ask what the person wants or you might be drinking coffee for two. This simple surprise might even start a new conversation that will make you a new friend.

2. **Home-cooking for the world.** Do you often find yourself eating out at restaurants or buying a meal on the run on your way or from work? Cook at home for a week, brown-bag it to work, make your morning coffee before you leave the house, and use the money you save to support a program that helps feed the hungry.

3. **Try a taste of something different.** Host a "taste of the nations" dinner party for your neighbors in which you cook different recipes from around the world. Accept $10-$15 donations on behalf of a charity that feeds the hungry. Provide your guests with printed information about this charity at the door so everyone can come.

My Story

OPRAH WINFREY

I will never forget the year I was about 12 years old, living with my mother who was single and raising my half-sister, my half-brother, and me in Milwaukee. We were on welfare, and she told us that we would not be receiving Christmas gifts because there was not enough money. I remember at the time that I felt sad and thought, What will my story be? What would I say when the other kids asked what I'd gotten? What will my classmates think when I go back to school and say, "We didn't have Christmas because we didn't have any money"? Just when I started to accept that there would not be a Christmas that year, three nuns showed up at our house with gifts for all of us. There was a turkey, a fruit basket, and some games, and for me, they brought a doll. I felt such a sense of relief that I had been given something, and that I would no longer have to be embarrassed when I returned to school. I remember feeling that I mattered enough to these nuns—whom I had never met and to this day still do not know their names—and what it meant that they had remembered me. I wasn't forgotten. Somebody had thought enough of me to bring me a gift.

Years later, in the spring of 2002, I stood in the kitchen of my new house and thought about that upcoming Christmas, envisioning how I wanted to decorate the house to make my first Christmas there special and memorable. I then started to think about the best Christmas I ever had, and I instantly recalled the nuns' visit and impact they had on my life. I have always encouraged giving, using your life, teaching what you learn, and extending yourself in the form of service. So, that day in my kitchen, I put that same challenge to myself. What could I do, by using the abundance that I had been blessed with, to make this Christmas more meaningful to someone else? I decided that I wanted to create that same feeling of importance and acknowledgement for as many children as I could possibly reach. I immediately thought of the children of South Africa, whose poverty and suffering I had seen firsthand on my previous visits. The people of South Africa and the strength of their spirit had always held a special place in my heart. I simply wanted to create one day in the lives of these children that they could remember as a happy one.

So, I came up with a plan and gathered forty people from my company, Harpo, Inc., to help. Together with my greatest mentor, Nelson

Mandela, we created a program that I called Christmas Kindness South Africa 2002. We worked together to identify gifts that would be culturally relevant, from black dolls—which none of these children had ever seen—and soccer balls, which is one of South Africa's favorite sports, to sneakers for every child, because so many of them don't own a pair of shoes. We wanted to help these children forget their troubles and have some fun, even if only for a short while. We created a fantasyland of parties—complete with Christmas trees, fairy princesses and jesters, games, and prizes—for the orphans, most of whom had never attended a party in their lives. It was at the first one of these parties that I experienced the single greatest moment of my life.

We gathered approximately one hundred and twenty-five children from different orphanages at each party. For every child, we wrapped colorful packages filled with toys, clothes, much-needed books, and school supplies. Each package was labeled with a child's name. We wanted all of them to know they were special, and for a lot of those children it would be the only gift they had ever received. Before I called out their names and handed them their gifts, I reminded them that they couldn't unwrap their presents until every child had come forward. Much to my surprise, they sat patiently—like no other children I had seen before—for what must have seemed like an eternity, listening for their cue. Finally, the moment they had been waiting for came as I called out, "One, two, three. Open your presents!" As the children ripped open their packages, their faces beamed as their jubilant smiles lit up the room. They cheered, sang, and danced in celebration. They hugged their gifts and hugged one another; the joy in the room was palpable, and it wasn't just about toys. It was a feeling—the feeling I knew from that Christmas so long ago when the nuns came to visit… I wasn't forgotten. Somebody thought of me. I matter.

I never knew that level of joy existed until that Christmas I spent with the children of South Africa. Their energy and elation were contagious. I felt it so deeply; it was overwhelming and it completely filled me. I realized in that moment that joy has a texture you can really feel. I saw myself in their eyes, and I carry their joy in my heart. I am grateful to God that I was able to see, touch, hear, and feel that kind of happiness by giving back to those who had so little. That Christmas we were able to bring joy to fifty thousand children, but there were more than a million moments of happiness.

Making other people happy is what brings me happiness. This principle of living has brought me enormous good fortune, long before I knew this is how the Universe works. I grew up being taught, "Do unto others as you would have them do unto you." The real lesson is what you do to others will indeed be done unto you. What you put out comes back; it's the third law of motion. So we're always rewarded in kind according to the depth of our deeds. I speak daily to ten million people all over the world with the purest intention of in some way lifting them up through hope, laughter, inspiration and entertainment. I, in turn, have been exalted by the blessings.

CHAPTER EIGHT

GRATITUDE

"Gratitude unlocks the fullness of life. It turns what we have into enough, and more. It turns denial into acceptance, chaos to order, confusion to clarity. It can turn a meal into a feast, a house into a home, a stranger into a friend. Gratitude makes sense of our past, brings peace for today, and creates a vision for tomorrow."

—Melody Beattie

CRAIG'S REFLECTIONS

It's easy to take the simple things in life for granted. Somehow, everyday blessings blend into the background. It's the exceptional experiences that we feel grateful for, not the "normal" ones. Until the day when everything changes in an instant. On September 10, 2001, I was in New York City, meeting with local charities just a few blocks from the World Trade Center. My trips are usually incredibly busy and this was no exception: there was too much to do in too little time. It wasn't until late that evening, with the day's work finally over, that I had a chance to catch my breath. Disappointed that I hadn't had time to enjoy the familiar sights and sounds of one of my favorite cities, I decided I could at least go for a walk.

New York has an energy of its own, and that late summer evening, I truly understood why. All around me the city was alive with activity as everyone headed in different directions. The Big Apple's fabled ambition, wealth, and power were on full display, in the sleek cars stopped by the curb, the bright windows of the bustling restaurants and the studied nonchalance of stylish young people out on the town.

As I cut through the financial district, I passed the Twin Towers, shimmering in the street lights.

Then came the next morning. Even before I heard what was happening, it was clear something was terribly wrong: there was an unfamiliar edge of desperation to the city's usual hectic pace. At a friend's house, uneasy, but unsure why, I turned on the TV news. Within seconds, I saw one, then another, plane crash into the World Trade Center. Time stopped. I was hit by the sickening realization that what I was seeing was real. I found it difficult to breathe as I stared blankly at the television screen. The horror hit me in waves, each more intense than the last.

A short distance away, people were injured, trapped, and dying. America was under attack. Again and again, the brutal images flashed by. The city was in a state of emergency. People were being told to stay inside and off the phones. Airports were closed, bridges clogged.

That evening there was a knock on the door. On the doorstep stood a ragged man looking frightened and shaken, covered with a thick layer of dust. His eyes were wide and strangely glazed and his body seemed to tremble. He turned out to be one of the few to have made it out of the World Trade Center alive. As my host and I later learned, this man had spent the day wandering the city in shock, trying to get through to his wife on his cell phone. When he finally reached her, tearful and happy beyond belief, she had reminded him that an acquaintance, my host, lived in the area. And so he stood there confused and full of apologies, unsure of what to say or do. Of course, he was immediately invited in. No sooner did he step across the threshold than he abruptly collapsed into a nearby chair. He would later say it was a miracle he was still alive.

The events that day rocked me to the core. Grieving for those affected, I realized that had things been different, I might have been at the World Trade Center myself. In the midst of my sadness and fear, I felt profoundly grateful to be alive. Twenty-four hours earlier, caught up in meeting after meeting, my biggest problem had seemed to be adding a few more hours onto the day. Now that world seemed so far away. Reeling from the tragedy, I realized that each and every hour I had was a blessing that not everyone would enjoy. I vowed never again think of time as a problem—but only as a privilege.

During the next days and weeks, I heard many variations on this same story. People in a city usually preoccupied with money, success and celebrity, expressed appreciation for what most of us so often take for granted—life. New York, the city defined worldwide as the city of extravagance, had suddenly become profoundly thankful for simple things. People's sense of the miraculous expanded. Just hearing a loved one's voice was reason for joy. So was running into a neighbor, or getting a one-line e-mail from a former colleague. Old resentments and divisions were for-gotten as people came together in an unprecedented display of solidarity. Citizens of every size, shape, and color rushed to Ground Zero to help. Survivors comforted one another in candlelight vigils. Across the city, annoyance and impatience gave way to kindness and respect: drivers weren't as quick to pound their horns, doors were opened en masse and strangers stopped to share the latest news. People were grateful for the smallest of blessings.

Tragedies have a way of forcing us to confront what is most important in life. As we would later discover, the resurgence of gratitude Craig wit-nessed in the wake of 9/11 was observed by others. In a study of col-lege students conducted shortly after the attacks, participants reported that along with sadness and anger, feelings of love, interest and gratitude emerged. These positive emotions didn't erase people's pain—those who experienced the highest levels of positive emotions were not any more immune to suffering than anyone else—but they did enable participants to better cope with their sorrow. Researchers suggested that as with non-bereaved citizens more generally, these students were "likely feel-ing grateful for their own safety and for the safety of their loved ones and motivated to count their blessings."[1]

This was no isolated case. In the aftermath of Hurricane Katrina, Marc still remembers how one active Free The Children supporter, hav-ing learned that his house had been badly damaged, declared, "I feel very blessed. Thank God I am alive." It wasn't only his words that were powerful, it was the conviction in his trembling voice. While many other survivors spoke of appalling hardships, they too expressed extraordinary thankfulness; their gratitude had grace. As one person put it, "As long as you have your life, you have everything."[2]

Like the cloth that clears the dust off of a long neglected painting to reveal the masterpiece beneath, disasters like 9/11, Hurricane Katrina and others have a way of revealing the true worth of good health, family, community, and daily life in all of its beauty.

Although it's definitely heartening when disasters bring out the best in people, none of us should need to suffer simply to feel thankful for all we have. We should cherish our blessings day in and day out, never losing sight of the abundance in our lives. We should prize life's treasures, always understanding their true value. Gratitude can help us do this and more. As we hope to show you, this important emotion is crucial in strengthening us both as individuals and communities. In connecting us with others, it can play a powerful role in helping us to make the transition from Me to We.

As a psychological state, gratitude involves a "sense of wonder, thankfulness, and appreciation for life."[3] The word itself is derived from the Latin *gratia*, which means "grace," "graciousness," or "gratefulness." All derivatives from this Latin root "have to do with kindness, generosity, gifts, the beauty of giving and receiving, or getting something for nothing."[4] This mini-etymology lesson provides us with an important clue about the true meaning of the term: it highlights the fact that gratitude is not only about being on the receiving end of the good things in life; it also is about our own generosity with others. At its best, gratitude is a contagious state of mind. It sends tingles up the spine that emerge in joy and bliss, leaving us touched in such a way that we want nothing more than to share the feeling with others. It is the poetry of the soul emerging from us in many ways, shapes and forms. Without it we cannot hope to recognize, revel in or renew the abundance that graces our lives.

Gratitude, Abundance, and the Scarcity Myth

Gratitude often seems in short supply these days. By and large, we live in a glass-half-empty society. Advertising tells us we lack things, and with new products coming out all the time, we lack more every day. Our focus on what's missing keeps us from seeing what we have, creating a kind of gratitude blindness. As a result, we come to experience what author and activist Lynne Twist has called a "chronic sense of inadequacy about life."[5] Whether it's money, time, caring, power, or anything else, it seems like there's never enough.

Busy with our work at Free The Children and Me to We, we have sometimes caught ourselves in this trap, lamenting the need for more time and resources for more projects. We find the words "if only we had…" cropping up in conversations when we least expect it.

As easy as it is to slip into this kind of thinking, there's nothing easy about the results. In this state, a perpetual need for more breeds a mentality of scarcity. Before long, actions become driven by the fear that there's not enough of anything to go around and never will be. This encourages hoarding, not only of money, but of time and energy. When you're consumed by the idea that you don't have enough for yourself, sharing seems impossible. The question is, what if we've been duped? What if the scarcity we think we know so well is actually a myth perpetuated by advertisers and strengthened by social norms? What if this myth overshadows the reality around us, hiding the true abundance that is ours to enjoy?

During the past decade, we've been both fortunate and unfortunate to have seen real scarcity up close. We've stood witness to war zones rife with images of torture and violence; we've seen slums and refugee camps where desperation and absolute poverty reign; we've been to jails where darkness is all that can be seen; we've seen hunger and people's desperate struggle to survive; we've seen plantations where people are enslaved, brutalized and commodified. These are expressions of true scarcity: scarcity of peace, justice, nourishment, stability, community, and freedom. Such experiences have gradually taught us to understand the scarcity myth for what it is, and recognize abundance when we see it. We have come to understand that the very act of waking up in the morning is a blessing. We have learned to be thankful for a full belly, for a roof and shelter, for family and friends and for the fulfilling work we do. It is gratitude that helps us move forward despite the great hardship in the world.

At each new turn in the road, we are constantly reminded of the old adage, "In order to help others, you must first help yourself." We respectfully disagree. It is not a question of first or second. We have witnessed people in desperate need reaching out to help others, gaining for themselves the motivation and ability to improve their own situation. As these individuals bettered their own lives, they sought to share their improved situation with friends, family, and community members. And in reaching out, they each gained a renewed sense of purpose, energy, and optimism.

We've found that when you reach out to help, you set in motion a cycle of abundance: giving to others helps you feel grateful, feeling grateful helps you to give. Unlike the myth of scarcity, this cycle leads to an individual and collective uplifting. When we speak of abundance, we are not referring merely to money. Most of us have a very finite amount of money in our bank accounts and we're not suggesting you spend your last dollar on good deeds. There are so many other ways to express your gratitude. Smiles, unlike bank accounts, are limitless. Reserves of goodwill need never run dry. You can give a smile to a loved one or coworker, devote yourself as a volunteer, provide hope to someone who is blue or commit a random act of kindness. These things need not come in finite amounts. Such contributions are driven not by cash but by our individual and collective compassion, courage, and ingenuity. They create a cycle of abundance that reaches beyond the financial, the only true antidote to the myth of scarcity.

One of our favorite stories about the cycle of abundance comes from our friend Kim, a successful freelance writer and mother of three. Volunteering at a barebones nursing home across town seemed like the last thing in the world this busy working mother had time to do. But wanting to help a few "forgotten souls" in her city find peace, Kim decided to try it anyway. Full of exuberance, her dog Boomer seemed like the perfect helper. And so, for an hour each week, they visited. On her first day, Kim wondered on her way to the nursing home if there really was any value in what she was doing. Dirty breakfast dishes sat in her sink. Work sat untouched on her desk. Mildew clung mercilessly to her shower. She had to race home to get one of her kids to a soccer game. Was this worth it? Within five minutes of her arrival, Kim knew the answer. In the days and months to come, she would experience this time and time again. As she and Boomer walked the halls of the home, visiting, listening, smiling, laughing, Kim's mood began to change. Her worries melted away.

And then there was Margaret. The skin on Margaret's face sank over sharpened cheekbones, yellow and translucent. Her hands showed her age the most—delicate blue veins traveling over tiny bones, angular arthritic knuckles, carefully tended nails. Once, she had been a concert pianist. She had hosted orchestras from around the world in her humble home. But after her husband died, she suffered several strokes and worried she would never play piano again. "I looked at my hand and it just wouldn't move," she told Kim. "I said to it, 'I will not let this happen. You will move.' And it did!" Upon seeing Boomer, Margaret would gingerly bend down and bunch up his soft face next to her own for a moment, touching her cheek to his glossy coat. Her smile alone lifted Kim up. After each visit, orderlies would take Margaret down to lunch. And every time she would show her appreciation for Kim's presence and for Boomer's wagging tail. "Thank you so much, dear," she would say as they wheeled her from the room. "Don't you forget to come back and see me next time."

In the end, these visits enriched the lives of all involved. For Margaret, scratching Boomer's ears gave joy and brought life to her delicate fingers, inspiring her to play the nursing home's piano, to cheer the hearts of the other residents. As for Boomer, he was on the receiving end of so much attention that he couldn't help but feel happy and grateful, his appreciation shown by the wag of his tail and the deep contented sigh he gave as he rested his head in Margaret's lap. Meanwhile, Kim was grateful for a new outlook. "With their gift of perspective and perseverance, Margaret and the others we visit help me to realize how lucky I am," she told us. "They remind me to feel grateful for small gifts like smiles, and laughter and kindness." Like so many others who volunteer, she has found that giving has helped her to appreciate all that she has, and taught her just how much she has to give. Through helping, she has come to recognize the abundance in her life.

As we think you'll agree, it's time to shatter the scarcity myth that forces us to believe life is a game of win or lose, and let abundance replace scarcity. We need to recognize the non-material wealth that surrounds us and share it generously. Let us coin a new phrase, then, one that affirms, "In order to help ourselves and others, we need gratitude to help light up the abundance in everyday life."

IT ONLY TAKES A SPARK

Social scientists have long appreciated the importance of gratitude. Psychologists have found that people who regularly experience this emotion enjoy a high degree of life satisfaction along with positive emotions such as happiness, vitality and hope, traits that not only help us to function as individuals, but also pave the way for rewarding relationships with others. At the interpersonal level, gratitude has been shown to be important in both establishing and strengthening relationships. Feelings of gratitude encourage people to focus on the benefits they receive from others, leading them to feel loved and cared for.[6]

Science aside, we all know the benefits of gratitude without being told. When someone does us a favor, we usually feel grateful. Often, we tend to appreciate him or her more. Think back over your own life. It likely won't take long to remember a time when you experienced this phenomenon. Think about your parents and how they nurtured your growth. Think of how you have in turn helped them as they have aged and needed your support. Think of all of the small favors you have enjoyed from others. Has a neighbor ever cleared snow from your driveway on a blustery winter's day? Has a friend picked up a book she knew you would love? Has your spouse cooked you dinner after a day of stressful meetings? If so, then chances are you weren't only grateful for what was done; you were likely grateful to whoever it was that went out of his or her way to brighten your day. Likely, you wanted to return the favor.

This particular phenomenon is called *reciprocity*, the idea that one good turn deserves another. When we feel grateful for something someone has done for us, we are often eager to "pay him or her back." While most of us take this social norm for granted, it can be seen as the glue that holds societies together by encouraging us to reward the good deeds of others, facilitating harmony.

Of course, gratitude is more than simply doing a good turn for someone who has helped you in the past. Studies show that this emotion tends to be connected with helping behavior more generally. At a basic level, the link between gratitude and helping can be seen as part of "the feel good, do good effect." Psychologists have made the case that negative emotions encourage people to focus on themselves, whereas positive emotions, like gratitude, tend to orient people toward helping others.

In 1972, Alice Isen and Paula Levin tested this idea in an interesting experiment in shopping malls in San Francisco and Philadelphia. Their goal was to compare the helping behavior of two groups of people: individuals who were happier than usual, and those who were just "normal shoppers." No doubt on a budget, they chose to make shoppers happier in a very simple way—by leaving a dime in the coin-return slot of a pay telephone. When the person left the telephone with their new dime in hand, they would see a man a few feet in front of them drop a folder full of papers. Only 4 percent of shoppers who had not found a dime stopped to help. However, 84 percent of the people who had just found a dime stopped to help pick up the papers![7] We love this particular study because it shows just how little it takes to make us feel like helping others. It also reminds us that if we brighten even one person's day, there's a good chance they'll pass along the good will. With even one small gesture, it is possible to start a cycle of abundance that will affect people in ways you could have never imagined!

GRATITUDE IN PRACTICE

> *"To speak gratitude is courteous and pleasant,*
> *to enact gratitude is generous and noble,*
> *but to live gratitude is to touch Heaven."*
>
> —Johannes A. Gaertner

We have learned that feeling and expressing gratitude is a skill that can be developed through practice. In the most basic sense, practicing gratitude involves training your mind to notice, savor and remember the positive aspects of life. It doesn't mean deluding yourself, certainly. It simply means making a conscious choice to abandon fears and insecurities and instead to develop a sense of wonder and appreciation for the world. We then see circumstances in terms of the opportunities they present, rather than the obstacles they create.

Research shows a little practice can go a along way. One study of gratitude journals offered these simple directions: "There are many things in our lives, both large and small, that we might be grateful about. Think back over the past week and write down up to five things in your life that you are grateful or thankful for." Pretty simple, right?

The examples listed by participants involved: "waking up this morning," "the generosity of friends," "God for giving me determination," "wonderful parents," "the Lord for just another day," and "the Rolling Stones."[8]

Our own choice wouldn't be Mick Jagger in tight pants, but we won't judge. For us, the interesting thing here is that these answers are nothing extraordinary. These are things that most, if not all, of us can be thankful for.

The practice of keeping this simple journal actually increased the extent to which the participants offered emotional support to others or "helped someone with a problem."[9] What makes these results all the more amazing is that this study involved adults with neuromuscular diseases. These were people in very difficult circumstances, losing control of their bodies and their independence, spending days and nights in pain and discomfort. Other studies on gratitude journals have featured healthy participants and achieved similar results. We chose to share this specific study because it makes an important point: if gratitude can help the desperately ill find the strength to reach out, it can certainly help those of us with less serious obstacles to contend with.

After all this, are you still having trouble coming up with a good reason to feel grateful? Take a moment to think about your day. Did you wake up in a bed? Did you enjoy running water, maybe a nice hot shower? Have you eaten yet, or had anything to drink? Have you been able to leave your home without stepping into a war zone?

If you bought this book, you are more fortunate than the roughly three billion people in the world who live on less than $2 a day. If you have an acquaintance who lent you this book, you are more blessed than the millions of people who, rightly or wrongly, feel they have no family or friends in the world. Even if you are reading this book in a coffee shop, dental office, library or school, you are still far ahead of about 800 million of the world's people who remain illiterate.

Let's face it: most of us lead charmed lives. Showing gratitude for the things we have helps us to appreciate and share our good fortune. This mental shift, though challenging, is but a small hill to climb before the road gets easier. As we learn to feel gratitude and to act on our good feelings through reaching out to others, we begin to live the Me to We philosophy.

In closing this chapter, we would like to share with you a special letter of gratitude that expresses thanks for one of those small moments that change lives forever. It was written by our friend Laurie, after her unlikely encounter with a young man named Andrew. We can assure you the events it describes really happened!

Dear Andrew,

Remember me? Maybe not. I was just another faceless mom in the suburbs. I would have been easy to forget—if I hadn't called the cops.

Well we haven't forgotten you. I don't think we ever will.

This may come as a surprise to you, but there are times we think back on our family life and divide it in two: "before Andrew," and "after Andrew." "Before Andrew," our family lived an uncomplicated life and our town felt cozy and safe. We moved here to get away from the troubles of the city. My husband and I both worked downtown and we saw troubled and homeless people there, but when we left for the day, we left all that behind. Here in this squeaky-clean bedroom community, all the lawns are cut, the bills are paid and the children tucked safely into bed. "Before Andrew," our three boys assumed everyone had a split-level home, two cars, a cottage, and a mom and dad who cared.

And then you came along.

I can still see you—your stocking hat pulled tight over greasy hair, your reddened gloveless hands shoved in the front pockets of your jeans, your wet boots squeaking with melting snow. I was watching my son Scott wobble on the ice with the other preschool skaters when you slipped through the arena doors. Your eyes, watering from the cold, met mine, and then quickly shifted away. You slid into one of the seats, slouched down, and stared at the floor.

I couldn't ignore you. I mean, how could I? I'm a mom. I see a boy who should be in school and my radar goes up. I tried to make a little conversation, see what's up, you know—"Cold out there, huh?" "No school today?"—that kind of thing. You mumbled a few things, "Yeah, it's cold," and then you hunched deeper into the seat. You just wanted warmth, some place to close your eyes; you hadn't bargained on me! I suppose I could have left you alone. What business was it of mine? But I looked at my happy healthy little boy learning how to skate. Then I looked at you, so obviously unhappy, not much older than my own 13-year-old son. And it was just a week before Christmas. Perhaps I was overwhelmed by the holiday spirit. I don't know. But my heart crumbled. I took a leap of faith. I asked if you'd like to come home with us for some warm lunch.

Little Scott didn't know what to make of you. He stared at you non-stop as we loaded up the station wagon and headed home. It was on the drive that you opened up, told me about getting kicked out of school, kicked out of your foster home, dad in jail, mom didn't care. You hadn't eaten in days. For two nights you stayed at your friend's place until his parents booted you out. Last night you slept in their cold, wet garden shed.

Well! When we got home you wolfed down those two cans of Alphagetti, and then zonked out on Scott's bed. I thought my husband would kill me. I picked up the phone and spoke quietly, as you slept in the room next door, telling my husband what I had done. He worried, of course. Who were you, what if you had drugs, or a weapon? He hurried home. I know you'll never believe this, but we felt we were doing the right thing, calling the police. While you lay slumbering, I spoke with your school principal. She said you had vandalized her car, then run away from the foster home, and missed your court date. The police had a warrant out for your arrest and they wanted to come and get you.

I looked at you curled under the covers, sleeping like a little child. You're a good kid—I could tell that—you just lost your way early in life. Now you were lonely and scared. But we had to do it and the police came to get you. What did you think, I wonder, when you left me at the door, tears running down my face? Did you hear me call out? "I'm sorry!" Did you understand? That night, we talked with the kids. We had a long discussion about how some kids don't have parents to take care of them, and sometimes get in trouble with the law. We even had to explain what a foster home was— they'd never heard of one. My other son, Christopher, took it really hard. He bawled his eyes out.

At night we sat on the bed with him and talked about how life isn't al- ways fair and how those of us who are lucky should do all we can to help those who aren't. Christopher just couldn't get over the fact that you were spending Christmas in a detention center, alone—no presents, no tree, no family. I was pretty shaken up, too—did we do the right thing? Then, we thought of something.

After school one evening, I took the kids to the mall. We had an amazing time picking out presents for you, figuring out what size to buy, searching through the shelves that were depleted from Christmas. We thought the CD Walkman would come in handy—you could keep it with you, wherever you went. Christopher hoped you'd like the CD he chose—he says it's the hottest group. Our three boys wrapped the gifts. My husband wrote the note.

It took a while to track you down. No one would tell us where you were, until the police officer who arrested you gave us a hand. You were in a group home downtown. We dressed up, believe it or not. It was Christmas Eve. As we parked in front of an old Victorian house, I looked at my family, a little out of place in this inner city neighborhood. Everyone seemed a bit nervous. Would you be angry? Would you even want to see us?

I was so relieved to see the happy look on your face! You seemed so much better off. You didn't have to go back to that foster home that you hated so much, and the teenagers you were living with now seemed a much better fit. My boys soaked it all in—the street noise, the strange sights, the life you were living so different from theirs. They were thrilled to see your eyes light up at the presents. That was best of all.

Christmas was so different after that.

You let us all experience how much better it is to give than to receive. On Christmas morning, I noticed the boys weren't so focused on what was under the tree. Opening the presents, they talked about you and wondered what you were doing. We've talked about you since, too. "After Andrew," my children know that life isn't always easy or good. They've learned that we are all here to help each other; that it is our job to care.

Every Christmas "after Andrew," the boys and I buy gifts for other disadvantaged kids. My husband admits to stuffing a lot more money into the Salvation Army kettles and to tossing a few extra groceries into the soup kitchen bins. And I think about you often. You'd be 17 now. I wonder if you've chosen a different path. I wonder if you have presents under your tree this year. I could have minded my own business that day. I'm glad I didn't. You gave us a Christmas gift that will stay with our family forever.

Take care of yourself,

Laurie

START NOW!

- Think of ten things in your daily routine you are grateful for. It doesn't matter how simple they seem: if they were taken away, you know you would miss them. Are you surprised what you think of?

- Make a list of people you are grateful for. Ask yourself:
  - » Who supports me?
  - » Who mentors me?
  - » Who's always there to help me reach my goals?

- Think about all the gifts that you have. Pay special attention to the simple ones many of us do not always remember—clean water, public education, relative wealth when so many live in poverty.

- If you have not already started to keep a gratitude journal, now is the time to give it a try! Every day, write down three to five things that you are grateful for. Make sure to put your journal somewhere you'll always see it—for instance, beside your bed or on your coffee table. Write down your thoughts before you begin your morning routine or when you have a quiet moment in the evening.

TAKE ANOTHER LOOK!

Poverty comes in many forms. It's important to remember that you don't have to travel very far to find someone in need. Think about both sharing with those close to home and reaching further to help those around the world. Be generous with your time and your money. Be generous with your resources and your gifts. And be thankful for the many things you have to share. Through sharing your gifts you can affect poverty at the local level and around the world.

- The Children's Defense Fund estimates that every 35 seconds, a baby is born into poverty in the United States.[10]

- In 2005, people spent more than $ 53.2 billion on lotteries in the U.S., yet it would only cost $6.7 billion per year to reduce by half the number of people without access to safe drinking water and basic sanitation.[11]

- The top 20 percent of the world's wealthiest people control 74% of the world's income.[12]

ME TO WE ACTION

1. **Mean what you say.** Next time you thank someone, make eye contact, smile, and really mean what you're saying. Then go further: place a note on a coworker's desk explaining why you're grateful for their presence in your life. Be creative and most of all, be thankful.

2. **Buy nothing for a week.** Commit to going an entire week without buying anything that you don't absolutely need. Rely on your own resources. Celebrate the fact that it's possible because we're already blessed with so much.

3. **Make the 0.7 percent commitment.** Poverty can be reduced if the world's wealthy countries honored their promises to devote 0.7 percent of their gross national income to development assistance. Exactly how much is 0.7 percent? Find out by making a commitment of your own. For one month, donate 0.7 percent of your paycheck to a good cause.

My Story

KATHY BUCKLEY

I began my life—my real life—the day I died.

Of course, I didn't know it at the time, but that's how it went. I finally saw the light when I was run over by a Jeep.

Before that, my life was about as peachy as you'd expect when you look like a telephone pole, can't hear, and think you're mentally retarded. Add to that sexual molestation, a few more near-death experiences, and a bout with cervical cancer, and you get the picture. Not the best life on the planet.

So why am I laughing now? I'll tell you.

For as long as I can remember, life seemed, well, confusing. Everyone else seemed to have it so together. Not me. I didn't have a clue. It would have helped if someone had told me I was deaf. No one knew. Instead, they thought I was a smart-aleck kid with a weird voice, an unfortunate perm (what was my mom thinking?), and an annoying way of staring at people's lips.

I didn't know that others could hear more than the low rumblings and "wah-wah" sounds that I heard. Grown-ups told me I spoke funny because I had a lazy tongue. I'd stand in front of the mirror and poke my tongue, trying to wake it up. Somehow, I managed to teach myself to lip-read.

At school, I was completely lost. How do you read the teacher's lips when she's writing on the chalkboard? In second grade, the teacher started teaching phonics. "Sound it out, Kathy!" Uh … I don't think so.

Finally, someone thought to test my hearing. I'd been at that school for three years before anyone clued in to the fact that I was deaf. (And they called me slow!)

Just one little problem. They forgot to tell me.

Instead, they gave me these big plastic earmuffs: Zenith Diplomat hearing aids. I hated them. They must have had a pound of plastic for each ear. It was the only time in my life I was actually top-heavy. I didn't understand why I had to wear these stupid things. They sent me to a school for the disabled. I figured it was because I was causing trouble and they didn't want me there anymore.

It wasn't so bad at the new school. I made friends with a sweet little blind girl. I used to trade sandwiches with her. At least, I thought she knew we were trading. Later, I learned she never saw me make the exchange—just thought she was getting boring PB-and-J, while I got yummy barbecued beef. Of course, I never heard her complain!

At the special school I learned how to speak well enough to be sent back to the public system. With my big hearing aids, funny speech, and a growth spurt that shot me up to six feet tall, I felt like an alien. I wore a thick headband to hide the hearing aids and stole candy from my parents to make the other kids like me. All I was doing was looking for acceptance, a place to belong.

By high school I'd learned how to deflect attention with wisecracks. I didn't think I was being funny. Joking was my defense mechanism to keep them from seeing my pain, from seeing that I was dumb. If they laughed with me, they couldn't laugh at me. I became my own one-woman improv group.

Academically, I was a disaster. I don't know what I was thinking when I signed up for French. Try lip-reading "oui, oui." I didn't make it in typing either. I'd sit at the keyboard with my fingers in the air, ready to go, while everyone else was typing away. Apparently there was a record player going, dictating what we were supposed to type. Music class? Get that girl outta here! I graduated with a one-point grade average.

It wasn't much better after graduation. I couldn't hold a job because I kept messing up. As an employee in the fashion industry, I was asked to cut fifteen patterns. I thought they said fifteen hundred and I was cutting for days. Job after job, I was fired, and I had no idea why.

I had a series of accidents—which I suspect were half-hearted attempts at suicide—and my mother kicked me out of the house at eighteen. I just kept thinking there was something wrong with me. Why couldn't I connect? "Fix me!" I wanted to cry. "Or just let me die." I kept imagining cutting my arm off and watching myself bleed to death. With a little blade I started scratching things into my arm. I just wanted the pain to stop.

One morning I decided to lie on the beach by myself. Suddenly, I saw a lifeguard's Jeep barreling across the sand. I thought to myself, "My God, the way that Jeep is tearing around someone is liable to get run over."

I never thought it would be me.

Run over by a lifeguard! Talk about not knowing your job description.

I felt terrible pressure as my body was pressed into the sand. This was very bad. But strangely, I felt okay—like I could finally be at peace—

for just a moment. Then, no! I wasn't ready for this. Suddenly there was noise and paramedics and someone shouting, "3:40, dead on arrival." A sheet was pulled over me. I couldn't move. I was strapped to a board, wearing a neck brace. I blew hard on the sheet to get it off my face. "I'm so sorry," someone kept saying.

I was in ICU for six days. It wasn't until later I realized what a gift I'd been given when I died—the gift of choice. I would use that gift much later to turn my whole life around. For the moment, all I knew was that I was alive—but might never walk again. I sat in the wheelchair looking out the hospital window and pleaded with God: "Please don't forsake me. I don't want to end up in a wheelchair for the rest of my life lip-reading nose hair."

One day, when I could finally use my legs again, I had a complete physical examination. Lo and behold, they diagnosed a hearing impairment! No, Kathy, the examiner said, you're not retarded. I tried my first pair of functional hearing aids. Keys jingled! The door squeaked! God knows how long that toilet's been running! I even heard myself pee. Scared me to death! I thought my liver had fallen out.

With the knowledge of my disability, I could feel those old labels start to fade. I found a job as a massage therapist. One morning a woman came in. She'd just been in a bad accident. Her body hurt; it was too tense to massage. Instead, I joked with her. "I was so mad at that guy for driving right out in front of me," she said. "Oh, be honest. You're pissed 'cause you missed your hair appointment." As she laughed, I could feel the pain and tension in her body fade away. That day, I saw the power of laughter. Until then, I'd just used it to keep people away.

Not long after, a friend dared me to take part in a stand-up comedy contest to raise money for children with cerebral palsy. What did I know about comedy? But then I remembered that day under the Jeep, and how I was given the gift of choice. Here was a choice I could make to help children. I'd do it. To my surprise, all the years of wisecracking paid off. I ended up in the semi-finals—me with my two weeks in the business up against 80 others who'd been comedians for three to ten years—and I placed fourth.

So you see, it was completely unplanned. I made a choice to reach out of my wallowing little world and ended up with a career making people laugh. I'm having a life I never thought I could have. I've written a book and an award-winning autobiographical play, and now have a successful career as a motivational speaker, sharing my stories of exclusion to help others.

Funny thing—every time I went onstage, I could feel something changing inside me. The monster that I used to feel crawling around in my stomach was withering away. With each speech, with each positive thought, or every time I reached out to another person, the monster got smaller.

I learned that wallowing is bad—but easy to do. And I learned that reaching out is good—and surprisingly easy too. It's as simple as stepping outside of "What about me" to "What about you…What do you need today that I can offer you? A smile, a hug?" If you put a smile on someone's face, you're going to feel better yourself.

What it comes down to, on a selfish level, is this: making people laugh gives me an opportunity to put a smile on my God's face. Every time I get to touch somebody's heart or their spirit, that smile may be God saying, "You did good today, honey."

CHAPTER NINE

EMPATHY

"The discoveries of how we can grow and the insights we need to have really come from the inside out. To have genuine empathy, not as a make-nice tool but as an understanding, is essential to the next step."

—Patricia Sun

The WE offices are located in an eclectic neighborhood in downtown Toronto. Since the move, we have grown to love the area's mix of ethnic groups, old Victorian and Irish immigrant roots, quiet parks, and bustling businesses. Although vibrant, it is also touched by homelessness and hunger, alcoholism and drug abuse.

Wanting to become active agents in the growth of our community, we sought out the advice of a friend of ours, a local social worker. What, we wondered, would be the best way to reach out? We were looking for solid steps, a list of answers, ideas that we could put into action tomorrow. But that's not what we got. Instead, our friend insisted we sit down for a moment. "Now, close your eyes," she instructed, "and try to imagine this situation:

"After a long day at your new office, you finally decide it's time to head home for the evening. You pack up your things, throw on your coat and head out into the night.

As the first blast of cold air hits your face, you realize the temperature is lower than the forecast. You're already dreading waiting for the bus, but you cheer yourself up thinking about how good it will feel to step into the comfortable warmth of your cozy apartment. As you walk to your stop, you're already envisioning your evening: first a nice meal, then a hot shower, then a few hours with the book you've been enjoying for the past three nights. How will it end? The suspense is already killing you.

There you are, walking along, oblivious to the world, when a shrill voice pulls you back to reality. Looking ahead, you see two women arguing out in front of the local women's shelter. One you recognize as a shelter representative, the other is very young and visibly upset. As you approach them, you see that the young woman has a child slung across her hip. Despite the weather, neither she nor her child is wearing a coat. As you walk slowly past, you hear the woman from the shelter say, 'I'm so sorry; I don't know what to do. We're already way over our capacity. We just don't have any more room.'

With tears now streaming down her face, the younger woman repeats her pleas even more loudly. 'But we don't have anywhere else to go! This isn't about drugs, I'm telling you. You don't understand.' She pauses, furtively checking over her shoulder, then lowers her voice and breaks down. 'We can't go back. He'll kill us!' You stare, aghast."

The question, as our social worker friend put it, is what happens next? Will you comfort yourself with the certainty that the woman really isn't as badly off as she seems? Will you continue to wait for the bus, trying to forget what you've just heard by turning your thoughts back to a pleasant evening of relaxation? Or will you be moved by the woman's plight to the point where you try to help her and the child? This situation may by hypothetical but, as our friend pointedly made clear to us that day, the answers you come up with offer some indication of how you might respond in a similar situation.

Whether it's walking down the street or seeing people in distress on the evening news, we all encounter situations that have a lot in common with the one above. Often, our reactions mirror those we have just discussed: we avoid, defend ourselves through resisting the pain of others' suffering, or act on our feelings of empathy.

AVOIDANCE: AVERTING OUR EYES

Avoidance happens when we look upon others' suffering and become overwhelmed by our own response to it. We know we feel bad and we know we want it to end. Since the quickest and easiest way to relieve our own pain is to remove ourselves from the situation, this is what we do, either physically or through distracting ourselves with something pleasurable. This is what happens when we see images of poverty and deprivation on television, and quickly change the channel. It's what prompts us to pick up our pace when we see a homeless person on the sidewalk shivering in the cold. Avoidance is usually the first of many reactions that people go through when facing such dilemmas in life. It is about our fear of the unknown, and fear of the responsibility of taking action where others fail to act.

DEFENSE: RESISTING THE PAIN OF OTHERS' SUFFERING

If avoidance is not possible, people are often motivated to defend themselves from the emotional pain of identifying with the suffering of others. This last line of defense is in fact a toolbox of strategies that we employ to keep from having to confront negative and distressing realities. These psychological tricks we play on ourselves—mostly without realizing it—are able to distort and change the meaning of what we see. This doesn't change the negative reality, but it does make us feel better.

How does this work when we see other people suffering? Simple. At the extreme, we dehumanize those people, distancing ourselves from their suffering. Most of us find it difficult to commit, or passively allow, acts that inflict harm on other people "just like us" so we convince ourselves that "they" are not like "us." We may have to label them as "the enemy," and attach a set of negative characteristics to their particular ethnic, religious or other social group. We may blame them for their circumstances, emphasizing or imagining all the weaknesses and failures of that group that have led to these circumstances. We may try to ignore the external factors, the political, ideological, economic, military, and other forces that shaped their fates from the outside. We might use derogatory names for the people of that social group, and adopt views of their group as being inherently undesirable, lazy, apathetic, violent, greedy, evil, or just backward, inferior, or less civilized. We may fall prey to subtler forms of prejudice, such as assuming that our group is better than their group, noticing the good things about our group and ignoring or explaining away whatever negative qualities exist, while emphasizing the negative qualities and downplaying the positive aspects of other groups.

Learning to view other human beings in ways that dehumanize or devalue them allows us to find comfort in vague notions. Since they are so different from us, maybe they don't suffer the same way we would in the same situation. Perhaps they have gotten used to living that way, or they are just "those kinds of people" and don't know how to live any other way. Thinking this way makes it easy to believe that people in unfortunate circumstances actually deserve to be there, that it's their fault they are in this situation.

You can see how these strategies blend together and reinforce each other. Seeing people in "us" and "them" terms makes it easier to dehumanize and devalue them, to assume that there are fundamental differences between us and them, and to blame them for their suffering. Thinking in "us" and "them" terms also makes it easier to reduce people to numbers, to conveniently forget about their individualities; we can see them as just an abstract mass and not as a group of separate, fascinating, beautiful human beings, like we are. In this way, people in poverty, people suffering from violence, prejudice, illiteracy, hunger—you name it—become more than faceless statistics. In our own charitable work, we have had the occasion to witness terrible suffering, and we struggle not to block it out, to see the child behind the challenge, and the person behind the number. It can be very hard.

EMPATHY: REACHING OUT WITH COMPASSION

Empathy allows us to look at another and see a reflection of ourselves or someone we care about. Whether you understand it as compassion, or as a sympathetic understanding of someone else's feelings, it is the flip side of avoidance and dismissal. When we are open to the empathy we feel for someone in distress, we experience an urge to reach out and help.

Empathy is crucial for living Me to We because it is one of the most important ways that we can establish an emotional connection with others. It is empathy that helps us to connect our own desire for happiness to that held by others, and to understand how similar we all are despite our differences. In our Me-focused society, we often close ourselves off from this emotion, but to make the shift from Me to We, we need to be willing to open ourselves up to it. Stepping outside of our comfort zones to say "I feel something here, and I want to explore how I can help" is not easy. But doing so we acknowledge the responsibility we have for one another.

Study after study of helping behavior provides overwhelming evidence that a key part of assisting others involves feeling empathy.[1] In our work with Free The Children, we have seen how important this emotion can be in inspiring people of all ages to reach out to others. We have seen how it can inspire a shy student to take up public speaking, motivate a busy professional to make time to volunteer, or induce an urban teen to spend the summer building a school in rural Kenya. We have seen it turn ordinary people into extraordinary activists. When we empathize with another person, we respond with kindness, treating him or her how we would wish to be treated ourselves.

When empathy is not actively suppressed, but nurtured and allowed to flourish, it blossoms into one of the most beautiful aspects of our humanity. It opens our hearts and our minds to the possibility of collective support and understanding. As this chapter progresses, we will share some ideas and stories with you that will help guide you through this process in your own life.

Theresa's Story: Empathy Unites

When we first began trying to understand the connection between helping and empathy, we decided to sit down with one of the most helpful people we know: a young woman named Theresa. As one of Free The Children's youth coordinators, Theresa spends her days inspiring young people and providing them with the support they need to help children around the world. She is the kindest of people, always willing to lend a hand for a worthy cause, big or small. Whenever anyone is having a difficult day, she is the first one ready with a hug and words of encouragement.

When we asked Theresa about her experiences with empathy, her first words were "I guess it's actually kind of a long story."

It turns out that as a young child, Theresa was diagnosed with a severe form of Juvenile Rheumatoid Arthritis. This debilitating illness affected every moving joint in her body, leaving her in excruciating pain. Often confined to a wheelchair, she made frequent trips to the hospital. The treatment was onerous: physiotherapy appointments, weekly intramuscular injections of gold (she truly is a walking treasure!), and blood work were facts of life.

Theresa told us that while her disability severely limited her physical movement, it did wonders to strengthen her spirit. She credits this incredibly difficult experience with helping her to relate to other people's pain and sorrow, and to appreciate the power of compassion. When, against all odds, she was able to triumph against this cruel disease, she made up her mind to devote herself to a life of service to others.

It was several years after her recovery that one of her most profound experiences with empathy occurred. While in Calcutta, she volunteered at one of Mother Teresa's homes, Sho She Bavan, a center for severely handicapped and sick children whose parents had either died or abandoned them. It was there that she met Amanda.

The first time Theresa saw Amanda, the little girl was lying on a bright red mat like the rest of the children. Although her eyes were alive, her tiny hands were curled up underneath themselves and her frail legs were molded into a hardened bunch. There was no doctor to diagnose Amanda's many painful symptoms, but Theresa recognized them immediately. They were similar to those that she herself had once experienced.

"All the horror stories the doctors told me would affect me had already taken an effect on her," she recalled. "The difference between us was that, whereas I had physical therapy on a regular basis and received medicine, Amanda didn't have the means for these types of luxuries."

Minutes after meeting Amanda, Theresa knew how she wanted to spend the rest of her time in India. Acutely aware of the pain the little girl was experiencing, she worked to make her as comfortable as possible, tending to her needs and showering her with affection. Although Amanda was unable to speak and would not have been able to understand English, the bond of understanding between them grew stronger by the day.

"When the time finally came to say goodbye, I carried her over to her bed, sang her one more song, and combed her hair." Theresa told us quietly. "As I started to walk away, there were tears in my eyes, but as I looked back, I saw that Amanda was smiling. It was in that moment that I realized just how similar Amanda and I were. It was love that cured an illness I had that the doctors said would leave me crippled and end my life early. And it was love that gave Amanda the strength to embrace the gifts of life, understanding and compassion."

As Theresa's encounter with Amanda shows, the extent to which we consider others to be similar to ourselves can be a powerful force in inspiring empathy. Yet, as Theresa now demonstrates in her work with children around the world, feeling empathy for others need not be dependent on having experienced exactly what someone else is going through. It is bigger than that. It involves a willingness to open yourself to, and care about others, and to help them in whatever way you can.

Understanding Empathy in Action

If anything, our chat with Theresa made us even more curious about the workings of empathy. Her unique life experiences had obviously shaped her understanding of this emotion, but what about the rest of us? How does empathy develop, and what role does it play in encouraging us to reach out? Can it thrive in people's hearts even when it seems to be lacking in society as a whole?

In our search for answers we turned to Dr. Jonathan White, a professor of sociology and political economy at Bridgewater State College in Massachusetts. As someone who specializes in both encouraging civic engagement and understanding the horrors that result in its absence, Dr. White has long been interested in empathy and its power to both do good and prevent tragedy.

Taking a seat in his bright and student-friendly office, lined with books from top to bottom, Dr. White told us that it is crucial to understand that the seeds of empathy are ingrained within each one of us. "It's natural for us to care and natural for us to be caretakers," he explained with his characteristic energy. "It's also natural for us to wish that others experience more happiness and less suffering and that this is just as much a part of our human nature as is our desire for personal happiness."

As we would learn, we experience empathy even as infants. As many parents and childcare workers have learned the hard way, when one baby in a nursery starts to cry, it doesn't take long for the others to follow suit. It has been found that it isn't just the loud noise that they are responding to—other types of loud noises do not elicit the same response—it is the suffering of others. Studies by child psychologists have backed this up, showing that even young babies and infants seem to be especially attuned to the social dimension, paying more attention to other people, and reacting noticeably to even the subtlest signs that others are in distress. This shows that empathy is so deeply embedded into human nature that it exerts an influence even in the first stages of life.

Upon learning that empathy is an emotion all of us experience from our earliest days, we became even more determined to ask about the role it plays in the darker aspects of our friend's research. After all, it doesn't take more than a quick look at history to see that while the seeds of empathy may be within us, there are times when it seems to all but disappear from the scene. We knew that as an expert on the history and sociophychology of genocide and political violence, Dr. White had had the chance to study empathy and its absence in the most extreme situations.

"We know that many of those who saved Jews during the Holocaust were actually ordinary people," Dr. White frankly told us. "They were farmers, teachers, business owners, and factory workers. Some were rich, some were poor, some Protestants, others Catholics. Many have done little else that is extraordinary, either before the war or since. One of the things that they all seem to have common, however, was an ability to feel empathy and act on it."

We must have looked puzzled. In fact, it seemed difficult to understand how average people found the courage to take such heroic actions.

"Let me tell you the story of a young woman named Gitta, and I think you'll see what I mean," Dr. White offered, carefully extracting some papers from the large pile precariously balanced on his desk.

Gitta Bauer was born in Berlin in 1919. When the Nazi Party began to gain popularity during the hard times of the 1930s, both of her parents opposed them. Many years later she would recall asking her father, "What's a Jew?" His reply would stay with her always: "Jews are people like you and me, only with a different religion. And that's it."

By the time Hitler came to power, Gitta was a young woman. She watched as the treatment of Germany's Jewish citizens grew worse by the day. In her words, "You didn't have to read Mein Kampf to know Hitler had it in for the Jews...You saw photos of Jews being marched through the street... Even if you didn't see it yourself, you had to be aware." The rights of German Jews were taken away, one after another.

As violence escalated, Gitta chose to act. As she explained it, "My aunt's friend had a twin sister who came to me in 1933 and said that her daughter was in danger. What else could I say but 'I'll take her into my home?' This was no big moral or religious decision... she needed help. We knew it was dangerous, and we were careful, but we didn't consider not taking her."

The girl whose life Gitta saved was 21-year-old Ilse Baumgart. Ilse lived with Gitta for nine months, until the end of the war. Decades later, Ilse's testimony led to Gitta being honored with a Yad Vashem medal for her compassion and courage in face of one of the greatest horrors of the twentieth century.[2]

"Gitta's story is one good example of the way that normal people took a stand for their beliefs," Dr. White told us. "Obviously, the details of each case are unique, but the process she went through is similar to many others."

As Dr. White explained to us at length that afternoon, the lives of people like Gitta hold important lessons about the way that empathy develops and moves people to action—lessons that we can all learn from. For us, the first and most obvious lesson is that you need to know about a situation before you can do something about it. This means refusing to turn a blind eye to injustice, just as Gitta did, and learning all you can about it.

Once you're aware of the situation, the next important step is to get to know those involved as people. While we don't always need to know someone personally, as Gitta did, it is crucial to learn about his or her life story. We all know the difference between reading about a large number of people dying from a disease, and listening to an interview with one person suffering from that disease and learning about its impact on her life. Ultimately, the empathy we feel from learning about the suffering of an individual helps us to generalize our empathy when we learn about what otherwise might feel like nameless, faceless statistics. When we are able to humanize the statistics, then we feel a natural empathy toward those who are suffering, much as a baby feels when she hears other babies crying. We've found that one way to begin developing a better appreciation of someone else's situation is to imagine how you would feel if you were in that person's place. There's nothing like trying to "walk a mile in someone else's shoes" when it comes to understanding the challenges he or she faces, and relating to his or her position. Equally imporatant is to then imagine walking a mile in your own shoes, but with the vision of how you can use your time, skills, and resources to powerfully and positively affect the lives of those you have gained newfound empathy for.

Feeling empathy encourages us to act, but to make a difference we need to do more than just listen politely to our inner voice—we need to actually follow through on its advice. In our own work, we have come to believe that this is one of the greatest challenges that people, and especially young people, face. Even when individuals experience empathy, they often grapple with the issue of whether they themselves can make a difference. When it comes to turning empathy into action, we need the inner strength to believe we can do something to make things better. Gitta knew that offering Ilse refuge would help her, but she also trusted enough in herself to know she could do this. She knew that she had the power to save a life. By following her heart and believing in herself, she was able to hide Ilse until she was no longer in danger. While her situation was extreme and her courage tremendous, we can all draw on her experience with empathy as we go about our daily lives. She did what she could to help one person. Ultimately, this is something all of us can do. We all encounter situations where we can make a difference in someone's life—indeed in many people's lives. It's up to each of us to choose how we will respond.

Nurturing Empathy Early

In Gitta's story, the importance she attributes to her father's egalitarian views is striking. When we asked Dr. White about this, he explained that this is common among many of those who saved lives during the Holocaust. Studies show that many rescuers attribute their respect for others to the lessons learned in childhood.[3] In fact, two lessons are critically important. The first is the lesson of empathy, of being open to the emotional resonance you feel for others, especially when they are in pain. The second is the lesson of what you might call "universal egalitarianism." This is the principle of equality for all people. This perspective calls us to focus on our shared humanity, to emphasize the similarities that unite us all, and de-emphasize the group boundaries and differences that divide us.

Rescuers had internalized the moral lesson that we all have an equal right to happiness and justice, and had coupled this with a strong sense of empathy. These were the people who had been able to resist the Nazi propaganda machine, who had retained their own personal convictions of the equal value of all people. When it was time for heroism, these were the people who rose to the challenge of their times and found the courage to save lives.

The message is clear: when our innate empathy is nurtured in our earliest days, and when this empathy is applied as broadly as possible, it can weather even the hardest of times. As a board member of several different non-profit organizations focused on youth, Dr. White was only too happy to offer his expertise. "Encouraging young people to foster their innate sense of empathy toward others is crucial," he explained, "as is helping them to understand the impact of their actions and inactions on others. Parents, who praise children for positive actions, promote good role models and set a good example themselves, are definitely on the right track. It is important to teach young people from an early age to empathize with human suffering. They need to know they have the power and responsibility to act upon their empathy in ways that will reduce and even eliminate this suffering. Creating a generation of responsible citizens is possible, and it is also necessary for us to thrive."

TIPS FOR NURTURING EMPATHY IN CHILDREN

1. **Discuss feelings:** On a daily basis, ask them how they feel and tell them how you feel. By doing so, you'll help them to see that others experience similar emotions: happiness, satisfaction, pain, frustration, anger, elation, surprise, empowerment, etc.

2. **Discipline appropriately:** Describing the emotional costs of a child's bad behavior helps children appreciate that their behavior affects others, and motivates them to be "good" because of the empathy they feel for others. Furthermore, using discipline that is grounded in reasoning and explanation, rather than power, sends the message that the more powerful must treat the less powerful with justice and respect.

3. **Praise and label positive actions:** Notice when a child does something good, and praise them for it. You might say, "I saw you helping your sister. That was really nice of you. You are a really kind person!" This encourages children to think of themselves as kind, and behave accordingly, because a precedent has been set.

4. **Use role models:** Children naturally identify with heroes. It is important to reinforce this tendency by praising "good" heroes, both fictional and real, who will act as role models. Children will seek to emulate the good deeds of others, leading them to internalize positive values and morals.

5. **Set a good example:** Children often model themselves after their parents, and are profoundly influenced by the example they set. This means that if parents are themselves kind, generous, selfless, empathetic, compassionate, etc., then their children stand to adopt the same values and behaviors.

6. **Provide a moral compass:** It's important to teach children the principles of good decision-making as well as the differences between right and wrong. Such discussions are vital in providing children with a sense of ethics and morality, internalizing rules that will later guide behavior.

EMPATHY CYCLES

When values learned in childhood last a lifetime, it's clear that the world's most powerful people aren't presidents and CEOs. They're the parents and teachers who interact with children every day and shape the values they will carry with them through to adulthood.

When children learn to develop their capacity for empathy early in life, they go on to treat others with empathy later. Empathetic children become empathic parents, who raise empathetic children. An empathy cycle is created, and it stretches far beyond a single lifetime. Just think: Mother Teresa's father set an empathy cycle in motion, as did Dr. Martin Luther King's mother. These parents helped nurture within their children an extraordinary sense of empathy, courage, and compassion, helping to transform the world through the acts of their children and the people they, in turn, have affected.

One of the most successful programs that we have discovered for encouraging empathy in children is called Roots of Empathy. Designed for schoolchildren from Kindergarten to eighth grade, this program allows children to learn not from adults, but from a baby! Over the course of the school year, visits from a local parent-infant team, guided by a trained instructor, allow students to observe the baby's development, and to learn how to interact with the little one in a gentle and loving way.[4]

It's clear that these visits have an impact. Through interacting with the infant, children gradually become adept at identifying its feelings and needs, and become sensitive to its temperament. Through learning about what the baby is experiencing, they develop an appreciation for someone whose reality is far different from their own. Roots of Empathy has been shown to reduce levels of aggression and violence among schoolchildren while raising social/emotional competence and increasing empathy. Graduates take their newfound lessons beyond the classroom, triggering empathy cycles that endure and are passed on to the next generation.

As you can see, empathy cycles are often set in motion by simple gestures of everyday kindness and love. Sometimes, however, they work in more mysterious ways. Some people believe in fate, others in divine intervention, others in the idea that what goes around, comes around. However you want to put it, some empathy cycles operate in ways that defy easy explanations. Such was the case with the Malfinder family.

We met the Malfinders in Sierra Leone, a country in West Africa where Free The Children works, which was long the site of a brutal civil war. As with so many wars, this one was driven by greed. Have you heard of blood diamonds? This is the name given to illegally traded diamonds used to finance violence and bloodshed. In Sierra Leone, almost $300 million worth of these illegal diamonds were smuggled out of the country in 1999 alone, fuelling arms purchases and, with them, the ambitions of local warlords.[5]

In eleven years of fighting, more than 7,000 children were forcibly recruited as child soldiers, with boys as young as seven and eight years old being threatened with death and sent out to kill.[6] Young girls were taken as "war brides" and given to soldiers, or used as domestic servants in the home or slaves in the mines. Traveling from town to town after the war, we heard of mass executions, murder, rape, and disfigurement.

The Malfinder family came from the province of Kono, one of the areas most devastated by the fighting. When we met them outside of their modest hut, each of their haggard faces spoke of intense suffering. It was the father that told us their story, speaking softly as his wife listened silently.

At the height of the violence, the Malfinders and their children had fled their home and began the journey to neighboring Guinea on foot, determined to find asylum. Traveling together with a group of neighbors, they had hoped for the best. But it wasn't to be. On the way they came across a band of rebel soldiers who were traveling from village to village, destroying everything in their path. The family hid in the brush alongside the road, desperately trying not to make a sound. But the youngest daughter, Hanna, who was six years old, was so afraid that she cried out. After a brief struggle, the rebels captured the three children—Hanna, nine-year-old John, and eleven-year-old Suzanne—and their grandmother. The parents managed to escape.

The rebels quickly decided that the grandmother was too old for manual labor, so she was shot to death. The children were then divided among them as trophies—the boy was given to one rebel commander and the two girls were given to another.

John was made to work as a slave in the fields for three years, helping to grow crops to feed the troops. As soon as he turned twelve years old, he was forced to become a soldier. When an amnesty was declared and he was reunited with his family after the war, John explained how he had helped to transport diamonds from the diamond mines throughout Sierra Leone to secret rendezvous points, where white men who spoke English would land their helicopters and trade guns for diamonds. Hanna and Suzanne were used as domestic servants. After two years in captivity, they gave up hope of ever seeing their family again.

But their father had never stopped looking for them. Having made it to safety in Guinea, he and their mother were tormented by thoughts of what their children were enduring. At great personal risk, he crossed back into the rebel-controlled territory in Sierra Leone each night, searching for his missing children. He knew that if he were captured he would likely be killed or worse, but he couldn't bear to think that his children were suffering.

Eventually, he located the home where his daughters were being held captive. Courageously, he met with the rebel commander and pleaded for their return. The commander, impressed with the father's determination and bravery, responded by saying that he could have one daughter back—the other would be kept as a slave.

The father broke down in tears at this point, unable to choose which daughter would be freed and which one would remain. He was facing the most horrible choice that anyone could ever be asked to make. He stood there in silence, paralyzed by the horror of the situation.

It was then that Suzanne, who was thirteen years old at the time, spoke. Knowing of the terrible fate that awaited her sister if she remained in captivity, Suzanne told the commander that she would stay if he let her younger sister go. Because of Suzanne's sacrifice, Hanna was granted her freedom and permitted to leave with their father.

After that, Suzanne was left with no one at all to turn to. Each night she dreamed of escaping, but she knew that if she were caught, the penalty would be death. Then, three months later, a glimmer of hope appeared out of the blue. While she was washing the clothes at the riverbank one morning, a woman approached her. Claiming to be a family friend, this woman promised to help Suzanne to escape. Suzanne was fearful of what would happen to them both if they were caught, but finally agreed to accept the stranger's help.

That evening, Suzanne snuck out of the house and traveled with the woman under the cover of night. They slept during the day, hidden in the bush. When they approached the Guinean border, the woman gave Suzanne all the money in her possession. It was a small amount, the equivalent of a single dollar, but this was a fortune in a place where almost no one had any money at all, where starvation was rampant and where a few dollars could buy a gun. She then embraced her, and wished her luck. Soon after, she vanished as abruptly as she had first appeared.

When Suzanne approached the impasse between the two countries, she saw that the Sierra Leonean side of the border was controlled by rebel troops. One of the young boys—a child soldier—recognized her as a domestic servant and stopped her. The boy demanded to know why she was so far away from the commander's home. Suzanne, certain that this child would kill her, showed him her money. She said it had been given to her by the commander in order to buy shoes for him in Guinea and that she was to bring them back across the border to Sierra Leone. No slave would have had any money, so the boy believed her story and let her cross. Suzanne walked safely into Guinea—and to freedom.

Weeks later, Suzanne found the refugee camp were her parents were staying and was reunited with her family. She never again saw the woman who had rescued her. When she later explained her story, it emerged that her parents had no idea who the woman could have been. Her description didn't match that of anyone they knew.

In her years of captivity, Suzanne had never once encountered anyone who provided her with aid. Yet she was granted her freedom three months after helping her sister. To this day, she still believes that the woman was an angel—a miracle—sent by God. Suzanne believes that God sent this angel to rescue her, inspired by her willingness to sacrifice her own life for another's freedom.

START NOW!

- Although it may be emotionally difficult, think back to a time when you could have helped someone but didn't.

- Try to identify why you made the decision you did. Was it easier to avoid the problem? Was it tempting to believe that the situation wasn't really as difficult as it seemed?

- Reaction like this can make it difficult to reach out—but the good news is that we can always improve.

- Pick an issue you care about and begin to nurture your empathy for those directly affected. Ask yourself:

  » Where can I go to learn more about the issue?

  » Where can I go to meet and talk to people facing the issue?

  » Can I speak with someone working to help those people to learn more about what I too can do?

TAKE ANOTHER LOOK!

We know that children around the world often can't get medical treatment when they're sick. But sometimes we forget that there are also millions of children in America who can't afford to see a doctor when they need to. What are some small ways you can make a child feel better when he or she is sick? Locally, creating a fun care package or supporting a clinic in a low-income neighborhood can work wonders. Globally, raising awareness or helping a charity to send medical supplies overseas can save lives.

- About 10 million children in the U.S. do not have health insurance.[7]

- More than 12 million children and adolescents in the U.S. are overweight.[8]

- In 2005, half a million children in Africa died of HIV/AIDS, yet fewer than 10 percent of HIV-positive mothers in sub-Saharan Africa have access to drugs that can drop the rate of transmission from mother to child to 2 percent.[9]

ME TO WE ACTION

1. **Don't walk by, say hi!** Next time you pass a homeless person on the street, ask yourself how he or she got there. Could you have been in the same position if you'd made different decisions, if you'd lost your job or had a loved one die? After asking these questions, do something to make a difference. Smile, say hi, or take to time to chat.

2. **Give an extra tip.** What's better than a good tip? In the service industry, almost all the customer feedback is negative. One nice comment can go a long way. Let a manager know how hard that waiter, mechanic, or health care provider is working.

3. **Give a gift that keeps on giving.** Next time you find yourself hunting for a birthday gift for that special someone, make a donation to an international charity in his or her name. Every year, more than 10,000,000 children never reach the age of five—your gift may help a child reach his or her next birthday.

My Story

JONATHAN WHITE

Running behind as always, but this time for an important date that I just couldn't be late for! I found myself at a checkout counter behind an elderly woman seemingly in no rush as she paid her groceries. A Ph.D. student with not a lot of money, I had hurried into the grocery store to pick up a bouquet of flowers and a pack of breath mints. I was in a huge rush, thinking of my upcoming evening. I did not want to be late for this date.

We were in Boston, Massachusetts—a place not always known for small conversation between strangers. The woman stopped unloading her basket and looked up at me. She smiled. It was a nice smile—warm, reassuring—and I returned her gift by smiling back.

"Must be a special lady, whoever it is that will be getting those beautiful flowers," she said.

"Yes, as a matter of fact, she is special," I said, and then to my embarrassment, the words kept coming out. "It's only our second date, but somehow I am just having the feeling that she's 'the one' and I've never in my life felt that before." Jokingly, I added, "The only problem is that I can't figure out why she would want to date a guy like me."

"Well, I think she's very lucky to have a boyfriend who brings her such lovely flowers and who is obviously so smitten with her," the woman said. "My husband, God rest his soul, used to bring me flowers every week—even when times were tough and we didn't have much money. Those were incredible days, he was very romantic and—of course—I miss him since he's passed away."

I paid for my flowers as she was gathering up her groceries and putting on her coat. There was no doubt in my mind as I walked up to her. I tapped her on the shoulder and said, "You were right, you know. These flowers are indeed for a very special lady." I handed her the bouquet and thanked her for such a nice conversation.

It took her a moment to realize that I was giving her the flowers I had just purchased. "You have a wonderful evening," I said. I left her with a big smile and my heart warmed as I could see her smelling the beautiful bouquet.

I remember being slightly late for my date that night and telling my girlfriend the above story. A couple of years later, when I finally worked up the courage to propose marriage, she told me that this story had helped to seal it for her—that was the night that I won her heart.

CHAPTER TEN

REDEFINING HAPPINESS

"I look to stop wishing, at least until the end of time
'Cause my last wish is that happiness be both yours and mine."

—Joe Opatowski

Joe's celebration was like no other. With less than a week's notice, they came in droves. All in all, there were six hundred people from across North America: young and old; homeless people and CEOs; bestselling authors and dignitaries. Everyone showed up with smiling faces, eyes filled with love, and a determination to party like they had never partied before. From the minute things kicked off, it was an event to remember.

Four rooms were set up, each with its own special purpose. The first was an oasis of tranquility, its walls covered with Joe's own words. People stood reading his messages in the soft light, bathed in the incense wafting through the air. On the opposite wall, a slideshow was set up, with images flashing by to the sound of soothing music. In one corner of the room stood a Zen garden of sand, etched with finger-drawn messages of empathy, gratitude, and love. In the far corner stood a wishing well where people revealed their thoughts, wishes, dreams. The scene was one of peace and introspection as people gathered together lost in thought.

The room next door shook with the sound of music, with people drumming to intricate African and Indian rhythms. A circle was formed around the drummers, and onlookers stood on the outside keeping time with noisemakers. Right beside this music room was the art room, where canvas-lined tables stood with markers and paint brushes, waiting for anyone filled with creative inspiration. In the middle of the room, a group of people with shoes off and pant legs rolled up danced on canvas with paint-covered feet to the beats coming from next door. Finally, there was the food room, where tables pushed against the four walls were lined with Mexican, Sri Lankan, Indian, Thai, Korean, and Guinean foods—all Joe's favorites. And, of course, there were smoothies made with strawberry, kiwi, blueberry, mango, and even some cabbage. Here, the chatter of first encounters mingled with the conversations of long-time friends, filling the air with happy stories. People spoke fondly of Joe, recalling all of the many happy times they had spent with him over the years. They spoke of deep late night conversations, happy out-of-the-blue meetings on street corners, days spent traveling together in distant cities, outrageous antics of one kind or another, and moments of shared inspiration. People spoke of early-morning breakfasts, poetry, hugs, passion, and even the titles on Joe's famous bookshelf. Everyone had a tale to tell.

Later that evening, this party of parties wound to a close with a dance. As a DJ blared music, people linked arms to form a huge circle. Everyone danced together to the changing sounds of Joe's favorite songs long into the night, celebrating the happiness he had brought them. When we think of true happiness, we think of the feeling that filled the room that night: one of pure joy without expectation or definition, a happiness simply felt and understood.

It may seem like this celebration could have been many things, a birthday party or perhaps a graduation bash. But it wasn't. It was Joe's going away party, in the most final sense of the term.

Joe Opatowski, brother, son, friend, mentor, and inspiration, is no longer with us.

His spirit, however, lives on in all those whose lives he touched. In death, as in life, he redefined happiness for both himself and all who knew him. If any one person can be said to have embodied the Me to We philosophy, it's him. One of the philosophy's earliest and most passionate proponents, he dedicated himself both to living the message and sharing it through his writings and speeches. For him, it was about finding the truest, deepest kind of happiness. In this chapter, we want to walk you through Joe's awakening, and share his legacy with you.

Many of us feel that we understand what happiness is. When we tell people how happy we are, we expect them to know just what we mean. But ask someone to explain this feeling, and he or she will likely fumble for words. Joe himself could never really define it. He found it, yes, but quite by accident. When he found it, he realized that it wasn't anything like he had imagined; it was better.

THE SECRET TO HAPPINESS: FINDING BALANCE

Joe didn't have it easy growing up. By the time he was in high school, he recognized most of the police officers who patrolled his neighborhood—they had all taken turns visiting his house over the years. Fights, and the screaming and yelling that accompanied them, were a matter of routine in his family. As time passed, things only got worse. Twice his mom disappeared, and he was convinced he would never see her again. Then someone from social services took his brother away to live in a foster home. Things needed to change.

At seventeen, Joe left home on a spur-of-the-moment decision. It was an act of desperation, but one he could not take back. After a few nights in coffee shops, a friend took him in until he found a landlord who would rent to a minor. To get by, he did whatever it took: market research and telemarketing in the afternoons, waiting tables and deejaying at night. To make ends meet, he even took up selling drugs. Through some miracle, he still managed to show up for school, keeping his role as the class clown and bargaining with his teachers for better marks. Some brushed him off as a delinquent; others thought he was a genius. Everyone agreed he had a way with words and a knack for getting people's attention.

Jordan didn't have much in common with the kids in Joe's crowd. Looking back, it's hard to imagine how the two of them ever struck up a conversation. But they did. When Jordan first started talking about a summer camp that would "change his life," Joe's eyes began to glaze over. It didn't sound like his kind of thing. But then Jordan uttered the magic word: *girls*. "There will be a ton of girls there," he promised. "They come from all over the world." Joe decided maybe this camp was worth a try after all.

The camp, hosted by Free The Children, wasn't what Joe had expected. Sure, he was interested in the girls—and Jordan had been right, there were lots—but he also found himself interested in what everyone had to say. As Joe got to know the other young people at this camp, he noticed something different about them. They cared. Not just about the social issues they were fighting for, but about everybody.

This camp was where we met Joe for the first time. Looking back, our first thoughts were something along the lines of "smart guy, great break-dancer, definitely charismatic." Did we expect him to stay involved? We figured it was anyone's guess. But when the camp ended,

Joe kept in touch with his new friends. He joined Free The Children's Toronto chapter, and began taking part in its activities. He helped raise funds to build a school overseas. From there, he started working with street kids and homeless people. He got to know them, learning their names. And the street kids returned the favor; they gave him a street name: Hugs. His life was changing.

Before long, Joe was sponsored to go with a group of young people to volunteer in the slums of Jamaica. A few months later, he found himself in Riverton, bouncing down a dirt road in a bus full of noisy and enthusiastic volunteers ready to "get involved." On either side of the road rose humongous piles of garbage. Suddenly, one of the piles moved. A flap opened and out climbed a young boy and a frail old man. The flap of garbage was the front door to their home. Everyone suddenly went quiet.

Climbing out of the bus, the group was instantly surrounded by local kids, all full of curiosity. As the children crowded around, Joe saw that most were wearing little more than rags. Not one had shoes. The little hands that reached out towards him were as boney as they were grubby. Joe knew what poverty was like back home, but it had never been like this. Seeing the hope in their eyes, he tried to think of something he could do. But what could someone like him, with so little to offer, possibly do?

In the end, he gave the only thing he could: piggyback rides. Almost before he knew it, everyone was smiling and laughing! It all seemed so unreal. Here he was in the middle of a garbage dump with some of the poorest kids on earth, and everyone was having a great time. Running around in the heat, Joe realized he was feeling something he hadn't felt in a very, very long time: happiness.

Finding happiness has preoccupied humans since ancient times. Although it's clear that it's something we all desire, too often a lot of us end up feeling like our best efforts fall short. Somehow, we're never happy enough, or as happy as we *could* be. Nevertheless, we remain captivated by the possibility of discovering the "Big Secret." You might say that our fascination has now reached the level of obsession: a quick Internet search for the secret of happiness turns up 79,900,000 links, all waiting to be explored. The thing is, before we try to *find* happiness, we need to ask ourselves what exactly it is we're looking for. Is it the excitement of going on vacation? Is it the joy of hearing someone say "I love you"? Is it the certainty that your actions make a difference in the world?

As we saw in chapter six, when Americans are asked about the biggest source of happiness in their lives, they talk about their loved ones and faith more frequently than anything else.[1] Still, despite the value that people claim to place on their relationships, it's clear that many are prioritizing spending power over time spent with loved ones. It may be a cliché to say that money can't buy happiness, but if you run into someone who has recently bought a new car, moved to a bigger house, or installed a state-of-the-art stereo system, more often than not he's smiling ear-to-ear. Seeing this happen time and time again eventually prompted us to wonder what exactly was going on.

We've found that understanding this situation requires drawing on the wisdom of none other the Aristotle. Although this philosophical heavyweight lived thousands of years ago in Ancient Greece, his insights about the nature of happiness have stood the test of time. While many people have expanded on his ideas over the years, he was the first to make a distinction between two very different kinds of happiness: *hedonic* and *eudaimonic*.

Hedonic Happiness

As a society, hedonic happiness is the kind we are most familiar with today. It's the sex, drugs and rock 'n' roll of happiness, firmly rooted in the five senses. It's the surge of pleasure we experience when we enjoy a delicious meal, the exhiliration of hitting the slopes for some great skiing, or the sheer bliss of basking in the sun at a beach for a week. Fundamentally, this kind of happiness is about Me and the feeling it provides for the individual. Like all life's highs, this type of happiness is as fleeting as it is intense. When it wears off, as it inevitably does, we remain as unfulfilled as ever, left to set off in pursuit of the next great thrill.

Eudaimonic Happiness

If hedonic happiness is the happiness of the senses, then eudaimonic happiness is the happiness of the soul. It is found in activities that are aligned with our fundamental human needs for meaning, connection and personal growth, and it brings a sense of engagement, contentment, and fulfillment. This is the happiness we feel when we spend time with loved ones, and when we grow as people. It is the satisfaction felt by the mother who teaches her daughter to read, by the community member who pitches in to clean up the neighborhood, and by the endless volunteers in soup kitchens, hospitals, drop-in centers, and camps across America. While it is vital for all of us as individuals, and therefore crucial for Me, by its very nature, it involves We in one way or another.

Unlike with hedonic happiness, time spent in eudaimonic pursuits fundamentally changes us, allowing us to flourish and grow as individuals and as communities. This is what happened to Joe when he began to reach out to those children in Jamaica. It had been forever since he had felt such a soul-stretching happiness, and it took him by surprise. He began to see that unlike the short-lived rush provided by his hedonic pursuits, the partying and clowning around, the eudaimonic happiness that came from making a connection with children in need provided a deep sense of satisfaction.

In our view, a full life involves striking a balance between hedonic and eudaimonic happiness. We're the first to admit that we enjoy life's pleasures as much as anyone. We have found—and continue to find—happiness in a nice meal, a good movie, a day off, and other simple things. While traveling, we enjoy trying new foods, sitting down at a local restaurant and asking for recommendations. We love it when we get a chance to explore the countries where we volunteer, enjoying the amazingly clear oceans off the coasts of India and Thailand, trekking in the beautiful outback and safaris in parts of Africa, or wandering the streets of vibrant Latin American cities.

Yet, we have also come to find happiness in other ways. Sometimes it's in the smile of a child we're mentoring in our organization. Sometimes it's when we travel overseas and see a mother holding a baby, knowing it will receive life-saving treatment from one of Free The Children's clinics. Sometimes it's meeting a new student, a proud parent, or a dedicated community leader, and realizing the world is being changed. Sometimes it's spending time with family and friends, joking around about our latest adventures.

Initially, whenever we traveled, we used to bring back a small piece of artwork to help remind us of our trip. After years of frequent travel, we had assembled quite a collection of knick-knacks, mostly small items that we would place on our desks. But when we started to lose track of which carving came from what country, we realized that these trinkets were not helping to bring back the best memories of our travels—the people we met, the friendships we formed, the good laughs, stories, and experiences we enjoyed together.

Since then, we have started investing in a different kind of memory, one that truly captures what our visits mean to us. Now, instead of picking up a painting or a small carving, we put aside some of our personal money to help someone in the country: money for medicine for someone who is sick, or for buying a school uniform for a child, or for giving a cow to a family as a permanent source of income. Whenever we look at the pictures of the people we've helped, we remember our time with them and the happiness the moment brought comes flooding back—the hugs, tears, and the joy we shared. Even years later, we can't help smiling.

Although hedonic pleasures have their place, it is crucial that we don't allow them to distract or discourage us from pursuing the deeper sense of well-being that only eudaimonic happiness can bring. When we pursue this kind of happiness, we reach beyond ourselves, moving from a mentality of Me towards an appreciation of We. In our experience, this is a process that begins when you find the courage to re-examine your goals and values, the patience to look for the meaning in what you do, and the inner strength necessary to live a life of purpose. This was certainly the case for Joe.

GOALS, VALUES, AND MEANING

In Jamaica, the heat can be overwhelming. After hours spent giving piggyback rides on that sunny afternoon, Joe was thirsty. Really thirsty. Spotting a street vendor, he went over and bought a carton of juice. As he raised it to his lips, he noticed a small boy staring up at him with big shiny eyes. His oversized T-shirt was torn and smudged with dirt, his tiny legs sticking out beneath. It didn't take Joe long to realize that this child was probably just as thirsty as he was, and would never be able to afford such a treat. Guiltily, he handed over the carton. "Here you go, kid, you can have it."

Expecting a look of gratitude, Joe was surprised to see the child's face turned serious.

The boy took a deep breath and then walked back toward the other children, carton in hand. Watching in disbelief, Joe saw this incredibly poor little boy pass the carton from child to child, making sure that each of his friends had an equal sip. When he had shared the juice with everyone, he walked over and offered the carton to Joe with a smile on his face. Then he took a sip of his own.

Witnessing such generosity, Joe's face grew wet with tears. In that instant, he saw that as bad as he thought he had it, somebody always had it worse. And in this case, that somebody—a poverty-stricken little boy—wasn't just *surviving*, he was *aliving*. He didn't have much to share, but he was sharing. He was doing what he could with what he had. It was a lesson Joe would never forget.

By the time he returned home, Joe was a changed man. Now he knew he wanted to do more than just get by. He was determined to share what he had learned in Jamaica, and, most important, to live it. His trip had encouraged him to begin rethinking his values and goals, and he continued this process, knowing he still had much to learn. Eager for inspiration, he began to study the lives of the world's greatest proponents of social justice: Martin Luther King Jr., Malcolm X, Nelson Mandela, Mother Teresa, Gandhi, and others, soaking up their wisdom. His life began to take on new meaning.

It wasn't long before Joe decided the drug dealing had to go. He brought his family together and told them that he would be there for them through the hard times. He shared stories about his Caribbean experiences and about his past life with anyone who would listen. He spoke to his friends, to youth groups, and to schools.

It was during one of these speeches that Joe cemented his commitment to his new life. He was standing up at the front of a school auditorium, with hundreds of eyes focused on him. Taking out the knife that he had secretly carried in his pocket (just in case) for as long as he could remember, he slapped it down on the podium that separated him from the crowd. "I used to think that a knife was the only way to get respect," he told his astounded audience. "But I don't think that any more."

When Joe abruptly turned and walked away from the podium that day, he left his old way of life behind for good. In relinquishing his weapon and all it represented, he walked away from the thrill of life on the edge, from the hedonistic happiness of the fast life and all of its dangerous yet seductive pleasures. At last, he knew beyond a shadow of a doubt that he had found a better way. He wanted to be a role model, and he saw that now he had to hold himself to a higher standard in order to reach this goal. He knew it was time to start living his values.

For many people, the primary goal in life is happiness. Yet, research indicates that happiness is most often a by-product of participating in worthwhile projects and activities that do not have as their primary focus the attainment of happiness itself. [2] Often, we gain the most by focusing not on ourselves, but on others. It is as Dr. Albert Schweitzer, one of the greatest humanitarians of our time, once declared: "One thing I know; the only ones among you who will be truly happy are those who have sought and found how to serve."

This message has important implications for happiness in our goal-obsessed society. Every day, the pursuit of our goals dictates how we spend much of our time, and what thoughts and emotions we experience.[3] We read book after book that promises to help us achieve our goals, but far fewer that encourage us to question what we're striving for. As a result, we often fall into a trap: the goals we strive for have little in common with the values we hold most dear. Remember the rich-but-poor phenomenon, living to work instead of working to live? Few people who succumb to it start out thinking they will. Although we try to be vigilant, even we are not immune. In our case, long hours at the office and hectic travel schedules have been known to take their toll when it comes to our love of sports. We both enjoy lots of different sports, including rugby, and we see games as a great way to spend time together having a blast. But between one thing and another, it can be hard to find the time. Chances are, you may be facing a similar challenge when it comes to something that's important to you. The problem is how easy it is to ignore the growing gap between our goals and values as we race to get ahead. There comes a time when we need to question why we're in the race.

We have found that when it comes to happiness—our own and others—all goals are not created equal. Looking over the research, we were intrigued to find that psychologists Tim Kasser and Richard Ryan conducted a series of studies on goal setting. They found that the more participants held goals and values related to financial striving, the less happy they were, *even controlling for the likelihood that they would achieve what they were aiming for*! In contrast, the more participants had goals and values related to relationships, community, self-acceptance and personal growth, the happier they were.[4] We believe that this study makes an important point: happiness comes not so much from achieving your goals as from having the right ones.

Overall, research has found that three types of goals that people strive for are consistently related to well-being. The first type involves intimacy, the desire for close, reciprocal relationships. Fundamentally, these kinds of goals involve creating connections with others. The second type involves spirituality. These types of goals involve a concern with ethics, and lead us to seek the divine in daily life. The third type involves a commitment to, and concern for future generations.[5] For us, such findings suggest that as Albert Schweitzer understood and Joe eventually discovered, happiness happens we recognize and appreciate our connection to others, and align our goals with the best of our values.

One hero who has taught us a lot about living by our beliefs is a woman named June Callwood. The author of twenty-eight books, she has also found time to found or co-found more than fifty social action organizations, including an AIDS hospice, a youth hostel, a hostel for women, a center for teenage parents, and a civil liberties foundation! After more than fifty years of public service, she still radiates hope. Now over eighty years of age and recently diagnosed with terminal cancer, she still zooms around in a little red sports car. Eager to discover the source of her amazing dedication, we arranged an interview with her. However, things didn't go quite as we expected.

"What motivated you to become involved in social issues?" we asked.

"I did it because it was the right thing to do," she said.

"But your whole life has been devoted to helping others. Was it because of your faith, a personal philosophy you hold dear, or some sudden tragedy in your life?"

"No," she responded, "only because there was a need and it was the right thing to do. No other reason."

June must have sensed our frustration in trying to discover her source of inspiration and commitment. So she explained to us that she had grown up in a small town not far from Detroit, in a tight-knit community where people took care of one another. When someone was sick or was having a tough time, neighbors brought food. When there was an accident or a death, people supported one another. Neighbors looked out for one another's children. Farmers helped one another through difficult times.

When June moved to the city, however, she was shocked to see the overwhelming presence of hunger, homelessness, and pain—and to find so few people responding. For her, all the work she had done since then was simply an extension of what she had learned as a child—that a community is like a big family and "taking care of each other is the right thing to do." Although we were initially surprised that her answer to our question was such a straight forward one, we have come to appreciate its power. In finding the strength to act on her values, June lives an important lesson: what we do should reflect what we believe. When we act in good conscience, we gain the satisfaction of knowing that we're truly doing the best we can.

From Goals and Values to a Life of Meaning

We have found that aligning our goals with our values gives meaning to our lives, just as it did for June and for Joe. As charitable work has become an important part of our own everyday existence, we have gained a new sense of purpose.

As human beings we need meaning: this is the foundation upon which we build our lives, live our values, and find joy in what we do. Psychologists have found that the extent to which a person feels that his or her life is meaningful is a strong predictor of life satisfaction and happiness.[6] "The opposite is also true: a lack of meaning is associated with anxiety, unhappiness and disengagement."[7]

While meaning can exist in many things, as the psychologist Dr. Martin Seligman has argued, finding it requires "an attachment to something larger than the lonely self."[8] While meaning may come from within, it depends on a connection to that which is beyond ourselves.

Research shows that by and large, our ability to find meaning in our lives is determined not by the circumstances we face, but how we choose to face them. Even in the midst of tragedy, meaning can be found. This is true even of the Holocaust. More than eleven million people perished during this period due to mass execution, starvation, and disease. While we see descriptions of Nazi camp guards, the torture, and the killings, there are also accounts of prisoners sharing their last piece of bread and walking through the bunkhouses to comfort their fellow captives.

The extraordinary examples of both cruelty and compassion show that the greatest of choices is the commitment to fulfill one's own sacred and unique task in life. By doing so, one could achieve one's highest potential.

The ME to WE philosophy is essentially a choice of how we live our lives. We have the freedom to choose how we respond to the worst of human situations, as we do to the minor problems of everyday life. Every time we witness pain, need, or injustice, we are challenged to be true to our values and to fulfill our most basic human instinct to help others. And at the core, what moves us to act is love. While *love* may be an overused word, it is an underused action. The ME to WE philosophy seeks to correct this imbalance, bringing us back to what is fundamentally human.

SUCCESS THROUGH HAPPINESS: LEAVING A LEGACY

As Joe's involvement with Free The Children increased, we offered him a job as a motivational speaker. With his amazing people skills, deep dedication and knack for being in the spotlight, he was the ideal person for the job. He accepted at once, telling us it was the opportunity of a lifetime. After graduating from high school, he began to travel across North America, speaking to more than 150,000 young people about issues such as youth violence, poverty, cultural diversity, and service to others, sharing the message of Me to We with everyone he spoke to. With his incredible charisma, amazing stories and unforgettable rap songs, he reached even the kids some said couldn't be helped. Even the most skeptical connected with his passion and humor. Being on the road wasn't always easy, but Joe loved his work. He used to say that if he could bring a smile to someone's face, if he could comfort one person with a hug, or encourage one young person to pursue his or her dreams, then he had been successful.

What does it mean to live a successful life? Our own favorite definition of success, often attributed to Ralph Waldo Emerson, gives us a clue: "To laugh much; to win respect of intelligent persons and the affections of children; to earn the approbation of honest critics and endure the betrayal of false friends; to appreciate beauty; to find the best in others; to give one's self; to leave the world a little better, whether by a healthy child, a garden patch, or a redeemed social condition; to have played and laughed with enthusiasm, and sung with exultation; to know even one life has breathed easier because you have lived, this is to have succeeded."

When we host leadership workshops with adults or youth audiences, we ask them to list the most successful people of our time. In hundreds of sessions, the names most frequently on the list are those of people such as Nelson Mandela, Martin Luther King, Mahatma Gandhi, Terry Fox, and Rosa Parks.

According to the norms of our current culture, these heroes would no doubt be considered failures. After all, they were never actually able to achieve their goals in their lifetime: despite the end of segregation racism still exists, colonialism has given way to neo-colonialism, and inequality is still rampant. Major gains have been made, yet there is still much to achieve. The thing is, these leaders lived by a community-based philosophy. They knew that they were not acting alone, and that their struggle would be carried forward by others.

At the individual level, we believe the truest mark of successful life lies in leaving a lasting legacy. This does not mean having a street named after you, erecting a statue with your face on it, or founding a company that bears your family name. Few can remember the names of history's kings and queens. Statues crumble. Even the pyramids are covered by the sands of time. In the end, a true legacy is a living legacy. Every time a person of color sits at the front of a bus, we see the legacy of Rosa Parks. Every time someone chooses non-violence over violence, we see the legacy of Mahatma Gandhi. If you have been important in the life of a child, you have left a legacy. If you have brought purpose, meaning, and thereby happiness to your family, you have left a legacy.

We cannot all be a Nelson Mandela or an Oprah Winfrey. The world could not function unless each one of us had different talents and skills. We need scientists, teachers, artists, garbage collectors, carpenters, and economists—everyone makes an important contribution to building a healthy society. Ultimately, each of us will be remembered for how we choose to use our gifts and talents, and by how we touch the lives of others. As the old Jewish proverb says, "When we come into the world, we are crying and those around us are smiling. Our goal should be to lead our lives in such a way that when we leave, we are smiling and those around us are crying."

In his own way, Joe Opatowski left the world smiling. On October 29, 2004 Joe had just completed a series of speaking engagements in New York state, sharing the message of Me to We in packed auditoriums. By all accounts he had had a great trip, his enthusiasm never waning. After his last speech of the day, Joe visited some friends and then decided to begin the journey home.

It will never be clear exactly what happened. It seems Joe was driving down a long stretch of road that night when his car was hit by an oncoming vehicle. He was killed on impact.

As people learned of Joe's death, hundreds upon hundreds of letters, e-mails, and telephone calls began to pour in from around the world. All were from friends. Some had known Joe for years, others had heard him speak or knew someone who had, but all were friends. People wrote of the times they had shared with him and of his impact on their lives. They wrote of his smiles, his famous hugs, his poetry and his endless passion. They wrote of how he had inspired them, and how they wanted to honor his memory.

We would like to end this chapter as we began it, with some of Joe's words. Always one to put his heart into every endeavor, he seemed to be able to understand how to achieve the happiness that so many of us strive for.

What would you do if today was your last day to live?
If everything you saw was a last time gift
There'd be no time to complain, and no time to worry
All of a sudden you'd live life in a flurry.
And I hate to remind, but you could die today
So if there's something on your chest, make sure that you say
And act now if you happen across an urge to do a cartwheel,
Everyone should be so lucky to see a feeling that is real
A feeling that is real? That brings us to another thought
What is love and what agenda has it got
If you play too much with fire then you're bound to get burned
But that's not what love is, I've just started to learn.
And that's what life is, entertainment for the soul
People claim happiness is the ultimate goal
And it's with those people that I tend to agree
But as humans we can't agree on vocabulary.
Some call it money, and others call it power
Some believe it's taking drugs, every single hour
And what's the harm to live today? People forget how to live
We've become convinced the getting is better than giving gifts
As children we were brainwashed through a lack of control

But today you hear your thoughts, so you can set your goals
My suggestion for your list, is that you learn how to live,
And do things that remind you of what happiness is,
And when your strength is built, make sure that you share
The best way to find happiness is showing others you care.

—Joe Opatowski (1983-2004)

START NOW!

- Take a piece of paper and tear it into ten pieces.

- On each piece of paper, write down one thing that you value.

- Which of these things bring you hedonic happiness? Which bring you eudemonic happiness?

- Choose five things you would be willing to sacrifice. Tear up these pieces of paper with as much gusto as you can muster.

- Take a few moments to reflect on how your life would be different without the things you have just given up. Now give up two more.

- Let go of one more.

- Now you will be left with two of the things that you value most in your life. They are both extremely dear to you. Choose one to keep and one to sacrifice.

- Think about these pieces of paper and what they represent. Which were easy to sacrifice? Which were hard? Which were near impossible?

- List the values you've learned are most dear to you and revisit the Start Now! Section in Chapter 3. Take a few moments to look back at your list of things that worry you and put an X beside those that don't line up with what you value most.

- Ask yourself how you can live your legacy by making the most of what you value and worrying less about those things you don't place as much importance on.

TAKE ANOTHER LOOK!

Have you ever thought about the legacy that you'd like to leave? One of the best ways to have a lasting impact on the world is to positively affect the life of a child. Young people are facing some tremendous challenges today, but they are also rising to meet these challenges and creating a more peaceful and compassionate world. By acting as positive role models and mentors, adults can help empower young people to live their dreams.

- Through the Experience Corps program, more than 2,000 Americans over fifty-five years old are volunteering in public school programs as tutors and mentors to youth.[10]

- If a person volunteers as a youth, he or she is three times as likely to volunteer as an adult.[11]

- The majority of parents with children under eighteen say it would be beneficial to have other adults whom they trust spend time with their kids.[12]

LIVING ME TO WE

1. **Share your skills and knowledge.** Perhaps the most profound way to thank a mentor is to pay it forward and become a mentor yourself. Do you play an instrument? Introduce a child to the world of music. Are you a talented photographer? Help a young person learn the ropes.

2. **Schedule meaning first.** At the beginning of each week, schedule blocks of time for activities that align with your values. This might be time with your kids or volunteering at your local food bank. Do not sacrifice these times.

3. **Know your clothes.** Set aside some time to look through your closet. Do you know how your clothes are made? Do the brands you buy help create sustainable incomes or trap underpaid workers in a cycle of poverty? When you decide to buy something new, make responsible choices. Me to We Style empowers you with ethical options at metowestyle.com.

My Story

LINDSAY AVNER

I knew what it meant. Mom was going to die.

I was eleven years old. Mom was sitting at the kitchen table, staring down at her cup of tea, running her fingers round the rim. It took her a few seconds to look up. I'd never seen that kind of look on her face before.

For as long as I can remember, breast cancer had stalked our family. Grandma died of it at the age of thirty-nine, Great-grandma passed away from the same disease. Several aunts on both my mom's and dad's sides died of breast cancer, too. There were no females left now, except Mom and me.

And now it had snared my mom, too.

From this day on, I thought to myself, there will never be another day where things will be happy and okay.

That's pretty much how it was.

I'd come home from school to find my mom throwing up in a bucket in her room, the house a mess, and no dinner in sight. I'd drop my backpack—and childhood—at the door and take over as surrogate mom. Me—who'd never willingly touched a vacuum in my life—cleaning house, doing laundry, and bathing and reading to my little brother Jory. Dad tried to help, but he had to work late to pay the medical bills and keep the family afloat, so it was up to me.

One day, it was all too much. Instead of heading out for recess, I stood in the girls' washroom and cried. Through blurry eyes, I could see a classmate approach. "You know, Lindsay," the girl said in that catty pre-teen way, "you can't just blame everything on your mom's cancer." With a toss of her hair she walked away.

That's when I crumbled. No one understands! I wept quietly to myself. I'm watching my mom's hair fall out, watching her die! I had never felt so alone.

The worst was the moment of fake hope, when the doctors told us the cancer was gone. Mom was going to be okay! We were going to be happy again! Mom started exercising, eating right, and her hair started to grow back. I struggled to get my own life back to normal.

Then the cancer came back. Ovarian cancer, this time—a basketball-sized growth that had to be removed immediately. Mom was rushed to

New York for surgery. This can't be happening! I was reeling. This is so unfair!

The chemo, the nausea, and the fear—it all came back again. "You've got to be strong," people said to me. "Gotta be strong for Jory. Gotta get through this."

Somehow, Mom made it. The doctors said it was a miracle: she beat cancer a second time. They were thrilled. It was time to make that slow climb back to normal. But not me. It was too late. You want me to be happy again, just like that? Nope. Not happening. I was bitter and tired and angry. The cancer was in my family, probably in me too and would eventually strike. It took my childhood, probably my future. I was a mess. When I wasn't in my room crying, I was thundering about the house, or moping with another friend who was upset over her parents' divorce. We had nothing in common except our sadness, so we sat and sulked.

"Come on, run with me." Mom was on my back again. She wanted me to run in the marathon for the local breast cancer fundraiser. Thought it'd be good for me. It would get me out of the house. I didn't want to go. I wanted to wallow.

But she kept at it, kept hammering away. All right then. Fine. I'll go. Just this once. To make her happy, I signed up for Run for the Cure.

Tying my shoes on the day of the race, I snuck a peek around. I saw old people, young children, women, and men. No one I knew. No one my age. I started to question why I was here. The gun blasted and the race was on. Through the blur I caught a glimpse of words on T-shirts: "I run for the memory of my sister," "I run for the memory of my Gran." I didn't want to see that. I looked to the sidelines where well-wishers handed out water bottles. "Only two more miles!" they cheered. "You can do it." Right. What if I don't want to do it? I turned up my Walkman and ran faster, watching my shoes flashing white on the road. I felt a stitch in my side, a nagging ache. Maybe I should quit?

And there it was—the finish line. Gulping for air, I lifted my face up to the sky, felt my aching muscles and my hammering heart. I felt good. I felt strangely energized. I think I even started to smile—but I swallowed it, quickly, when I saw who was behind me. There, approaching the finish line was me—Lindsay—a little girl with freckle-speckled cheeks and dark curly hair. The little girl was the spitting image of me when I was small. And across her tiny T-shirt, the black printed words: "I run for the memory of my mom."

Suddenly, I couldn't breathe. Standing in the middle of the cheering crowd, I realized that little girl could have been me! My mom was still alive, and I couldn't imagine life without her. I rose on tiptoe, scanned the crowd to find her. I wanted to run to my mother, to hold her tight.

Things were different after that. I saw that I wasn't alone, and I saw that there was hope, and courage, and companionship if I just reached out. That's it, I vowed, I'm getting off my butt and taking charge of my life!

I decided to organize the first Race for the Cure—High School Challenge. My friends were skeptical at first. But like my mom, I kept plugging away until I won them over. More than three hundred and fifty teens showed up at that first race—way more than I'd ever dreamed. It was amazing: everyone pouring praise on me, strangers writing letters, confiding in me. Who'd have thought? Within two years, it grew to fifteen different races around the country, from New Jersey to Hollywood, with eleven schools in Los Angeles alone.

And me? I'm running regularly now. It's made me stronger, more able to help my mom should she need me again, more able to fight cancer myself should it ever dare to ambush me. I'm planning a career in breast cancer advocacy. And I'm telling everyone I know that you just have to keep on trying. Everyone goes through bad times. It's not easy. You have to pick yourself up and keep on going. I know I'll keep going, keep running—for myself, for my mom, and for the cure.

CHAPTER ELEVEN

CREATING COMMUNITY

"As I looked down (on the earth from space), I saw a large river meandering slowly along for miles, passing from one country to another without stopping. I also saw huge forests, extending along several borders. And I watched the extent of one ocean touch the shores of separate continents. Two words leaped to mind as I looked down on all this: commonality *and* interdependence. We are one world.*"*

—John-David Bartoe

They say home is where the heart is, but how often do we act that way? Our friend Jeff McLeod knew that in his city there was at least one place where nothing was further from the truth.

"The Hood" was built on land donated by the city council to veterans to thank them for fighting in the war. As the fortunes of residents waned, so did those of the area. Over time, a neighborhood defined by pride and courage became known for drugs and crime. Jeff, a student, spent much of the school year studying. In the summer, he operated a painting franchise. He hadn't really thought about this social decline until he received a phone call from a former employee.

Karaline, a student in urban planning, was working on a project in The Hood that aimed to improve community morale by sprucing up the neighborhood. She invited Jeff's painting company to get involved with the community and work for change. Jeff had never been part of this kind of project, but he liked the idea. In no time, he was on the phone to local businesses, friends and neighbors. After a series of talks with the local community association, a project took shape. Jeff's paint supplier donated paint and equipment and his crew volunteered their time. A local nursery donated shrubs, and a landscaping company agreed to help out for free. City residents offered their time and energy. Finally, local homeowners were invited to apply for a home makeover.

The place that was chosen belonged to an eighty-five-year-old war veteran. The city's first radiologist, he had installed the community's first ever X-ray machine. He had been given his plot of land in 1950 and had built his own house. But the place was now an eyesore, the yard was overgrown, and junk was everywhere: a sink stood abandoned at one side of the yard, an old tin boat leaned up against the house, the garden was a mass of weeds.

When Jeff told the elderly winner that his house had been chosen, the old man broke into a huge smile. Frail as he was, he was dead set on cleaning the yard before everyone arrived. He wasn't sure what colors to paint his house, so he asked Jeff to choose.

The project got underway on the hottest day of the year. When Jeff arrived at 9 a.m., thirty volunteers were already sprucing up the yard. The owner's son had hung speakers out of the windows and everyone was working away to sweet sounds of old Motown. Two neighborhood girls, age seven and nine, were painting the garage. When reinforcements were needed, more people pitched in. When supplies ran out, companies donated more. Everyone did what they could, enjoying BBQ breaks at lunch and dinner. Intrigued passersby joined in. Even the mayor stopped in and the local TV station and newspaper came by.

When all was said and done, a rundown house was transformed into a home that not even its owners could recognize. Amazingly, the total value of the work cleared $10,000. "Just being there you could feel the sense of community pride that was growing as neighbors worked side by side," Jeff said. Without realizing it, Jeff and his community had participated in a North American *minga*.

WE ARE CREATURES OF COMMUNITY

Humans are creatures of community: it's in our bones. The first people to walk the earth survived not because they had better credit ratings than the competition, but because they worked together to find food and shelter. Whatever you call it, a network or a web, it was a community of hunters and gatherers who shared skills and knowledge about which berries were edible, where water could be found and how to bring down an animal using only a simple weapon. Those who cooperated fared better than the rest.

A look through the history books reveals that even as humans settled the land, sowing crops and raising animals, they relied on one another to bring in harvests, to build places of worship, to raise barns. Villages and towns sprung up as people traded skills and services for goods. With a more stable food source and fewer natural dangers to face, populations grew. Village life, in which everyone knew one another and played a necessary role in shaping the growth of the town, satisfied the need for community.

By the Industrial Revolution in the early 1800s, urbanization had taken hold. Towns and villages became booming metropolises. As time passed, people no longer grew their own food, made their own clothes or built their own houses. Few fixed their own plumbing or disposed of their own garbage. As occupations became ever more specialized, people began to rely on the work of others to obtain the necessities of life, offering money in exchange for what they needed.

In our own era, there has been a similar transformation.[1] Increasingly, we no longer see people for who they are, but rather only notice what they do. The person behind the wheel of the school bus is "the bus driver," not Peggy. The doctor is "the doctor," not Steve. And the farmer, well, we rarely see or hear about the person who grows what we eat—we just assume he or she is doing all right. Thanks to advances in technology, we can now order groceries over the Internet, or hire a contractor over the phone, all without leaving home or needing to cooperate with anyone else.

With everything available at the touch of a fingertip, it's easy to think we're free from the need to depend on anyone else these days. But when you think about it, the growing specialization of society makes it next to impossible to live life without the work of others, both within the local community and around the world. The very fact that most of us no longer grow our own food, build our own homes or know much about how the water we drink becomes fit for drinking is all evidence we can't survive alone. We need community more than ever before, just as our communities need our special skills and talents to cope with the demands of a complex world.

HOW TO CREATE COMMUNITY: LESSONS FROM CAMP

In seeking to understand the dynamics of Me to We communities, we have come to realize there are three ingredients: shift in mindset, goals that unify, and civic engagement. Combined, they offer a tried-and-true recipe for success.

One of the most interesting studies of community building to date was conducted by the social scientist Muzafer Sherif and his colleagues in 1954.[2] The setting was a two-hundred acre Boy Scout of America camp surrounded by Robbers Cave State Park in Oklahoma. It was just like any other camp except for one detail: Sherif and his associates consistently manipulated the social environment in order to observe the effects on the boys' social relations. Their experiment called for twenty-four well-adjusted twelve-year-old boys, all in the same grade and from similar lower middle-class Protestant backgrounds. They were as similar as could be. Yet despite this, researchers discovered quickly that it didn't take much to create disharmony. At the outset, they randomly split the group between two cabins. At once an "us vs. them" mentality emerged. Allowing the boys to choose names for their groups—the Eagles and the Rattlers—only strengthened the sense of division. Before long, the two intensely competitive groups were trading insults. Chaos ensued when sports or games pitted Eagles against Rattlers; lunchroom fights became common. The animosity became increasingly difficult to control. Sound familiar? We ourselves recall similar, if milder versions of this situation at camp when we were younger. These same kinds of divisions exist in classrooms at schools where cliques are the order of the day.

Having created an atmosphere of animosity, the researchers were faced with a problem. It had been easy to create divisions; the question now was, could they make peace? First, they tried to bring the groups together more often. But no matter how enjoyable the activities, the results were disastrous. "Picnics produced food fights, entertainment programs gave way to shouting matches, and dining hall lines disintegrated into shoving matches."[3]

Eventually, Sherif and his colleagues engineered a series of situations where the boys would have to work together. First, the staff reported that the camp's water supply had been cut off (ostensibly the work of vandals). Facing thirst and a shutdown of the camp's plumbing, both groups went to inspect the sight and were left to repair the faucet. Working cooperatively instead of competitively, there was little or no ill will. When the water finally came through, there was shared rejoicing. "The Rattlers did not object to having the Eagles get ahead of them when they all got a drink, since the Eagles did not have canteens with them and were thirstier. No protests or 'Ladies first' type of remarks were made."[4] It was the breakthrough researchers had been looking for.

The water tap challenge was one of many activities designed to encourage group cooperation. The situation didn't change overnight, but relations between the two groups steadily improved. Name-calling died down, boys from different groups began to eat together again and new friendships were formed.

Compassion at Home and at Large

Decades later, the Robbers Cave study continues to offer a profound example of how to create community. As Sherif and his colleagues discovered, overcoming divisions to create a new kind of community requires a change of perspective. To make friends of enemies, the researchers had to help the boys *think* about each other in a different way—as members of one larger team instead of two competing ones. This shift in mind-set is fundamental to creating a Me to We community.

Granted, it isn't always easy. We have a tendency to relate to and to care for people on the basis of how close they are to us: first comes "Me," then come loved ones and family, next the community immediately surrounding us, or perhaps our ethnic or faith group, then maybe our town or city and then our nation. Always in last place is the international community, for which we feel the least responsible. The closer people are to us, the more likely we are to consider them part of the community and to reach out to help. We describe this approach as one of the "spheres of compassion."

Spheres of compassion make it easier to respond to the poverty of local children than to hungry children on another continent, even though the suffering of both is heart-wrenching. The spheres explain why we would do whatever we could to save our own family from danger, but watch war and devastation on TV and feel the problem isn't urgent. It could be that our spheres have something to do with the old idea that "charity begins at home." But where exactly is home? We now live in an interconnected world and it's time to embrace this reality: home is the global village. We need to break down our spheres of compassion. We must recognize we are all part of one large group: humanity.

Unifying Goals

How do you shift mind-sets to create a truly inclusive community? As Sherif's study made clear, it's not as simple as bringing people together and hoping for the best. Just sitting side by side is not enough to diminish old prejudices: just look at neighborhoods where people live row on row. Consider cities where people rarely move between neighborhoods. Look at bordering nations that are unrelentingly hostile.

Just as Sherif's team turned water into gold, we learned the secret to changing people's community vision when we first encountered a *minga*. The experience taught us that communities form and grow, not when people sit next to each other, but rather when they discover *unifying goals*, goals that benefit everyone and can be realized only through collective effort.

CRAIG'S REFLECTIONS

As surprising as it may sound, one of my most powerful lessons on unifying goals occurred in the Middle East, a region plagued by conflict. Invited to a human rights film festival, I traveled to Israel and the Palestinian territories to run workshops to bring together children from both communities.

During my tour, I traveled into the Negev desert to spend time with the Bedouins, a traditionally nomadic people who have roamed the land for as long as anyone can recall. I visited their homes, tents and shanty houses, which had neither electricity nor running water. I learned that the community lacked employment, health services and quality schooling. Children explained that many other people—presidents and dignitaries included—had come and gone from the community leaving behind hollow promises to help. One well-known individual, accompanied by hoards of eager reporters and camera-flashing photographers, had promised to send computers for the children to use in their school. However, as with everything else, they never arrived. These children confided that what they really wanted were pencils. Could I send some pencils? Returning to Israel and the Palestinian territories, I was haunted by what I had seen and heard.

The following day I met with a group of Israeli and Palestinian children. It was very clear who was who—both were wearing traditional dress, standing stiffly at opposite ends of the room. I decided to break the ice with a simple question: "How are you?" This remark—a normal conversational gambit in North America—promptly gave rise to anarchy! Children on each side began to shout angrily about their historical grievances. The workshop hadn't even started and we were headed for trouble!

Quickly shifting gears, I told the children about what I had just witnessed at the Bedouin camp. The shouting subsided as both the Palestinian and the Israeli youth listened closely. As the morning progressed, the group agreed to temporarily set aside their differences and to spend the rest of their workshop planning together how to help the Bedouin. In the end, they decided to gather and distribute pencils and other school supplies with the help offered by Canadian youth.

Goodwill had replaced hostility by the end of the session. These Israeli and Palestinian children had discovered common ground with people whom they had always perceived as "other," or as people to be feared. Coming together to help those in need helped them to respect each other by creating a sense of shared purpose that rose above religious and political differences, one that was basic to them all as human beings.

Unifying goals need not be complicated. In fact, the best are often simple. Fundamentally, they involve recognizing the many things that unite us, things like wanting peace and security and a good life for our children. Communities are built through this recognition and the shared understanding it creates.

CIVIC ENGAGEMENT: THE MORE WE ARE TOGETHER

Civic engagement is what brings people together to achieve unifying goals. It's what happens every time you volunteer or attend a PTA meeting, or take part in a community parade. It may involve something as simple as joining a book club, meeting with members to share opinions and ideas over coffee. It can involve church bake sales for the food bank, volunteering at a local center for battered women or joining a global campaign to increase aid to the world's poorest countries. Such actions bring us together to create positive social change that we can all see, experience, and enjoy.

One factor that is both a cause and consequence of successful civic engagement is social capital. In his acclaimed book *Making Democracy Work*, Harvard professor Robert Putnam defines social capital as "features of social organization, such as trust, norms and networks that can improve the efficiency of society by facilitating coordinated actions."[5] He's talking about community networks—clubs, teams, leagues and any other sort of informal gathering that brings people together. In such group activities, people learn about one another, forge bonds of trust and feel a shared sense of responsibility for their collective well-being. Social capital involves investing in community in the same way bankers invest in the economy. The returns from social capital, however, produce results far more valuable than money. They help us achieve unifying goals.

One group of youth in Scarsdale, New York, set and surpassed an unusual goal—one measured in tins of food. Like most kids on Halloween, the students hit the streets knocking on doors. But instead of candy bars and bags of chips, these students went trick-or-treating for non-perishable food items. On Halloween 2005, they were eager to beat their 2004 record of one thousand and one hundred cans. So in the days before October 31, the Scarsdale Youth in Action Group handed out flyers and spread the word among friends, family and at local elementary schools. Thanks to their efforts, the group collected nearly two thousand cans for local food banks.

"WE Scare Hunger is an amazing experience," said one trick-or-treater. "It's a chance to be with friends, to interact with the community and promote a good cause. Not only that, it's just ... fun. There's nothing like strolling with friends down the street with a cart full of cans."

Now the group is at work on a project farther away from home. Through Free The Children's development model, the students want to provide marginalized women and their families in developing countries with the support to start small businesses and earn sustainable incomes, which would allow parents to send their children to school instead of to work.

While the students are serious about the goal, their fundraising efforts have been anything but! Among the many money-generating efforts, the youth organized a hugely successful carnival that included donut bobbing, pie tosses, musical twister and tennis ball bowling. The carnival brought out more than one hundred young people to help raise money. What's more, some inspired carnivalgoers went on to start their own Free The Children groups.

On March 1, 2006, the Scarsdale students joined with youth across North America participating in the WE Are Silent campaign—standing in solidarity with exploited children across the world who have no voice while collecting pledges to fund development projects. This group took the idea and ran with it. Although pledged to silence, group members spread the word with specially designed T-shirts and information sheets. Thirty students each raised about $300. In the end, the Scarsdale group raised nearly $7,000 for Free The Children's development work.

As the Scarsdale success story shows, community is no longer just about neighborhoods, cities or even countries. Today, the world is literally at our doorstep. We can watch satellite images of far-off events and hop on a plane to travel halfway around the world. We can communicate easily with people in other countries by phone or over the Internet, and we have access to goods from the four corners of the world. Meanwhile, migration and immigration are changing demographics like never before. Look at the last names in phone books. Listen to the languages spoken on your streets, in your workplace, on public transit.

Intimidated by the pace of change, some people have retreated, returning to what some sociologists call "tribalism": an exclusive vision of community based on characteristics such as ethnicity. This creates inflexible definitions of "us" and "them" that are misleading and dangerous, serving only to maintain barriers and feed prejudice. What if we could reach beyond such barriers? What if we could create community based on something much deeper? What if we could imagine a community that includes everyone?

In our view, this new vision of community is not the stuff of fairy tales—it is both possible and crucial. When we look at the greatest challenges in the twenty-first century, it is clear no individual, group or nation can meet them alone. We now need each other more than ever. For all of our differences, we must acknowledge challenges and unifying goals that can be addressed only through collective effort and civic engagement on a global scale. In our view, few examples demonstrate this better than global threats to the environment, looming disease pandemics and the persistence of international terrorism.

The Environment: The Heat is On

There may be debate about the severity of the environmental experiment humans are conducting on the planet, but one thing is certain: the earth's climate is changing more than it has in recorded history.[6] Although many prefer to believe the issue is not yet critical, the effects are already being felt around the world. The International Federation of the Red Cross and Red Crescent Societies, which publishes an annual *World Disasters Report*, calculates that between 1994 and 1998, reported disasters averaged 428 per year. Between 1999 and 2003, this number was two-thirds higher, with 707 natural disasters each year."[7] Climate change isn't something that might happen in future—it's happening right now with devastating results.

What does this mean to the average American? Climate change seems likely to bring more droughts, floods and weather-related natural disasters—not just in faraway places but in America itself. The tsunami in Southeast Asia and the devastation Hurricane Katrina brought to New Orleans may be just the beginning. The prospects are frightening, but luckily many experts agree we can still make changes for the better—if we all work together. The key lies in recognizing that we share the planet and all have a responsibility to protect it. Let's face it: we all need an environment that will sustain life, both our own and those of generations to come.

Disease: The world needs a checkup

Each year when flu season hits, most people avoid shaking hands or holding stair railings. Few of us stop to think about global poverty, but we should. Headlines suggest that Avian flu is likely to cause the next world catastrophe. And although it seems like it emerged from nowhere, the disease actually owes its existence to very specific conditions. Infectious disease experts confirm it's no coincidence that this latest threat first appeared in East Asia, a part of the world plagued by unmet needs.

In many developing countries, mass poverty in the countryside drives struggling peasants into city slums, where disease thrives in cramped living spaces without proper sanitation. First the animals get sick, then it's passed to humans. We know only too well how viruses born amid deprivation can affect the developed world, moving from person to person, carried between countries and continents by those who have unwittingly become infected.

Remember SARS? One unknowing passenger arrived in Toronto from Hong Kong carrying a disease that virtually shut down our home city and paralyzed its health-care system and its economy. Once started, pandemics—and their consequences—are incredibly difficult to stop. If we are to avoid the human and economic costs of disease, we must recognize that good health is something everyone should enjoy, and work to make this a reality not only in our local communities, but around the world.

Security: Strength in Helping Numbers

In the twenty-first century, terrorism has become a global challenge. Our work routinely takes us to countries deemed dangerous by the State Department because of terror networks, so the issue hits close to home.

Check out this list: Somalia, Afghanistan, Sudan, Sierra Leone. On the UN's Human Development Index of the world's poorest countries, Sudan ranks 141 out of 177 and Sierra Leone ranks 176,[8] second to last. The situations in Somalia and Afghanistan were too unstable to even collect necessary data. What is so special about these four countries, aside from the fact that they are impoverished and struggling states? They were all, at one time, visited by or home to Osama Bin Laden.[9]

Poverty doesn't make terrorists, but terrorists can and do profit from and exploit the weaknesses of states suffering *from* poverty. When countries are plagued by extreme poverty, high unemployment, poor health and chronic corruption, extremist groups like Al-Qaeda find a safe haven. States do not have the ability or the resources to keep out these terrorist groups; they are preoccupied with larger issues of survival. They need our help, for the sake of their safety as much as our own.

PROMOTING PROSPERITY AND WELL-BEING: COMMUNITY CAN MAKE ALL THE DIFFERENCE

Global issues may seem too big to handle, but solutions can come one small victory at a time. Economics may be called "the dismal science," but Professor Muhammad Yunus has used his expertise to harness the power of community to create prosperity for one person after another.

We'd like to end this chapter with his story, which is an amazing illustration of what is possible when people work together, an inspirational example of resourcefulness and ingenuity, it shows how good ideas can begin in one community and travel the world.

In 1976, Professor Yunus met a village woman in his native Bangladesh whose situation made him stop and think. Twenty-two-year-old Sophia Khatoon was working seven days a week making bamboo furniture. She bought bamboo from the local trader on credit—on the condition she would sell the finished product back to him at the price he set, minus interest on her loan. Despite all of her skill and hard work, she made almost nothing. It seemed she was destined to be trapped in a cycle of poverty.

The professor calculated she was paying the trader 10 percent a day in interest—3,000 percent a year! Yet if she could just pay for her own bamboo, she could get a fair price for her wares. The problem was, she didn't have the 50 taka—roughly $2—it would take to get started. With no collateral, she could not qualify for a bank loan.

Professor Yunus decided to lend her the money himself. Within just a few months, Sophia had paid him back in full and was earning seven times more income than before! Aware of others in the same of situation, he began to provide loans to others and watched their success. Because no existing bank was interested in lending money to the poor, in 1983 he founded one that was: Grameen Bank.

Today, Grameen Bank is owned by those it serves: the poor. It lends out roughly half a billion dollars a year to 3.5 million borrowers, almost all of whom are women. It does not require collateral, but does stipulate that each borrower must join a five-member borrowers' group. These groups offer support and encourage members to behave responsibly. Amazingly, the repayment rate is around 99 percent—much higher than most other banks in the world.

Grameen Bank demonstrates the important ways community can promote the well-being of its members. With 2,399 branches and works in 76,848 villages, the bank operates at the local level, depending on trusting relationships among local women who work together to help group members with challenges.[10] The women use loans to start small businesses and form collectives, lifting themselves and their families out of poverty and becoming a resource for other women.

Today, the ideas behind the Grameen Bank are transforming the fight against poverty around the world. Learning a lesson from Bangladesh, here in North America, organizations such as Project Enterprise in New York City offer microloans and financial service to those who are living at or below the poverty line.

Plagued by bad health after an on-the-job accident, Annette found it difficult to hold down work and support her three children. She had a licence to sell insurance and dreamed of starting her own business, but had no capital for start-up costs. With business training, networking opportunities and a loan from Project Enterprise, she was able to buy a computer, a fax machine and business cards. This was the beginning of the ACM Agency. It opened with only two clients, and today it works with more than eight hundred people! Annette now serves on the board of Project Enterprise to help others who are struggling, giving back to the community that gave her a start.[11] Stories like this show that when people work together, social capital can become financial capital, ending poverty one person, one family and one community at a time.

Community, at its core, is about cooperation: on ideas, on social issues, on rearing our youth, on encouraging our society to create workable solutions to the challenges of our new century. Nurturing Me to We within our communities involves rediscovering the essence of what holds us together. It challenges us to move beyond the Me mentality of individualism to strengthen We in its many incarnations by working together for our collective well-being. It involves reconnecting with the communities members we know, and connecting with those we don't or are isolated from, whether it is the bus driver who takes us to work, the homeless person whom we pass everyday, or someone in need who lives halfway around the world. It's about figuring out what strengthens us as a family, a circle of friends, a group of co-workers, a neighborhood, a nation and a world and making it a reality. Fundamentally, living Me to We means creating communities that really are large enough to include everyone.

START NOW!

- By engaging in local mingas that can work to strengthen our families, our communities, our nations, and our world, we can realize our unifying goals.

- In the Start Now! Section at the end of chapter 1, you identified an issue that you care deeply about. Now imagine you're calling a minga to get people to help with your issue. Make a list of how you could call one in your community. Ask yourself:
  - » Who could help me? Friends? Parents? Coworkers?
  - » What tasks would I need help with?
  - » How would I call my minga? By sending out a group email? By making a presentation to my faith group? By posting a hand-printed notice in my office?

- It's amazing how many people in our lives are ready to help out ... all they need is someone to ask them. Give it a try and see for yourself!

TAKE ANOTHER LOOK!

Communities have historically privileged some people over others on the basis of things like age, sex, and ethnicity. These types of practices can make a community exclusive instead of inclusive, and ageism, sexism, and racism can take their toll. The Me to We philosophy offers a bolder, more inclusive vision of community, one that embraces diversity. Join the movement: expand your community by reading about a neighbor's religion, listening to a new American's stories, or learning from a young person.

- The number of hate groups operating in the United States rose from 762 to 803 in 2005, capping an increase of fully 33 percent over the five years since 2000.[12]

- An estimated 1 in 15 marriages in the United States was interracial by the turn of the century, up from 1 in 23 in 1990.[13]

- There are nearly 7,000 living languages in the world with 516 nearly extinct languages.[14]

LIVING ME TO WE

1. **Get involved.** To unify your community you need to get involved. Read the local newspaper, register to vote—and vote—or form a coalition to address issues that matter to people in your neighborhood. If none of these ideas appeals to you, don't worry. Before you turn the next page, brainstorm more options. There are as many ways to build community as there are people who belong to them!

2. **Learn about a faith that is not your own.** Read a book about a faith that is practiced in your community but with which you are not very familiar, or invite someone who practices this faith to talk with you about his or her beliefs.

3. **Host a movie night with a message.** Raise awareness about an issue affecting our global community by gathering family or friends together to watch a movie about a world issue. When the movie ends, talk about it. For the adventurous, bring food and music from that part of the world. The list of movies is endless, but here are a few to get you started: *City of Joy, Salaam Bombay, Blood Diamond, Hotel Rwanda, The Constant Gardener.*

My Story

HER MAJESTY QUEEN NOOR OF JORDAN

I was an unlikely candidate for the job of queen. Like many girls of my generation, I hadn't the slightest interest or knowledge about royalty. Far from dreaming about fairy-tale weddings, once upon a time I planned to join the Peace Corps to fight inequity around the world.

I was a student activist who marched with Martin Luther King Jr., and protested the Vietnam War. Although this may seem a strange starting point for a journey to a palace, it sparked my involvement with the civil rights, anti-war, and environmental movements of the 1960s and 1970s. These ideals and concerns are much the same ones that have motivated my work in the Middle East and around the world over the past thirty years—whether as a global humanitarian activist and UN expert advisor or as an advocate for cross-cultural understanding and founder and chair of the King Hussein Foundation.

When I was ten years old, my Arab-American father made a rare and remarkable confession to me. We had recently moved to Washington, D.C., from California, and he had suddenly become an intensely stressed-out workaholic. At that time, he had just given up a lucrative career in the private sector to become President Kennedy's head of the FAA and the highest-ranking minority member in the history of the United States government. The son of an enterprising Arab immigrant, he had succeeded through sheer willpower and indomitable self-discipline, and he was clearly suffering from considerable anguish about being in debt for the first time in his life on a government salary.

Nevertheless, I clearly remember him saying to me, "I am so much more fulfilled by serving my country." It was an insight into the rewards of public service that would have a profound impact on the rest of my life.

It was also through him that I connected with my Arab heritage. Several years earlier, when we were still living in California, my mother explained to me about my European ancestry on her side and my father's Arab roots. I remember sitting alone afterward, staring out the window at the limitless expanse of the Pacific Ocean. It was as if my world had suddenly expanded. Not only did I have a new sense of identity, for the first time I felt connected to a larger family and a wider world.

Years later, equipped with a degree in urban planning, I looked for ways I could serve by contributing to improving the lives of people in the Middle East and the developing world. Work in Iran and the Arab world broadened my early perspectives on social justice and peace, and provided the initial spark for my leap of faith into the life of an extraordinary public figure.

King Hussein understood his family lineage as direct descendants of the Prophet Muhammad (PBUH) and his temporal role as king as conferring upon him the responsibilities of a public servant rather than the entitlements of a ruler. This sense of humility, equality, and responsibility for empowering others is a central tenet of our Muslim faith. The Prophet said, "No one of you is a true believer until he wants for his brother that which he wants for himself." That conviction was the unifying thread of our work to promote opportunity, justice, security, and peace.

I began my own public service in Jordan by trying to identify ways to fill gaps in our development programs in areas related to human security—poverty, women's empowerment, education, environment conservation, and cross-cultural understanding. I shared a conviction with my husband that, even in a conflict region such as ours, when human needs and aspirations are prioritized in a society, that society is better able to resist and topple tyrants and extremists. That when people have hope and opportunity, they will sacrifice and invest in a stable and peaceful future for their families.

And when we invest in young people, miracles can happen.

From the first time King Hussein and I learned about the Seeds of Peace program, we knew that it embodied a number of our most cherished hopes and dreams for the future. When we first sent a group of Jordanian boys and girls to participate in this ambitious summer-program experiment, we prayed that its idealistic vision might help to heal the rifts that have so long divided the Middle East. Yet in our enthusiasm, even we never anticipated the extent to which the Arab and Israeli youth participating in this initiative might be able to change the face of a generations-old conflict.

As this program has continued to thrive and grow over the years, I have never ceased to be inspired by the example that the young people involved in Seeds of Peace offer to us all. In the midst of the most harrowing circumstances, they find the courage to come together across conflict lines to confront their prejudices and fears. Together, they are breaking down the barriers of ignorance and intolerance that perpetuate the vicious cycle of strife generation after generation.

When they return home, these committed youth continue to hold out their hands and hearts to one another. They maintain contact across embattled borders via phone and email to comfort their friends in the midst of violence, talking about peace or even just saying "hold on" over the sound of gunfire on the other end of the line. They risk the scorn of angry neighbors for the chance to meet and talk and grieve together. Sometimes, they risk their lives. But in taking these risks, they inspire their families and neighbors to take a chance on hope and humanity. With each and every act of bravery and compassion they find within themselves, they truly do plant the seeds from which peace will flourish in the years to come.

CHAPTER TWELVE

ME TO WE DECISIONS

———————

"When Thomas Edison invented the light bulb, he didn't start by trying to improve the candle. He decided that he wanted better light and went from there."

—Wendy Kopp

Our grandmother has struggled with hardship all her life, but it certainly hasn't dimmed her spirit. One of her greatest joys is storytelling, and whenever she speaks of her early years, there is one story she tells more often than any other. No matter how many times we've heard it already, we always love to hear it again.

Our grandmother grew up accustomed to the hard farming life: winters were cold, crops sometimes failed, her family was large, and there were many mouths to feed. She had early schooling but never considered high school. It was normal for a woman to marry young, start a family of her own, and settle into life as a housewife. And so she did. But luck was not on her side. Her husband died young during the Depression, leaving her with four children, no income, and a half-finished house.

That's when things *really* became difficult.

She had to find work, but as a woman she had few options. She cleaned homes, scrubbed walls and bathrooms, and scrimped and saved every penny she could. Luckily, she was resourceful, and when she had enough pennies saved she bought a used typewriter and taught herself to type. When she was ready, she got an interview for a secretarial position at a local car manufacturer. When she saw the woman behind the front desk with her carefully manicured nails, she looked down at her own fingers, red from the scrubbing and hard work, and her courage almost failed her. But she stared it down and she was called in to the interview.

The first question was about her education. Did she have a high school diploma? Knowing that her education was insufficient, she looked the manager straight in the eye and told him that, yes, she was a high school graduate. A couple of years earlier, the local high school had burned down, and with it all the records. There was no way for them to know the truth. She was fighting to feed her children, surely this lie was forgivable. Still uncertain, the manager asked to see her skills. So she sat down at a typewriter and started clicking away, just as she'd taught herself to do. Not one mistake. That was all the proof they needed. She got the job. It was one piece of the puzzle solved.

But between holding down a full-time job, tending to the house, and raising four kids, she still had her hands full. Perpetually short of money and without a refrigerator, she used to spend every evening making the long trek to the grocery store to buy food for her children. Arriving home late, she hurried to cook dinner before falling into bed, completely exhausted. Her hectic schedule meant that her children hardly had a chance to see her.

One day her boss, Mr. Williams, noticed that she looked particularly pale and tired. Through a few careful questions he learned about her nightly shopping trips and found out that she couldn't afford to buy a refrigerator to keep food from spoiling. Despite her repeated protests, he immediately called the local appliance store and arranged for a refrigerator to be delivered to her house that very day—using his own credit!

With great feeling, our grandmother recalls how much this one act of generosity meant to her and her family. No longer compelled to walk to the grocery store every evening, she was able to spend time with her children and even get a bit of rest. Determined to repay Mr. Williams for his kindness, she diligently saved $5 a week until she had repaid the cost of the refrigerator.

Now here's the best part: although all of this happened more than sixty years ago, she still tells this same story about Mr. Williams every Christmas, Easter, summer vacation, and during random visits. She still waves her hands at the same parts, laughs in the same way when she describes the new refrigerator arriving, blesses Mr. Williams once again for his kind deed, and smiles when she recalls how she was able to spend more time with her kids. After more than half a century, this single act of kindness has become a legend!

By now Mr. Williams has probably passed away, yet we still wonder if he ever truly understood the impact that his generosity had on the life of our grandmother and on the lives of our parents and us grandkids. We hope he did, but we suspect that he didn't. All too often, we never truly understand the extent to which our choices affect the lives of others.

The story of Mr. Williams lives on in our family's history, but it is a story to which everyone can relate. Each of us has met a Mr. Williams. Each of us has a family story or a personal memory of the kind deeds of others. When it comes to living Me to We, the importance of such every-day kindnesses should never be underestimated.

ME TO WE DECISIONS

As Eleanor Roosevelt once said, "One's philosophy is not best expressed in words. It is expressed in the choices that we make, and those choices are ultimately our responsibility." Decision making can be seen as the culmination of all that we have learned so far about living Me to We. It is both the logical and most practical next step on the journey from Me to We. At this stage there are important choices to be made. Some are made once in a lifetime, others arise daily. Whenever and wherever they occur, these choices allow each of us to decide what kind of lifestyle is best suited to our most cherished needs, interests, and values.

Starting down this path involves becoming more conscious of our choices and more aware of the opportunities around us. As unbelievable as it sounds, psychologists have discovered that most of the time, what we do and how we see the world around us occur without our conscious intention or control.[1] Most of us spend much of our lives on autopilot, guided by the habits that we have developed in the past.

Living Me to We challenges us to take control of our decisions and our lives. It involves not only making an effort to become more aware of our everyday choices and the impact they have but also to active-ly make decisions that promote well-being, both for ourselves and the larger community. It encourages us to stand up for our highest ideals, whether the decision in question is small and seemingly mundane or large and potentially life-altering.

Small Everyday Choices

As insignificant as small everyday choices seem, they have important consequences. Take the choice to turn off the lights in your home. Electricity is something that most of us in the developed world take for granted. We're used to having this incredible force at our fingertips, controlling it with the simple flick of a switch. Though we expend little energy turning off the lights in our homes, we expend huge amounts by leaving them on. Why? Because a large proportion of the electricity we use is generated by natural gas- and coal-fired power plants that produce enormous amounts of air pollution. When the air quality is poor, many people are affected. In our travels we've visited elderly people in North American nursing homes who can sense how bad the air is before they hear about it on the news—they can feel it with each short breath.

A friend of ours suffered this same fate not in his later years but at the very beginning. As a young boy, he spent much of his life in an oxygen tent, or hooked up to a breathing mask. Every day was a struggle. His asthma attacks were a slow, gasping suffocation, a terrifying experience for any person, young or old. For our friend, pollution made things worse; attacks were more frequent and lasted longer. Though today his lungs are stronger, he still feels it when the air is bad. He fears the day when his youth passes and the creeping suffocation returns, a painful reminder of the struggle he thought he'd won in his teenage years.

No one person or company is solely responsible for poor air quality and the suffering it causes. No one person is responsible for the fate of an estimated sixty thousand Americans who die prematurely each year from air pollution.[2] All this results from the accumulated actions of many, many people. With this in mind, it is easy to understand that small choices have large impacts. For instance, deciding to use energy-efficient lightbulbs and turning lights off when you leave a room (and encouraging others to do the same) doesn't just translate into lower electricity bills—it helps everyone breathe a little easier. If every U.S. homeowner replaced one household lightbulb with a more efficient one, it is estimated that "we would save enough energy to light seven million homes and prevent greenhouse gas emissions equivalent to those from one million cars."[3] For us, statistics like these really drive home just how much difference one small choice can make.

Other small but important choices include things like carpooling and reducing food and paper waste. Carpooling with three neighbors over a distance of 12.43 miles per day would reduce your CO_2 emissions by 75 percent and save approximately $311 per person annually.[4] If every American threw away one small bite of turkey at Thanksgiving, that would total eight million pounds of wasted food.[5] That's a lot of food when so many go hungry in America and around the world! How about paper use? The University of Illinois's paper-recycling program saved 18,200 trees and enough energy to heat and air-condition 542 homes for a year.[6] All of these choices are small, but there's nothing small about the results!

Pinnacle Moments and Addressing Root Causes

Of course, living Me to We doesn't involve only small everyday choices. We all have pivotal moments in our lives when we face major decisions, and it is vital that we respond to these situations by drawing on the best of ourselves. Sometimes opportunities arrive unexpectedly, and we are forced to make split-second choices that will affect both ourselves and others for years to come. However, most of us also face decisions at critical junctures that are more predictable. Choosing what to study. Starting a career. Facing that dreaded midlife crisis. Deciding what to do in retirement. For us, our first decisions to travel overseas proved to be crucial turning points. Little did we know how our early experiences in Asia would affect us, but there is no denying their impact in shaping our lives and work. Seeing poverty up close for the first time forced us to question our most basic ideas about the world and our own places in it. While these experiences were difficult, they ultimately moved us to try to help.

Adopting a Me to We mindset at pinnacle life points is crucial, because the decisions we make at these times set the pace for years to come. For example, if you choose to work for a company whose ethical practices you find questionable, then you will be presented with a scenario where your values won't necessarily gel with the company's mission. Or if, once you retire, you decide to travel the world aboard your dream yacht, you will not be able to make the kind of impact that you would by staying closer to land and volunteering. Major life choices like these require a commitment to acting in accordance with one's values whenever possible.

Good decision making requires foresight, something well understood by America's native peoples. *Haudenosaunee* means "people building a long house." To us, the name evokes images of *mingas* and barn raisings. That is appropriate, because *Haudenosaunee* is the preferred name of the Iroquois, a people who implicitly understand the importance of Me to We decisions in everyday life. Collectively, this union of Great Lakes natives can lay claim to a very compelling idea called the Seventh Generation principle. In practice, this principle requires all chiefs to consider the impact of their decisions on the seventh generation. In essence, this innovative idea empowers not only the Iroquois's grandchildren, but even their great-great-great-great-great-grandchildren with the ability to live in a socially productive society that is as healthy, or more so, as that of the generations before it.

The Iroquois understand that to build solutions to everyday life challenges, you need to address not only the symptoms of any particular problem but also its root causes. This is the kind of thinking that allows us to understand that there would be fewer smog warnings if more of us took public transit. It challenges us to confront the fact that there would be little need to sponsor a child overseas if his or her family was not forced to sell food crops at a low price because of unfair trade agreements or our own desire to buy imports as cheaply as possible. It challenges us to address the many factors that underlie the challenges we face.

Me to We decisions strike at the heart of much of what ails society: poverty, hunger, homelessness, the destruction of our environment, corporate scandals, government misconduct. Addressing such societal problems can seem daunting, but it all boils down to one simple question: What is my vision for an ideal world?

If we are to craft a world that is just, compassionate, sustainable, and free of violence and hate, we must take every opportunity to make decisions that reflect our vision. If we don't take the initiative, we will continue to live in a world where a citizen casts a ballot and chooses the party that best serves him or her and not the entire country; where a corporate employee doesn't want to risk losing a pension by blowing the whistle over cancer-causing agents in products; where a government official seeks reelection by pandering to special interest groups. Such short-term choices lead to insufficient funding for public education, high rates of childhood leukemia, and a political system awash with "soft money."[7] We all know there's a better way, and it's up to all of us to make it happen.

How can you begin to make Me to We decisions? Luckily, it's simple! When faced with a decision, fight the urge to respond instantly, out of habit. Instead, pause for a moment and ask yourself a few questions: How will this choice affect me and my family? What impact will it have on the community and the world? How will it affect future generations? These are perhaps the simplest and most powerful questions that any of us can ever ask ourselves. As you begin to act on the answers that emerge, keep in mind that every decision counts. As Robert Kennedy said, "Each time a man stands up for an ideal, or acts to improve the lot of others, or strikes out against injustice, he sends forth a tiny ripple of hope, and crossing each other from a million different centers of energy and daring, those ripples build a current that can sweep down the mightiest walls of oppression and resistance."[8]

START NOW! AND TAKE ME TO WE ACTION

Life is full of opportunities and choices, no matter who you are, what you do, or where you live. Starting your own journey from Me to We can be as simple as picking up the morning newspaper. When we spoke with Archbishop Desmond Tutu, who received a Nobel Peace Prize for helping to bring peace and reconciliation to South Africa after the fall of apartheid, he called the morning paper "God's prayer list delivered straight to my door." At first, we were surprised: what with the current state of the world, the morning news can make for difficult reading! But for the archbishop, the paper's stories about local and global issues offer a menu of issues to choose from—and a map of possibilities for change. We have never forgotten his comment, because it helped us to truly see the opportunities all around us.

Throughout this book we have presented a collection of facts about a number of social issues along with a variety of actions all of us can take to begin living Me to We. In the upcoming sections of this chapter, we would like to share more options for action. Our intention is not to try to persuade you to take totally new actions all at once, but instead begin trying to inspire you to start with the ones you find most appealing. We would like to encourage you to begin to see your life through the lens of Me to We—to notice everyday opportunities to build your ideal world.

A Better World Begins at Home

As we have explained, we didn't grow up as the children of activists. The lessons our parents taught were passed along quietly, sometimes without us really being aware of what was happening. In retrospect, it was the smallest things that often made the biggest impression.

With our mother, lessons usually came in the shape of a conversation. When some parents come across a homeless person while out with their children, they cross to the other side of the street. Our mother used to stop. Without fail, she would strike up a conversation. It was never more than a few sentences: Was it cold last night? What is your name? Where are you from? Have you been in the city a long time? Sometimes we were impatient, not quite understanding why we couldn't just continue to the mall or wherever else it was we were going. But years later, we understood the lesson. By acknowledging that person's presence and exchanging those few words, our mother taught us to see the humanity in every person and the value of respecting everyone, no matter who they are.

IDEAS FOR ACTION IN YOUR FAMILY

1. **Spend quality time together.** Set aside a day each week for a family activity. This works best when activities rotate around each family member's interests, with each person having the chance to choose an activity that all will enjoy. To cement family bonds, make this a TV-free day.
2. **Volunteer.** Volunteer as a family at a local food bank or soup kitchen, a conservation area, or a museum. By reaching out to your community, you'll help others and, as a family, you'll get to know one another better and have a greater appreciation for each other's strengths.
3. **Enjoy a different kind of vacation.** For your next vacation, consider taking a family volunteer trip. Whether you travel locally or go abroad, such adventures offer everyone a chance to experience new things, build life skills, and make a meaningful difference in the world.

A Better World Begins with Friendship

In a fast-paced world, it can be all too easy to fall out of touch with our friends, let alone make new ones. For two young professionals, an evening spent reminiscing about the excitement of their university days led them to find their own unique solutions to this dilemma. It all started when Katherine and Holly began to lament the lack of opportunities to spend quality time with their friends. The minute they learned that their other friends felt the same way, they decided to become "friendship activists." It was time to set things right.

Gathering close friends together, they spent the next several months planning a charity Halloween party called the Masquerade. Their goal was simple: they wanted to create the perfect fun evening for catching up and support a great cause at the same time. Planning was the best part, because it gave them a reason to get together regularly and enjoy one anothers' company. When at last the much anticipated night arrived, it was a resounding success! Everyone had a wonderful time seeing old friends and making new ones.

Not only did the Masquerade fulfill its primary mission with flying colors, it became an annual tradition. What's more, Katherine and Holly now gather with six other close friends to plan friendship parties throughout the year. The result? Years filled with laughter, collective learning and, above all, fun. In one fell swoop, with one simple idea, this dynamic duo of "friendship activists" created a new community tradition.

IDEAS FOR ACTION IN YOUR FRIENDSHIPS

1. **Plan a regular get-together.** Start a weekly, monthly, or bi-monthly tradition with your group of friends. You can invite people over spontaneously, rotate event organizers, hold potlucks, or do whatever else works. Just remember to keep everything simple and stress-free!

2. **Start a new hobby with a friend.** Together with a friend or friends you can learn to play a musical instrument, paddle a canoe, scuba dive, speak another language, dance the flamenco, cook Thai food, make pottery, do yoga, paint like Monet, fly kites in the park... the list of possibilities is endless!

3. **Build your community.** A full 40 percent of those who volunteer do so because someone invited them to![9] Ask a friend to join you in a community-building activity. You can build a community garden,

mentor a group of local youth, do both at once, or come up with a creative idea of your own. The choice is yours.

A Better World Begins in the Workplace

From the first day Jason Bentham opened a sporting goods store in his own struggling neighborhood, he was destined to become more than just another shopkeeper. When he discovered that the store's clientele was mostly made up of neighborhood youth, many of whom faced challenges like poverty, peer pressure, and gang violence, Jason knew he could relate to them.

He put up a basketball hoop outside his store where local youth could play in a safe environment. Since that moment, JB Sports has become a gathering place for the community's young people: a positive space where they can find advice and inspiration, a spot to study, or a place to shoot hoops. As Jason watched the youth grow up, he noticed an intriguing trend. The kids who hung out at his store didn't get into trouble; the ones who stayed away did. Parents noticed too, and they stopped by to meet and thank him, not only for giving their children a place to hang out but also for helping the boys with their résumés, providing them with references, and even tutoring kids during their exams!

As Jason's wife told us, he measures his success by the smiles on the young people's faces, the confidence in their step, their grades in school, and the jobs they have been able to land as a result of his support. Through his efforts, young people who might otherwise have turned to less socially responsible activities have found a sense of purpose and belonging. Although Jason's community work at JB Sports is informal, it is a thriving part of the community web—a small, flourishing business with a big heart.

IDEAS FOR ACTION IN YOUR WORKPLACE

1. **Share skills with your community.** Offer your skills to local nonprofit, charity, or community organizations to help ease the burden of tight budget constraints. If you're an accountant, help with the books. If you're a webmaster, design a webpage. Whatever your skill, share it with your community.
2. **Mentor a young businessperson.** Identify an individual in the community who is interested in learning about your business or specific

skill set. He or she will be delighted to learn new skills, and it will give you an opportunity to pass your knowledge on to the next generation of leaders.

3. **Support a good cause.** Arrange for a percentage of your paycheck to be automatically designated as a charitable donation. When a group of colleagues comes together, your contributions will add up to a sizable donation of funds and support for your workplace's chosen good cause.

Actions Your Company Can Take

Just as individual employees can live Me to We in the workplace, so too can your company. Whether you're a CEO, the owner of a small business, or an employee, you can encourage your company to join the growing number of organizations that are committing to community and reaping the benefits of corporate social responsibility (CSR).

1. Engage in cause-related marketing. Choose an issue your company, employees, and shareholders care about. Work together with a charitable organization in your community to raise awareness about your issue—and promote your brand at the same time.
    ▸   Every time someone used his or her credit card, American Express made a one-cent donation for the Statue of Liberty's restoration. As a result, the number of new cardholders soon grew by 45 percent and card usage increased by 28 percent.[10]

2. Conduct an environmental audit on your company to assess ways of reducing pollutants, increasing energy efficiency, and cutting operational costs.
    ▸   3M decreased pollutants, energy, and waste, and from 1975 to 1999 the company prevented 807,000 tons of pollutants, saved more than $827 million, and achieved energy efficiency improvements of 58 percent per unit of production.[11]

3. Provide one half day a month of paid volunteer time for employees and use holidays as an opportunity for employees to get involved with an important community cause.
    ▸   Companies that already offer a half day a month of paid volunteer time include the Body Shop, Fannie Mae, and Wachovia.[12]

4. Invest in the human capital of your employees by providing them with stress leave, flexible work hours, family days, health promotion through gym passes, etc.

   ▸ Microsoft's healthy living seminars are expected to lead to a savings of $1.92 for every $1.00 invested due to decreased employee drug costs, reduced visits to the emergency room, and lower risk of diabetes and heart attacks.[13]

5. Encourage and match your employees' donations to charity.

   ▸ Companies that already do this include AOL Time Warner, IBM, and PepsiCo.[14]

6. Demonstrate your commitment to CSR by reporting on your company's community involvement, engaging management, and recognizing employees' community-building efforts.

   ▸ A full 45 percent of Global Fortune 250 companies produced an environmental, social, or sustainability report in 2002, up from 35 percent in 1999.[15]

A Better World Begins in Your Faith Group

Trafalgar Presbyterian Church was a congregation united by faith but divided by culture. With a colorful mosaic of people from all sociocultural backgrounds, communication was often a challenge. At the best of times people found it difficult to understand one another; at the worst of times they were frustrated in their efforts to develop a sense of community spirit.

Then, they found music. Or, more accurately, music found them. Andrew Donaldson whisked into town, a man on a mission to bring the community together. His plan was simple: to use the community's diversity to its advantage. A talented musician with a passion for world music, Andrew teaches church members songs from different countries at every Sunday service. His innovative approach now helps parishioners to experience and enjoy one another's cultures.

It's for good reason that folks at Trafalgar like to call Andrew Donaldson their "worship enlivener." Cultural differences that once provoked divisions have become a source of inspiration, as members of the congregation experience the beauty of diverse musical traditions together. As Reverend Kristine O'Brien explains, the strength of his approach lies in the sense of inclusion it creates: "A woman who can't read is delighted to find a way to sing at church. A family from Ghana feels at home. A mother from Japan learns English through singing. A thirteen-year-old boy plays the violin among adult musicians. The congregation's development work in Uganda is supported, encouraged, and furthered through music." That's music to our ears.

IDEAS FOR ACTION IN YOUR FAITH GROUP

1. **Organize a service committee.** Focus your committee on a specific mission, educate parishioners about a particular issue, or discuss volunteer initiatives that your congregation could support. This will not only raise awareness but also energize your faith group with a community-building cause.
2. **Create an interfaith coalition.** Learn about other faith groups by creating an interfaith coalition to address a specific community challenge. Whether fighting gang violence, poverty, hunger, or homelessness, or building intercultural dialogue, join together to find common solutions.
3. **Adopt faith-based giving.** Follow in the footsteps of many faith groups around the world and support a local aid organization through a tithe or with a yearly fundraising drive or charitable donation. Bring your community together for an event to celebrate the occasion, whether a party, a sporting event, or a family picnic.

A Better World Begins in Your Neighborhood

The Quesada family landed in Grand Rapids, Michigan, seeking a better life. Ileana, the mother of the household, found a factory job. It wasn't much, but it was enough to scrape by. Then tragedy struck. On her way home from work, Ileana was hit by a car and left with two broken legs. She soon found herself laid off. The Quesadas were left in dire financial straits.

Alina met Ileana at a friend's house not long after her accident. When she saw that Ileana was wearing a tank top and shorts despite the cold November weather, she asked a mutual friend what was going on. When she found out that she could not afford warm clothes, she left without a word. Alina returned with half of her wardrobe, telling Ileana that these clothes were now hers. This was no small sacrifice: Alina was a new immigrant herself, struggling to get by and with a baby on the way.

But things didn't stop there. Later that day, Alina's sister Maria stopped by to borrow some clothes and saw that half of her sister's closet was empty. When she found out why, Maria wasted no time clearing out half of her wardrobe as well as that of her husband. When her husband came home and noticed that his favorite sweater was missing, he wanted answers. After Maria's explanation, he picked up the phone.

Several calls later, a plan was set in motion: a group of local families would adopt the Quesadas for Christmas. The Berman family brought kitchen supplies, the Fossel family handled furniture, and the Cooks got the cleaning and bathroom supplies. Maria and her family took on the task of filling the Quesada pantry. The children were put in charge of presents. It was both a family and community effort. That Christmas the Quesada family received their gifts with tears of joy and laughter. Today, Ileana has a new job, and so does her husband. Though there are still struggles, the Quesadas are doing fine.

IDEAS FOR ACTION IN YOUR NEIGHBORHOOD

1. **Lend a hand. Help your neighbors:** offer to babysit once in a while, drive them to the airport, ask if they need groceries, share tools (split the cost of new ones), share skills and introduce them to new neighbors.

2. **Create or join a community association.** Become involved in a community association to forge friendships, build community spirit, and find local solutions to local challenges. Get started by forming a community welcoming committee to reach out to new neighbors and inform them of your mission.

3. **Build intergenerational connections.** Encourage children to ask their grandparents or other community elders about what life was like when they were growing up generations ago, and support their efforts to learn about the history of the area in which they live.

LAUNCHING A ME TO WE GROUP

Have you ever joined a book club? If so, you probably have fond memories of hot coffee, fresh-baked cookies, lively discussions, and newly formed friendships. People love such gatherings because they represent a great opportunity for bonding with others over a shared love of literature. A Me to We group is no different, but its impact has the potential to reach far beyond your living room, and its theme is not literature, but life.

The world's first Me to We group began in the Free The Children office when four friends—Russ, Amy, Dan, and Chris—started meeting once a week over lunch to find fun ways of living Me to We. They started small, with weekly goals like "introduce yourself to a neighbor you haven't met" or "give a note of gratitude to one of your coworkers." At each new sit-down session, they shared last week's stories of actions and then brainstormed ideas for the next week. It was a simple formula that worked wonders. As each person's confidence grew, the group's good deeds became more ambitious. "It didn't take long for us to borrow courage from each other and start taking on more acts of kindness," Russ told us. "All of us started not only doing the small things but moving on to larger acts. Almost before we knew it, our everyday priorities began to change."

Like all communities, no two Me to We groups are exactly alike. They can be formal or informal or something in between. Your group may call itself a Me to We group and meet each week, or you may choose to add a Me to We component into an existing group, club, or family event. Whatever form your group takes, it can provide inspiration and support as you embrace this approach to life.

Around the world, people are now hearing about Me to We through speeches and word of mouth. In a collective effort to learn more, share stories, and support everyone, a virtual community has sprung up through the Me to We website, www.metowe.org. This is the world's largest Me to We group to date. Through all of the feedback we've received, it has evolved into an amazing online tool for the global Me to We community. When you visit, you'll find daily challenges, positive Me to We stories, blogs from people living Me to We in their everyday lives, and much, much more. It is there to help you find the courage to take the first step, because, as Russ and company discovered, after that, Me to We isn't only fun, it's life-changing.

START NOW!

- ▸ In this chapter we've explored a variety of ways you can begin making the shift from Me to We. Now it's time to take action!

- ▸ Make a list of at least five small, medium, and large actions you can take to begin living Me to We. Ask yourself about:

  - » Small, daily decisions: Could you smile at the people you pass on the street? Could you think of other small, simple ways to reach out?

  - » Medium daily decisions: Are you prepared to go a bit further in your efforts? Are you prepared to go a bit further in your efforts? Are you ready to take public transport more often or to volunteer for a few hours a week with a local charity? What other options do you find appealing?

  - » Pinnacle-moment decisions: Have you arrived at an important turning point in your life? Are you ready to explore more fulfilling career options? Is there a social cause to which you would like to make a substantial commitment of time and energy? Are you ready to make another major change?

- ▸ As you consider each of these kinds of decisions, your list will likely grow. Start acting on the small actions right away, and begin to move up to the larger ones gradually.

TAKE ANOTHER LOOK!

Girls and women have faced barriers to education, employment, and politics for generations. They've also found the strength to overcome a number of these barriers. In North America, women eventually won the right to be considered "persons: and to vote in elections. Globally, girls and women still face many barriers simply because they are female. Let's learn from the wisdom that mothers, grandmothers, and sisters have to share, then move from Me to We by supporting women's rights here and around the world.

- The first female U.S. Senator was appointed in 1922. Today there are 26 serving female senators.[16]
- In early 2006, 12 of the world's 192 heads of state were women.[17]
- 57 percent of adults with HIV in sub-Saharan Africa are women. Young women between the ages of fifteen and twenty-four in the region are three times more likely than young men to be infected with the virus.[18]

LIVING ME TO WE

We're keeping the actions coming! It's not difficult—the ways to change the world are endless!

1. **Clean house for a cause.** Go through your home and collect things your family no longer uses. Do you have clothing you rarely wear? Are there toys your kids don't play with? Donate them to a local women's shelter or another service organization. If there isn't one in your community, organize a yard sale and donate the profits to charity.

2. **Take aim at violence.** Children in North America play with war toys or violent video games, but in some places children the same age use real guns to survive. Talk with a young person in your life about giving up war toys. Collect pledges from family members to provide funds for each toy disposed of. Suggest using the money raised to help former child soldiers receive scholarships for school.

3. **Write for rights.** Around the world, women's rights are violated every day. In some places, including North America, women are paid less than men for doing the same work, or are victims of domestic violence. Research an issue that affects women, then write a letter to a political leader asking for urgent action.

My Story

JOHN AND JORDANA

We decided to write our stories together to illustrate how people of different age groups—John is a retired educator and Jordana is a 15-year-old student—can help one another through volunteerism.

John Gaither

Ahh, those were the days! I was a sprightly twenty-seven-year-old, a newly trained teacher with energy and idealism. It was the 1960s and I had just gotten my Ph.D. I was going to change the world. We all were back then—that and live in a yellow submarine.

Being so young, I got plenty of advice. Teach at an elite private school, they told me. Lecture at a university. Find a job with money and prestige. I didn't listen. Forget money and prestige—I decided to live the simple life with a wife, a child, and a Volvo. I wanted to slog it out in the trenches with the country's battered high school teachers. That was the life for me!

In the end, it really was the life for me. Sure, there were days I regretted my decision. Try teaching a class of Grade 9 or 10 students that learning should be a lifelong experience! But still, I loved the life and I loved the kids—especially the days when a student's eyes lit up as I told stories that related to them and made education—I shudder to use the word—relevant.

The years rushed by. I became the head of my department, then a vice-principal, then finally a principal—and that's where I stayed. I didn't want to be an administrator. I wanted to be near my students. But, as with every job, the years took their toll. Teaching used to be really enjoyable, and being a principal was the reward for being a good teacher, a problem solver, and a community builder. But as education became more politicized, getting up Monday mornings became more difficult. The end of summer came too fast. I grew tired of the budget meetings, the funding cuts, teacher strikes, union lockouts, and work-to-rule. I loved the kids, hated the politics.

I started to dream of retirement. Sitting in traffic on a weekday morning, I would find my mind wandering. I would imagine spending time with my grandchildren, quiet evenings with my wife, traveling, or rediscovering some great books. I told myself that I wouldn't sign myself up for any committees, substitute teaching, or anything requiring a schedule.

I remember my first day of retirement: it was glorious! I cooked a great breakfast for my wife and me, leisurely read the paper, cleaned a bit of the house, and wrote a few letters to friends. On the second day, I cooked a great breakfast, leisurely read the paper… and on the third day, I cooked a great breakfast… This is retirement? I tried to tell myself that it was just the transition, that those golden moments were just around the corner, that I would enjoy them soon enough. But something was missing.

A former colleague asked a favor. A group of students were going to Jamaica to work with children in the poorest neighborhoods of Kingston. They were short one chaperone. Would I interrupt my newfound "bliss" and return to the students, just this once? One trip. That's all. My bags were packed and by the door.

The trip was very inspiring. I was moved not only by the poverty I saw but also by the commitment of the young people on the trip and the education they received through this experience. When I returned home I offered to work one day a week with a local youth organization. The experience was so positive that I was soon volunteering nearly full-time, working with students across North America to assist them in becoming involved in their communities and in the world.

Now, it seems, the tables have turned. Some days I am the teacher; others days I am the student. These young people have reawakened my commitment to social justice issues by challenging me to learn more about the situation in the world today, where women and children are exploited and suffer because of corruption, sexism, and greed. Most importantly, they have given me the opportunity to continue to participate in helping to find solutions. In return, I help them administer their charitable projects overseas. I've gone from running one school to helping oversee the construction of schools in twenty-one countries!

So why do I volunteer? Because it allows me to continue to call upon and to use my skills as a teacher and an administrator working with and for youth in a way I never thought possible in retirement. Volunteering has changed my perception of retirement as the end of a career because I now celebrate it as a new beginning with new challenges and many rewards.

Strange. I'm back working with students, but it doesn't feel like work. Some days, I feel like I am twenty-seven again. I find my spirit renewed every day by the caring young people I meet—people like Jordana Weiss.

Jordana Weiss

We would have been pals, Emma and I, I'm sure of it. We'd have talked about the books we both loved, tried on hats together, giggled over our funny Buddha collections, and planned how we would someday change the world.

But we never got that chance. Instead, I like to think we're soulmates. It makes me feel as if I will never truly be alone.

Up until my thirteenth birthday, I'd never heard of Emma Johnstone. It was an important time in my life—my bat mitzvah—and I was having a blast. All my family and friends gathered together to dance, to feast, and to celebrate. But to be honest, I really wasn't into the party—I was more concerned about the presents. See, they weren't for me. I didn't need more jewelry and trinkets. What I really wanted was to build a school in the developing world. I'd asked my guests to bring monetary donations instead.

When the party was over, we sat down and eagerly tallied up the gifts. My guests had been incredibly generous—but we had not raised enough money to build a school. We were only halfway there. Disappointed, I tried to figure out what to do with the money. And that's when I learned about Emma.

Emma lived a three-hour drive away from me, near a lake in the countryside, and from what I hear, she was an amazing girl.

Her nickname was the Divine Miss Em. They say she had a sense of the divine about her, an awareness that there's more to this world than what we see. Her teachers liked how she didn't get caught up with the usual silly-girl shenanigans—you know, who's cool, who's not, and who's going out with whom. She liked everybody, and everybody liked her, as I'm sure I would have too. I can tell just by looking at her picture, at the way her laughing eyes seem to leap right out ready to tell me a secret, or something to make me smile.

It seems that everyone in that little town has a story about Emma—how she always brought spare change for the homeless when she visited the big city, how she refused to wear clothes that relied on Third World child labor, how, on her free days, she'd wander over to the nursing home to talk with the old people. And whenever she sent anyone a note or a poem, she'd add this Mother Teresa quote beside her name: "Love never measures. It just gives."

Of course, I didn't know about this back then. All I knew was that thanks to Emma, we were able to build that school after all. It wasn't until later that I got the full story, and when I did, I knew that Emma would always have a special place in my life.

It was a few months before my thirteenth birthday, and the summer before Emma started eighth grade. Emma's family was in the city waiting nervously for her dad's bypass operation. She and a friend were sending out emails, asking for prayers for him. After working at the computer for a while, they were wilting in the heat so they decided to go for a swim to cool off.

The girls hit the pool that day and, in the blink of an eye—while everyone's thoughts were with her dad—Emma Johnstone simply slipped away.

It was such a small pool, with water only a few feet deep. Who'd have thought there'd be danger there? The girls had been splashing around when the phone rang. When her friend returned from answering the call, she found Emma's lifeless body in the water. It's hard to understand what really happened that day. The inquest later found that Emma didn't do anything stupid or high-risk. She was a competitive swimmer, after all. It seems she just slipped off the ladder and somehow got stuck.

Over the next few days Emma's family lived through shock, anger, and disbelief—a kind of hell known only by people who have been there. Somehow, though, Jan and Gord—Emma's mom and dad—saw through their fog enough to know that Emma would not want people to send flowers. She would want something more "divine." She would want to reach beyond the pain to help others. The Johnstones decided to ask for donations to build a school in a developing country. Emma would have liked that.

The funeral was hugely attended and everyone had a role, from big sister Alex to the pre-teen buddies who wrote the service. And the money poured in.

But it wasn't enough.

John Gaither had been in contact with the Johnstone family and knew how desperately they wanted to build the school in their daughter's name. He also knew how disappointed I was in not raising enough money to build a school.

He asked me if I would like to add my bat mitzvah money to the Johnstones'.

Would I mind? To be able to help poor children and maybe Emma's family too—I was thrilled!

John helped us to find the right location—a small downtrodden village in Ecuador, a cold and foggy outpost where the only schools and hospitals were hours away, where transportation was by foot, the farmland unforgiving, and the children poorly nourished. The new school would be named after Emma. By the following summer it was ready—the Emma Johnstone Escuala—in Llilla, Ecuador. I was invited to join in the official opening.

With a lump in my throat and butterflies in my stomach, I made the long journey south, first by plane, then by truck, and finally by horseback. The whole way I carried a picture of Emma, a photo her dad had taken in the sunshine of her yard, a smiling girl with eyes that won't stay put. I carried Emma's picture along a rocky path to the top of one of the world's tallest mountains, to a cluster of thatched huts, to the arms of the colorfully dressed villagers huddled in the clouds.

It was there, so close to the heavens, that Emma's soul, and her school, were blessed. As the village children sang softly in their native voice, their leader sprinkled a mixture of incense, herbs, and tobacco into a metal pan filled with burning coal. Fragrant black smoke wafted up and around us. The leader spoke of Emma's goodness and her generosity. With her words, the smoke became Emma's spirit. She waved the smoke over three tiny pine tree seedlings—one for Emma, one for me and the other volunteers, and one for Llilla's new school. She circled the smoking pan over the trees as they were placed in the ground near the school, gathering Emma's spirit to its heart. She bade Emma to watch over the children there. Then she asked me to bless the remaining incense and to return it to Emma's parents.

I watched the smoke drift northward, twining in the soft breeze like a rope binding us all together—Emma, the Ecuadorians, and me. I realized that no matter where we live, we can all understand tragedy, feel others' pain and hunger, and want to help.

When I returned home, my family drove across the rolling farmland to meet Emma's parents and deliver the incense from the ceremony. Pulling into the driveway of Emma's tiny old house by the lake, I was struck by how different her life had been from mine—and yet, in many ways the same. Emma's dog trotted across the yard to greet us—the same color and breed as mine back home. In her bedroom under the eaves, I found Emma's collection of hats, books, and Buddhas, eerily similar to mine.

But those were superficial similarities. There was something more. Emma's parents called it an "essence" that used to shine from Emma's face, which they could see shining from my face now. They told me that, and I could feel my eyes fill with tears, the same tears I saw in theirs.

It has been two years since my bat mitzvah. I believe that souls that are alike are attracted to each other. I believe that Emma's soul found mine, teaching me that, though our bodies will not be here forever, our actions will, and the lives we touch today ensure that our own lives carry on. Emma and I were strangers once; we are soulmates now. Together, we have been able to do great things.

CHAPTER THIRTEEN

WELCOME TO THE MOVEMENT

"It was just a day like any other day. The only thing that made it significant was that masses of people joined in."

—Rosa Parks

On December 1, 1955, a soft-spoken seamstress was heading home after a long day at work. The bus she boarded had separate places for black and white passengers, like every other bus in town. Seating at the front was reserved for whites. Blacks, who made up the majority of the bus system's patrons, were consigned to the back. When a lone white man stepped aboard a short while later, the driver demanded that four black passengers stand so that he could have an entire row of seats to himself. Much to his consternation, only three of them got up.

As Rosa Parks would later recall, "When he saw me still sitting, he asked if I was going to stand up and I said, 'No, I'm not.' And he said, 'Well, if you don't stand up, I'm going to have to call the police and have you arrested.' I said, 'You may do that.'"[1] It was a simple but powerful gesture of protest in a place where people had been killed for less.

Rosa Parks was subsequently arrested and convicted of violating the segregation laws that still held sway in Montgomery, Alabama. The chain of events she set in motion would eventually extend far beyond her hometown: her gesture marked a major turning point in the growth of the civil rights movement of the 1950s and 1960s. Blacks in Montgomery boycotted buses for 381 days while launching a successful Supreme Court challenge to the Jim Crow laws that enforced their unequal status. In the process, a twenty-six-year-old Baptist preacher named Martin Luther King Jr. emerged as a leader capable of inspiring a nation.

So it was that Rosa Parks, an unassuming seamstress fed up with being treated as a second-class citizen, came to be heralded as the "Mother of the Civil Rights Movement." Streets and subway stations have been named in her honor, and Time magazine has declared her one of the one hundred most important people of the twentieth century. In the end, her simple choice to stand up for her beliefs by sitting down made history.

Of course, history highlights the headlines. What is all too often forgotten is that famous actions like Parks' rarely occur out of nowhere. More often than not, such public triumphs are fruits not only of individual courage but also of collective perseverance and hard-won struggles fought by many people no one has ever heard of. What most popular accounts leave out is that Rosa Parks had been an activist long before that fateful winter day. Her journey began twelve years earlier, when she answered the questions in her head with a decision to fight the injustice she felt in her heart. Her courage began when she attended her first National Association for the Advancement of Colored People (NAACP) meeting. It continued to grow as she became secretary of her local chapter, and attended workshops to learn from fellow civil rights activists.

Rosa Parks' famous gesture speaks to both the importance of individual action and the actions of the thousands of unsung heroes who supported her. As Dr. Martin Luther King Jr. wrote, "Mrs. Parks' arrest was the precipitating factor rather than the cause of the protest... The cause lay deep in the record of similar injustices."[2] It was through the struggles and lessons of others that Parks learned of a similar bus boycott held fifty years earlier in Montgomery, and of another in Baton Rouge, Louisiana, two years previous. She was also well aware that not a year before her own arrest, fifteen-year-old Claudette Colvin had unsuccessfully staged the very same protest.

What made Rosa Parks' case different was not so much her action as what happened next. When she claimed her rightful seat that day, many others took up her cause, people like Montgomery NAACP head E. D. Nixon, a mentor to both Parks and Martin Luther King Jr., and Jo Ann Robinson, whose women's advocacy group distributed leaflets to stir the masses following Parks' arrest. Far from diminishing the power of Parks' actions, this shows that although her perseverance and courage caught the attention of a nation one fateful day, these were lessons learned over time, supported by the hard work of many, many people.

As news of her case spread, the drive for change grew as people began to speak about the situation in fields and factories, on their front porches and around kitchen tables, in town halls and churches. Small groups came together, discussed and debated, struggled and strived, organized and spoke out. Every action taken by an individual and group to stand up against segregation and systemic discrimination contributed to the successes of the civil rights movement, the work of which is still not finished but has profoundly altered the course of American history.[3]

THE MAKING OF A MOVEMENT

The precise reasons for the success of the world's most celebrated social movements are hotly debated in academic literature and activist circles, but their beginnings are incontestable: somebody did something. When studying the history of social movements, we usually remember major events like the storming of the Bastille during the French Revolution, the March on Washington when Martin Luther King Jr. gave his impassioned "I Have a Dream" speech, or the Rivonia Trial when Nelson Mandela was sentenced to life imprisonment. However, we have an unfortunate tendency to overlook the daily actions and sacrifices of the thousands of ordinary people who provided the foundation upon which the world's greatest social movements were built.

Ultimately, this narrow view is as intimidating as it is misleading. When such grand events are considered in isolation, they begin to seem so huge and important it's hard to imagine ordinary people ever being able to take part. The standard they set begins to seem impossible to meet, and the individuals involved all seem to be blessed with superhero-like reserves of bravery and wisdom, not to mention time and energy.

The costs of this misunderstanding are too high to allow it to continue—it makes it impossible for any mere mortal to ever measure up! There's no room for uncertainty, imperfections, setbacks, or household chores for that matter. Luckily, the true stories behind most social movements offer a far more accessible and empowering picture. It's one in which ordinary people gradually come to believe in the need to address a challenge in society and come together to work for change, one small step at a time.

Do a little digging, and you'll find that small steps lie at the heart of nearly all large movements. This is certainly true of one of America's most important movements for equality: the movement for women's rights. In July 1848, Elizabeth Cady Stanton, a young wife and mother living in upstate New York, sat in her parlor with four women friends enjoying afternoon tea. She lamented the fact that the American Revolution, which was fought to put an end to tyranny, had not gone far enough. The rights of women were still not being adequately protected, even though women had played an integral role in ensuring the success of the war. Her friends agreed with her.

As in Rosa Parks' case, these five women were not the first to have such discussions; history has recorded that many others held similar views. However, this group took action, facing their fears head on and leading a call in 1848 for the first women's rights convention. It proved to be a critical move as it provided a forum where supporters of women's rights could meet, share ideas, and devise strategies to achieve their goals.

If the social movements of the past have an important lesson to offer, it is that modest steps, one after another, can lead to great things— one conversation, one meeting, one decision at a time. As Paul Loeb reminds us when considering Rosa Parks' legacy, her journey "suggests that change is the product of deliberate, incremental action, whereby we join together to try to shape a better world. Sometimes our struggles will fail, as did many earlier efforts of Parks, her peers, and her predecessors. Other times they may bear modest fruits. And at times they will trigger a miraculous outpouring of courage and heart—as happened with Parks' arrest and all that followed. For only when we act despite all our uncertainties and doubts do we have the chance to shape history."[4]

FINDING THE COURAGE WHEN IT COUNTS

Making the right choice isn't always easy. As you begin to make Me to We decisions, you may find yourself challenged to move outside of your comfort zone. You'll find that it takes courage to live the Me to We philosophy— courage to extend a helping hand, to deal with possible rejection, and to bring idealism and passion into your life and others'.

When you face your next opportunity to stand up for the kind of world you truly believe in—whether by joining a global campaign, choosing the right candidate, reaching out to a stranger, or improving the life of a loved one—the decision you make to exercise your own personal courage will be paramount.

In finding our own courage we have been inspired by a remarkable boy we once met. We would like to share his story with you, as he may inspire you to find your own inner strength as well. Santosh is living proof that great bravery can reveal itself at unexpected moments.

We met Santosh in Sierra Leone, which, as we have discussed, was plagued by an eleven-year civil war. Thousands of children were forced to fight in this conflict. The way they were "enlisted" was one of the most horrific things we have ever heard. When rebels first entered a village, they would round up the teachers and execute them. The teachers were the community's "wisdom keepers," and the rebels believed they had the knowledge and capacity to rally the citizenry against their violent ideology.

The second thing the rebels would do was gather all of the village's young people together in a large room or open space. The rebel commander would typically start off with an impassioned speech about the need to free Sierra Leone from the tyranny of the government and then offer the young people two choices.

Their first choice was to join the rebel army. The young people who chose this option would be told to line up single-file. One by one they would be led to the commander, who, with a dull razor blade, would make a deep gash up by their temples, and then rub a mixture of gunpowder and cocaine into the open wound. Once this mixture hit the bloodstream, the youth would become psychologically imbalanced. The young person would then be taken back to his or her home by a rebel soldier, who would force the child to kill his or her mother or father. This "test" was intended to sever the children's ties with the community for good, forcing them to accept the rebels as their only family.

Choice number two was a lot less complicated: anyone who refused to join the rebels would have his or her hand chopped off. This is how the rebels ensured they would never be able to fight on the side of the government.

Santosh was "head boy," what we might call student council president, in his middle school when the rebels came to his village. He was sitting on the ground in front of his school when he heard about the two choices facing the young people of his community. After a moment he stood up, and in a loud voice he said, "Mr. Rebel Commander, I am student council president. You have now put me in charge as you executed our teachers." Though it took every single ounce of courage in his body to stand up and walk in front of his peers, this is exactly what he did. As he walked, he held his right hand high in the air and began to wiggle his fingers.

When Santosh came up on stage, he stood on his toes so all of his classmates could see him. He took a deep breath and shouted, "Mr. Rebel Commander, my name is Santosh. Our village believes in peace. Please leave now!"

The rebel commander was incensed that this young boy would dare to give him such an order. He took out his huge machete and mockingly asked whether Santosh preferred a "short sleeve" or "long sleeve." Without waiting for an answer, he brought his machete down on his right hand, chopping it off. With a cruel smile, he then handed the boy his severed hand.

Even though he was young, Santosh had enough wisdom to keep his stump high up in the air. He walked away, and he didn't look back. He walked out of his village, and still he kept walking. When at last he came to the dividing line between Sierra Leone and Guinea, he literally fell into the arms of the UN soldiers who were stationed at the border. He was taken to a field hospital run by Doctors Without Borders, where he underwent a series of operations.

Santosh later came to Freetown during the establishment of the shaky cease-fire. When we spoke with him, he told us he was lucky. "Santosh," we said with great respect, "lucky is not a word we would use to describe you after everything that has happened!" He told us that he was lucky not because of his injury but because he was finally going back to school. Knowing that nearly all of the public schools in the country had been destroyed during the war, we were curious about how he would become a student.

"I'm paying my own way, and going to private school," he explained. "I've taught myself to use my left hand, and now I make beautiful wooden statues that I sell to the United Nations troops that come to my village. With the money I've saved, I can now go to school!" We were humbled by his resilience and ingenuity.

"Santosh, standing up for peace that day and losing your hand must have been the most painful decision you have ever had to make in your life!" we said gravely.

"No," he declared. "The most painful decision came just last week. In the market, I met the man who chopped off my hand."

After the war, there was a general amnesty in Sierra Leone. Santosh told us the most painful decision of his life was his choice to extend his left hand to shake this man's right hand as a sign of peace.

ME TO WE: A MOVEMENT FOR THE TWENTY-FIRST CENTURY

When people think of movements, they usually envision marches and demonstrations, public protests, petitions, and the changing of laws. While such activities have often played a central role in social movements of the past, they are not goals in and of themselves. In The Movement Action Plan, a theory of, and guide to social movements developed by renowned activist Bill Moyer, social movements are defined as "collective actions in which the populace is alerted, educated, and mobilized, sometimes over years and decades, to challenge the power holders and the whole society to redress social problems or grievances and restore critical social values."[5] A movement is thus built upon values, and its most important goal is to bring about a fundamental shift in the psyche of a people.

In writing this book, we are seeking to encourage just such a shift in the social psyche. In our own lives, the shift from Me to We has had profound consequences. In exploring the impact of the Me mentality that underlies our culture, the consumerism, the pursuit of wealth, and the ruthless individualism it breeds, we have come to see that these pre-occupations lead us away from the stuff of fulfilling happiness and deeper success: family, friends, community, and service. In turning to the truths remembered by communities around the world, we have come to understand that the urge to reach out to others is grounded in the best of what makes us human: an innate need for connection that we must fulfill in order to reach our full potential. We've seen that making the shift from Me to We has many personal and social benefits, and investigated how this transformation can be set in motion. We've explored how it can be encouraged in our hearts and minds through nurturing gratitude and empathy and redefining happiness, and we've examined how it can be shared through cultivating a spirit of community in the groups to which we all belong.

We've found that as you begin to deepen your experience with these skills, you can't help but begin to act in ways that promote the shift from Me to We in your own life and others'. For one person, this might mean deciding to spend less time at work and more time with family and friends. For another, it might mean spending this year's vacation volunteering instead of relaxing on the beach. For someone else it might mean supporting a global campaign to end poverty or fight AIDS, or helping a neighbor through a tough time. It can be as simple as providing a friend with a shoulder to lean on, getting to know your colleagues at work, devoting a few hours a week to volunteering, or supporting companies that respect and protect the environment. It can involve speaking up for someone who can't, joining an interfaith coalition, learning more about a global issue, or making the time to talk to your partner and children about the things that matter. These might seem like small decisions, but once made they have a way of multiplying. Kindness is contagious, as anyone who has ever enjoyed a favor, received help, or been "given a break" knows only too well. When something good happens, most of us have a tendency to "pay it forward": a well-timed word of encouragement inspires us to praise someone else, a kiss from a loved one reminds us to be a little kinder to the next person who crosses our path, a pleasant surprise leads us to brighten someone else's day. It doesn't take much to set this cycle in motion, but once started it's difficult to stop!

As a social movement, Me to We will take shape as a growing wave of kindness, compassion, and caring. It's a quiet, personal movement that spreads as ordinary people begin to embrace a new understanding of themselves and their relationship with the rest of the world. It's about living our lives as socially conscious and responsible people, engaging in daily acts of kindness, building meaningful relationships and strong communities, and considering the impact on We when making decisions.

As the Me to We movement gains strength, we will see people talking to one another more, making a greater effort to get to know their neighbors, holding more potlucks, and spending more time with their kids. We will see people shifting their patterns of consumption in favor of socially responsible products and taking more of an interest in social issues. We will see kids and adults alike starting to care less about the lives of TV characters and Hollywood stars and more about those of the people around them. We will see fewer blank, hollow expressions as people travel through their daily lives, and we will hear more laughter, see more smiles, and notice people having more conversations with strangers. This may not seem as dramatic as the social movements of the past, but the result will be just as powerful and important—a shift in the way people think and a change in their values, beliefs, attitudes, and, yes, daily decisions. Although such changes may at first seem small and subtle, the result will be nothing less than the transformation of our society's most basic values and the creation of a more compassionate world.

HOW ONE PERSON CAN MAKE A WORLD OF DIFFERENCE

In sharing our ideas about why and how to live Me to We, we're inviting you to join people around the world in helping this movement flourish and bringing its vision to life. The fact is, one person can make a world of difference.

Whenever people ask us how long it really takes to change the world, our answer is always the same: a couple of minutes. Whenever we see disbelief creep into the faces of listeners—which we almost always do—we share a story about an old friend of ours, Ed Gillis.

When Ed was in high school, he was desperate to be class president. But he was shy, a bit awkward, and above all, goofy. In other words, he was about as far away from being in the "cool" crowd as anyone could possibly get. His chances of getting elected were slim. Nevertheless, he was determined and ran for office every year over the next three years. Not only did he lose every time, but he became the butt of everyone's jokes. As we all know, high school can be a cruel place, and kids even made up a vicious little chant they used to taunt him with.

By his senior year Ed was getting discouraged, but he made up his mind to run one last time. He headed to the main office to pick up an application form as he had every other year and began to fill it out. His thoughts were interrupted when a group of kids broke out in a fresh rendition of their traditional chant. Ed was tired. He'd had enough of being pushed around and made fun of. In a fit of anger, he crumpled up his form and threw it at the nearest trash can. He missed by a mile. As he turned to leave, he collided with another student—one of the most popular guys in his class. He had hit a new low.

"What do you think you're doing?" asked Ed's classmate.

"I can't take it anymore!" Ed burst out. "Every year I run for president, and not only do people not vote for me, they go out of their way to make me feel horrible! Now I've had enough, I quit!"

This could have been the end of the conversation. But instead of walking away, Ed's classmate stood there. "You can't quit," he told Ed firmly. "Your being in the race is just about the only school tradition we have."

"What's the point?" said Ed miserably, "Even if I do run, no one will vote for me."

"You have my vote," his classmate replied, looking Ed straight in the eye.

Ed was shocked. Here was someone who had never even seemed to notice he was alive, encouraging him to keep trying and offering his support! After a moment, Ed went back and picked up his crumpled application form from where it had fallen on the floor. He decided that he would run after all and worked on his speech late into the night.

The next day, in front of the entire school, Ed began to speak. His voice was shaky at first, but he gained confidence as the minutes ticked by. He started to hear giggles and laughter, then the whole audience laughed together. They were laughing. But not at him—at his jokes. They liked his speech! His years of using humor to make up for his shyness had paid off. As he walked offstage, he felt better than ever before. That year, he became class president. Though he was happy he won, he was happier still to have discovered that he was a gifted public speaker.

The most amazing part is, Ed wasn't the person who originally told us this story.

It was a mutual friend, Melody, who filled us in on the details. Whenever she tells this story to high school students, she recounts how becoming class president was only the beginning for Ed. She explains how, with his newfound confidence, he went on to pursue several degrees in international politics and eventually joined a speaking tour that traveled across North America addressing more than 150,000 students. "Aren't you wondering why I know so much about Ed?" she asks with a smile at the end of every presentation. "I know because he's my mentor," she says proudly. "I'm one of the thousands of young people he has inspired."

Ed's chance encounter with a sympathetic classmate didn't last long, but it was enough to tip his life in a direction it might not otherwise have taken. Chances are, Ed's classmate didn't even realize just how much of a difference his words would make, or how many people would ultimately be affected by them. Nevertheless, his encouragement changed not only Ed's life, but also those of the thousands of students Ed has since inspired. Their importance will continue to live on as these young people in turn inspire others, who will inspire others. And all because of something that happened years ago to a high school student, in a couple of minutes. We love this story because it's a perfect illustration of how change happens: through small, everyday actions that bring people—and the communities in which they live—to a tipping point.

EVERYONE HAS A GIFT TO CONTRIBUTE

People often associate social movements with charismatic leaders who give passionate speeches. These are the people whose names make it into the history books: Martin Luther King Jr., JFK, Nelson Mandela, etc. However, as crucial as such visionaries may be, movements require much more than a small number of talented public speakers. To succeed, they need the active support of people with diverse talents and interests who play different but equally important roles. Alice Paul, the famous women's rights organizer and author of the Equal Rights Amendment passed in 1923, was right when she declared, "I always feel the movement is sort of a mosaic. Each of us puts in one little stone, and then you get a great mosaic."[6] Like a mosaic made up of countless brilliantly colored pieces, a movement thrives when everyone contributes his or her own unique gifts.

Many of us have difficulty recognizing our skills and talents as the gifts they truly are. Craig learned this lesson a few years ago while he was doing a television interview on a show that was focusing on "accomplished youth." The other young interviewee was nineteen years old, had already completed his master's degree and PhD, and was working at an important job at a pharmaceutical company. Throughout the interview, he kept mentioning that he was "gifted," a fact that he had discovered in third grade when he passed a special IQ test. Thereafter, the boy's parents told him that he was "gifted," his teachers spent extra time with him because he was "gifted," and the media labeled him "gifted." He must have said the word "gifted" at least five times during the interview. Finally, the host turned to Craig and asked, "Well, are you gifted, Craig?" Craig looked at her and shook his head.

Later that day, Craig was still thinking about this interview when he went back to the Free The Children office. As he looked around at the remarkable people who work with us, he realized that he had given the host the wrong answer. Craig saw our webmaster, whom we all consider to be incredibly gifted when it comes to designing websites visited by millions of people around the world. He saw our young writing staff, gifted in translating their passion and energy into words to inspire others. He saw our amazing adult volunteers, who are gifted mentors, giving tirelessly of their time and expertise. The more he thought about it, the more Craig realized he couldn't think of anyone he knew who wasn't gifted.

In our society, we are often led to believe that only an extraordinarily few people qualify as "gifted." In truth, everyone has a unique gift to share with the world, whether it's for creating beautiful works of art, healing the sick, being a compassionate listener, fixing things that are broken, raising money, being a good friend, or finding solutions to problems. Some people are excellent teachers, others have a talent for inventing things, others are great at playing baseball, running companies, designing clothing, organizing events, or writing computer programs.

When it comes to encouraging the movement from Me to We, all of our gifts are valuable. This is because we are all gifted in some way, but not in every way. We are naturally interdependent, like pieces of a puzzle that fit together to create a larger picture. It is only by using our gifts together that we can realize the vision of Me to We and create a better world.

Are you still uncertain about your own gifts, or stumped about what kind of contribution you can make? Take a minute or two to think about what you love to do or what interests you. Understanding yourself well enough to know what lights you up is the first step toward discovering your gifts, whether they involve sports, art, cooking, or working with children. Is there some activity that you think you could be good at or might really enjoy? Get out there and give!

Once you have identified your gifts, you need to decide how to use them. The good news is that when it comes to living Me to We, opportunities are limited only by your imagination! If your gifts are empathy and listening, you can be known around your school or workplace as someone whom people can always talk to, or you can volunteer at a support center for drug addicts, abused women, or street youth. If your gift is business- or accounting-related, you can help low-income families with their tax returns, or volunteer to help a local charity improve its infrastructure and efficiency or prepare for an audit. If your gift is research, you can help develop a social justice campaign around an issue that you feel passionate about. If your gift is sports- or arts-related, you can donate your time and talent to a local charity for a fundraising event, concert, or exhibition. If you are caring, brave, friendly, perceptive, organized, funny, patient, motivated, likable, handy, trustworthy, calming, disciplined, sensitive, or anything else, you can help in your own way. Everyone has a gift to contribute!

As you begin to use your gifts to make the shift from Me to We a reality, you may at times feel self-doubt and wonder if you will truly be able to make a difference. Don't worry! As we have learned, no one has all the answers. We were once in Stockholm at an international conference, where thirty of the most eminent minds of our time, including the Dalai Lama, had come together to discuss a number of pressing social issues. At one point, someone stood up and asked this revered spiritual leader an incredibly elaborate question. The Dalai Lama listened carefully and took some notes. After a long moment he looked up and responded, "I don't know."

There was a moment of silence. Sneaking a glance around the room, we saw that nearly everyone was smiling! We had all expected the Dalai Lama to come up with some pearl of wisdom that would enlighten us. Instead, with three simple words he dispelled the myth that someone must be all-knowing and all-powerful in order to influence the world. This great leader taught us a vital lesson that day: there is no magic answer. There are only people, a growing multitude of people, reaching out to help others with dedication, passion, and sincerity. And there is magic in that.

THE IDEAL TIME AND PLACE TO MAKE A DIFFERENCE

If there is one message to share about the Me to We movement, it's that it can't afford to wait for a distant "ideal" time and place. Now is the ideal time to begin living Me to We, and wherever you are now, you're in the ideal place—personally, socially, physically. It doesn't matter if you are rich or poor, sick or well, if there's pressure on you at work, or if things in your life are going as smoothly as you think they should. It doesn't matter where you live, who your friends are, or what your childhood was like. In the end, the decision to reach out to others is related not to our personal circumstances or level of ability but to our choices and priorities.

It was José who taught us the truth of this simple message. You might imagine José to be a well-known community leader or leading researcher, an award-winning author or some other kind of authoritative social commentator. He isn't. Craig met José when his work with Free The Children took him to the streets of Salvador on the coast of Brazil. With the help of a translator, he started talking to a boy who was shining shoes on the side of the street. This is how he met José.

After Craig had gained his trust, José brought him back to his home, a bus shelter he shared with other street children. As Craig sat among the children, they each told him the story of how they had ended up on the streets. Some had been sent away from home because the rain didn't fall, the crops didn't grow, and there was simply not enough food for the whole family. Others had run away from homes where they were being physically or sexually abused by their parents, relatives, or people in the community. Finding themselves alone in the city streets, they looked to one another for a sense of security, sharing the food and money they had gathered, watching out for one another, and coming to one another's aid. They had little in the way of material possessions, but they did have one another.

At one point during Craig's visit, the kids asked him if he wanted to play a game of soccer with them. "Sure," he agreed, "but where will we find a ball?"

"No problem!" José piped up. Suddenly, one of the boys dashed off around the corner. He returned a minute later, holding a plastic water bottle he had found amid the garbage on the street. He let it drop to the ground and started kicking it around: now they had their ball! Most of the children had only two possessions: a pair of shorts and a T-shirt. They did not own shoes—they were all barefoot. But that didn't keep them from the game. They played for hours that day, until finally, in one of the scuffles, someone fell on the bottle and crushed it. Everyone sank down on the side of the street, exhausted and totally content.

Craig had to leave the next day, and as he said goodbye to his new friends, José came forward. He wanted to give Craig a gift by which to remember the street kids. He stood there for a moment, looking down at his hands, thinking. Suddenly, he broke into a smile. He took off his T-shirt, a red and white soccer jersey bearing the logo of his favorite team, folded it carefully, and handed it to Craig.

Craig was dumbfounded. José stood there shirtless, not expecting anything in return. To him, Craig had already given them all a precious gift. Most people just ignore the street kids, spit on them, beat them up or worse. Instead, Craig had shown them respect. Craig was an outsider, of a different color and nationality, yet these street children embraced him as one of their friends, a member of their community. Craig said he couldn't accept the shirt, but José insisted, proud to have something to offer. After a moment, Craig took off his own T-shirt, folded it, and handed it to his new friend in return.

Craig still has that soccer jersey. When he came home, he framed it and hung it on the wall in his bedroom to remind him of the lesson that

José had taught him: if everyone had the heart of a fourteen-year-old street child, there would be no more poverty, injustice, or suffering in the world.

We sometimes speak of Me to We as a sea of change. It is much more than this and much simpler. Me to We is about everyday people like José who choose to give when they have very little, to speak above the crowd and act when they are unsure of the outcome. Me to We is about ordinary people doing extraordinary things. It is about liberating the mind from the world's injustices and serving as an example to others. Action is never easy. It takes courage and insight, but its rewards are transformative: stronger families, supportive communities, more ethical places of work and business, greater connections with others and with our values, and a heightened sense of life purpose and happiness. With every new act, Me to We gains strength. Although we may not reach the end of this thousand-mile journey in our lifetime, as Lao Tzu declared, we have to take the first step. With each word, act, and helping hand, we make the world a more just and compassionate place.

The adventure has already begun, and it will continue when you put down this book and move from thought to action.

START NOW!

▸ As you finish this book and prepare to take the next steps in your journey from Me to We, the challenge lies in capturing your energy and maintaining your momentum as you continue to transform your life and the lives of others! How are you going to do it? Ask yourself:

» How can I remember changes I would like to make in my daily life? Could I write a letter to myself containing a list of the changes I want to make and why, and then open it in a month to see if I'm on the right track?

» How will I overcome challenges and give myself a boost when I need it most? Could I post an inspirational message or picture on my mirror?

» Where can I find support? Could I email a friend asking him or her to be my Me to We buddy? Could I share a list of things I plan to change and ask for help staying on target? At the gym, a physical trainer helps us to stay on task—why not use a Me to We buddy in the same way?

TAKE ANOTHER LOOK!

People come to embrace the Me to We philosophy in a variety of ways. As with Craig, it can happen over a bowl of cereal, when an injustice ignites your commitment to social justice. Or as with Marc, it can happen because of a simple question, one that leads you to reconsider your place in the world around you. If this book has inspired you, find an issue and take a stand.

▸ Americans gave $248.52 billion to charity and other causes in 2004, more than 75 percent of which came from individuals.[7]

▸ Today, 32 percent of all municipal garbage produced in the U.S. is recycled— nearly double the amount recycles 15 years ago.[8]

▸ Since 1992, there has been a 40 percent decrease in armed conflicts worldwide.[9]

LIVING ME TO WE

1. **Spread the word!** Act now by sharing the energy you're feeling! Send your friends an email, or purchase a card from shop.metowe.com. Pick up the phone and call your relatives. Close this book and turn your passion into action!

2. **Join a Me to We club or start your own.** Join a local service organization in your community and introduce a Me to We component. If you can't find one you like, start your own Me to We club. Gather colleagues for coffee and a chat, and brainstorm ideas to move from Me thinking into We acting!

3. **Invest in the future.** This year, invest in ethical retirement and mutual funds, or support companies that lead their fields in environmental and social responsibility. Now breathe easy as you, your society, and your planet reap the dividends.

My Story

ANONYMOUS

We would like to conclude with a final story. This is the story of an individual with remarkable skills and talents. This person has vision, energy, and passion. This person has the power to change the world by reaching out to others—but was awaiting a call. One day, the call came. It didn't take much—there was no epiphany, no cloud opening. All it took was a gentle push.

With a little inspiration, this individual will go on to do great things, contributing to a better world in a unique and personal way. Although these remarkable actions won't make front-page news, they will be permanent etchings in the sands of time, forever remembered by the people who will be touched by them.

The positive energy, born of this one person, will spread like a ripple inspiring others to join a powerful movement to help others. This individual will embody the Movement from *Me to We* and make his or her life more meaningful, fulfilling, and happier than he or she ever dreamt possible.

Who is this person? We hope it will be you.

We don't know how this story will end, but we know how it can continue—with a simple gesture—one first act of giving that will set off a chain of events. We hope that you will gently push another person along this same journey, by now passing this book to someone special in your life.

ENDNOTES

Chapter 3

1   The World Values Survey, "Background," worldvaluessurvey.org/organization/index.html.

2   "Nigeria Tops Happiness Survey," BBC News, news.bbc.co.uk/1/hi/world/africa/3157570. stm. Of course, there are different ways of measuring happiness, and different methods give somewhat different rankings of countries. For example, one of the publications from the World Values Survey on this topic ranks countries in terms of their citizens' "subjective well-being," which is a more comprehensive measure of well-being, than simple self-reported happiness. Using this strategy, Nigeria falls to 19th, with the U.S. at 15th. However, although the specific countries differ, the basic point we are making stands. For example, in terms of subjective well-being, the U.S. is still behind Venezuela (thirteen), El Salvador (twelve), Colombia (eight), Mexico (two) and Puerto Rico (one). These rankings are from worldvaluessurvey.org.

3   Gregg Easterbrook, "The Real Truth About Money," *Time*, January 17, 2005, www.time. com/time/archive/preview/0,10987,1015883,00.html.

4   Jean Chatzky, *You Don't Have to be Rich: Comfort, Happiness and Financial Security on Your Own Terms* (New York: Portfolio/Penguin Books, 2003), 18.

5   P. Brickman, P.D. Coates, and R. Janoff-Bulman, "Lottery Winners and Accident Victims: Is Happiness Relative?" *Journal of Personality and Social Psychology*, 36 no. 8 (1978), 917-927.

6   Roger Highfield, "Wealthy Need Poor Friends to be Happy, Study Finds," *National Post*, (Canada) August 15, 2005.

7   Worldwatch Institute, "State of the World 2004: Consumption by the Numbers," worldwatch.org/state-world-2004-consumption-numbers.

8   Robert Putnam, *Better Together: The Saguaro Seminar on Civic Engagement in America* (December 2000), 76. The Saguaro Seminar is an ongoing initiative of Professor Robert D. Putnam at the John F. Kennedy School School of Government at Harvard University.

9   J.M. Darley and C.D. Batson, "'From Jerusalem to Jericho': A Study of Situational and Dispositional Variables in Helping Behavior," *Journal of Personality and Social Psychology*, 27 (1973): 100–08.

10   Amitai Etzioni, "The Post Affluent Society," *Review of Social Economy*, 62, no. 3 (September 2004): 407-20.

11   Mark Sweney, "American Idol Outvotes the President," *The Guardian*, May 26, 2006, theguardian.com/media/2006/may/26/realitytv.usnews.

12   Bureau of Labor Statistics, "Volunteering in the United States, 2006," Economic News Releases, bls.gov/news.release/archives/volun_01102007.pdf.

13   Live 8 website, "What happened," live8live.com/whathappened/.

Chapter 4

1   International Council of Shopping Centers, "The Impact of Shopping Centers in the United States," ed.gov/about/offices/list/ovae/pi/hs/hsfacts.html.

2   American Council on Education, "Working Their Way Through College," Government Relations & Public Policy, Online News, acenet.edu/news-room/Pages/Working-Their-Way-Through-College-.aspx.

3   3 UNESCO Institute for Statistics 2005, "Children Out of School: Measuring Exclusion from Primary Education," p. 3, uis.unesco.org/Library/Documents/oosc05-en.pdf.

Chapter 5

1   His Holiness The Dalai Lama, *An Open Heart: Practicing Compassion in Everyday Life* (Boston: Little, Brown, 2001), 9.

2   Al Ma'oon 107:1–7.

3   Mishna Avot 1:14.

4   Mishna Torah 10:7–14.

5   All quotes reflecting the Ethic of Reciprocity are cited from Golden Rule Poster by Paul McKenna, Scarboro Missions, 2000. Available online: scarboromissions.ca/Golden_rule/texts.php.

6   David Korten argues that "Smith believed the efficient market is composed of small, owner-managed enterprises located in the communities where the owners reside. Such owners normally share in the community's values and have a personal stake in the future of both the community and the enterprise." David C. Korten, *When Corporations Rule the World* (Bloomfield, CT: Kumarian Press, 2001), livingeconomiesforum.org/WCRW.

Chapter 6

1   R. F. Baumeister and M. R. Leary, "The Need to Belong: Desire for Interpersonal Attachments as a Fundamental Human Motivation," *Psychological Bulletin* 117, no. 3 (1995): 497-529.

2   Lowell Lewin, quoted in Allan Luks and Peggy Payne, *The Healing Power of Doing Good: The Health and Spiritual Benefits of Helping Others* (New York: Fawcett Columbine, 1992), 68.

3   "Happiness Study," *Time* magazine/SRBI, December 13-14, 2004.

4   S.L. Bruhn and S. Wolf, "Update on Roseto, Pennsylvania: Testing a Prediction," *Psychosomatic Medicine* 40 (1978): 86.

5   American Heart Association, "Heart Facts 2003: All Americans," heart.org/HEARTORG.

6   Luks and Payne, *Healing Power of Doing Good*, 31.

7   Meredith Minkler, "People Need People: Social Support and Health," in Robert Ornstein and Charles Swencionis, eds., *The Healing Brain: A Scientific Reader* (New York: Guilford Press, 1990), 88–97.

8   Health Canada, "Volunteering as a Vehicle for Social Support and Life Satisfaction," 2005, phac-aspc.gc.ca.

9   Ibid. These claims are confirmed in a review of scientific studies. See James House et al., "Social Relationships and Health," Science 241 (July 29, 1988): 541, cited in Luks and Payne, *Healing Power of Doing Good*, 3.

10   Luks and Payne, *Healing Power of Doing Good*, 7.

11   Ibid., 10.

12   Physiologically, it reduces stress and tension and breaks the cycle of negative effects caused by emotional stressors on physical well-being, such as high blood pressure and

muscle tension. Moreover, the endorphins are natural opiates that relieve pain by interfering with the release of substance P, the body's chemical transmitter of pain messages to the brain.

13 Luks and Payne, *Healing Power of Doing Good*, 16, 38.

14 Mark Bricklin et al., *Positive Living and Health: The Complete Guide to Brain/Body Healing and Mental Empowerment* (Emmaus, PA: Rodale Press, 1989), 115.

15 S. Brown, R. Nesse, A. Vinokur, and D. Smith, "Providing Social Support May Be More Beneficial Than Receiving It: Results from a Prospective Study of Mortality," *Psychological Science* 14, no. 4 (July 2003): 320-27.

16 M.A. Musick and J. Wilson, "Volunteering and Depression: The Role of Psychological and Social Resources in Different Age Groups," *Social Science and Medicine* 56 (2003): 259–69; N. Morrow-Howell et al., "Effects of Volunteering on the Well-Being of Older Adults," *Journals of Gerontology* 58B, no. 3 (2003): S137-45; M. A. Musick, R. Herzog, and J. S. House, "Volunteering and Morality among Older Adults : Findings from a National Sample," *Journals of Gerontology* 54B, no. 3 (1999): S173-80; C. Davis et al., "Benefits to Volunteers in a Community-Based Health Promotion and Chronic Illness Self-Management Program for the Elderly," *Journal of Gerontological Nursing* 24, no 10 (1998): 16-23.

17 S.L. Brown et al., "Providing Social Support."

18 National Runaway Safeline, "Home Free," 1800runaway.org/youth-teens.

19 U.S. Census Bureau, "65+ in the United States: 2005," Current Population Reports, census.gov/prod/2006pubs/p23-209.pdf.

20 Foreign Press Centers, U.S. Department of State, fpc.state.gov/documents/organization/32920.pdf.

Chapter 7

1 Robert Putnam and Lewis M. Feldstein, *Better Together: Restoring the American Community* (New York: Simon & Schuster, 2003), 98–118.

2 R. E. McKeown, et al. "Family Structure and Cohesion, and Depressive Symptoms in Adolescents," *Journal of Research on Adolescents* 7, no. 3 (1997): 267-81; M.D. Resnick, et al., "Protecting Adolescents from Harm: Findings from the National Longitudinal Study on Adolescent Health," *Journal of the American Medical Association*, 278, no. 10 (1997): 823-32; B. M. Wagner, M. A. C. Silverman, and C. E. Martin, "Family Factors in Youth Suicidal Behaviors," *American Behavioral Scientist* 46, no. 9 (2003): 1171-91.

3 B.H. Fiese, et al., "A Review of 50 Years of Research on Naturally Occurring Family Routines and Rituals: Cause for Celebration?" *Journal of Family Psychology* 16 (2002): 381-90.

4 Luis J. Rodriguez, "History of Luis J. Rodriguez," luisjrodriguez.com/history.

5 Jane Jacobs, *The Death and Life of Great American Cities* (New York: Random House, 1961), 56.

6 This study is described in Philip G. Zimbardo, "A Situationist Perspective on the Psychology of Evil: Understanding How Good People Are Transformed into Perpetrators", in Arthur Miller, ed., *The Social Psychology of Good and Evil: Understanding Our Capacity for Kindness and Cruelty* (New York: Guilford, 2004), zimbardo.com/downloads/2003%20Evil%20Chapter.pdf.

7 Philip G. Zimbardo, "The Human Choice: Individulization, Reason, and Order Versus

Deindividualization, Impulse, and Chaos.", in W. J. Arnold and D. Levine eds., *Nebraska Symposium on Motivation* (Lincoln: University of Nebraska Press, 1969), 287.

8   Zimbardo, "A Situationist Perspective."

9   Original experiments were conducted between 1927 and 1932 at the Hawthorne Plant of the Western Electric Company in Cicero, Illinois, by Harvard Business School Professor Elton Mayo and associates F.J. Roelthlisberger and William J. Dickson. Many articles and chapters in books have looked at the effects of the study. See Henry A. Landsberger, *Hawthorne Revisited: Management and the Worker: Its Critics, and Developments in Human Relations in Industry* (Ithaca, NY: Cornell University, 1958); Richard Gillespie, *Manufacturing Knowledge: A History of the Hawthorne Experiments* (New York: Cambridge University Press, 1991). We must note that the specific cause of the Hawthorne effect is not known and has been extensively debated ever since the original experiments. There is no way to tell whether the reason for the workers' improvement truly was because they were made to feel special, as initially proposed, or whether there were alternative explanations (many have been proposed over the years), or methodological flaws that led to the findings. However, the Hawthorne studies remain a powerful demonstration of the general point that social factors are important determinants of employee morale and productivity and that by treating people differently in the workplace, you can improve preformance. The Hawthorn studies remain important as landmarks in the history of organizational management.

10   *Business Ethics*, "100 Best Corporate Citizens: America's Most Responsible and Profitable Major Public Companies" business-ethics.com/whats_new/2002_100_best_corporate_citizens.html.

11   Susan J. Ellis and Katherine Moyes, *By the People: A History of Americans as Volunteers*, rev. ed. (San Francisco: Jossey-Bass, 1987).

12   Volunteers of America, "Historical Facts," voa.org.

13   Tom Large, "Big Tsunami Donors Rank Poorly in Generosity League", Reuters Tsunami Aidwatch, 2005.

14   "Aid Flows Top USD 100 Billion in 2005," Organization for Economic Cooperation and Development (OECD), April 4, 2006, (see table 1, chart 1), oecd.org/officialdocuments/publicdisplaydocumentpdf/?cote=PAC/COM/NEWS(2006)9&docLanguage=En.

15   Food Research & Action Center, "National School Lunch Program," frac.org/html/federal_food_programs/programs/nslp.html.

16   Laura Cummings, "The Diet Business: Banking on Failure," BBC news, February 5, 2003, news.bbc.co.uk/2/hi/business/2725943.stm.

17   World Food Program, "How WFP Works to Stop Hunger," wfp.org.

18   Food and Agricultural Organization, "The State of Food Insecurity in the World, 2005," p. 18, fao.org/3/a-a0200e.pdf.

Chapter 8

1   Barbara L. Fredrickson, Michele M. Tugade, Christian E. Waugh and Gregory R. Larkin, "What Good Are Positive Emotions in Crises? A Prospective Study of Resilience and Emotions Following the Terrorist Attacks on the United States on September 11th, 2001," *Journal of Personality and Social Psychology* 84, no. 2 (2004): 373.

2   "Faces in Our Midst: Homesick or Happy, Katrina Evacuees Reach First Holiday," *Washington Post*, November 24, 2005, washingtonpost.com/wp-dyn/content/article/2005/11/23/AR2005112302114.html.

3   R. A. Emmons and C. M. Shelton, "Gratitude and the Science of Positive Psychology,"
     in C. R. Snyder & S. J. Lopez, eds., *Handbook of Positive Psychology.* (New York: Oxford
     University Press, 2005), 460.

4   P. W. Pruyser, *The Minister as Diagnostician: Personal Problems in Pastoral Perspective*
     (Philadelphia: Westminster Press, 1976), cited ibid.

5   Lynne Twist, *The Soul of Money: Transforming Your Relationship with Money and Life* (New
     York: W.W. Norton, 2003), 45.

6   R. A. Emmons and M. E. McCullough, "Counting Blessings Versus Burdens: An Exper-
     imental Investigation of Gratitude and Subjective Well-Being in Daily Life," *Journal of
     Personality and Social Psychology* 84, no. 2 (2003): 377-89; D. K. Reynolds, *Naikan Psycho-
     therapy: Meditation for Self-Development.* (Chicago: University of Chicago Press, 1983).

7   Alice Isen and Paula Levin, "Effect of Feeling Good on Helping: Cookies and Kindness,"
     Journal of Personal and Social Psychology 21, no. 3 (March 1972): 384-88. Interestingly,
     similar results have been found for other mood-boosters, such as doing well on a test,
     receiving a gift, thinking happy thoughts, listening to pleasant music. A wide variety of
     helping behaviors have also been studied, including giving money to charity, donating
     blood, helping someone find a lost contact lens, tutoring another student, and helping
     coworkers on the job. For further information, see M. Carlson, V. Charlin, and N. Miller,
     "Positive Mood and Helping Behavior: A Test of Six Hypotheses," *Journal of Personality
     and Social Psychology* 55, no. 2 (1998): 211-29; J.M. George and A. P. Brief, "Feeling Good—
     Doing Good: A Conceptual Analysis of the Mood at Work-Organizational Spontaneity
     Relationship," *Psychological Bulletin* 112, no. 2 (1992): 310-29; A. M. Isen, "Positive Affect,"
     in T. Dalgleish and M. J. Power eds., *Handbook of Cognition and Emotion* (New York: John
     Wiley & Sons Ltd.) 521-39; P. Salovey, J. O. Mayer, and D. L. Rosenhan, "Mood and Helping:
     Mood as a Motivator of Helping and Helping as a Regulator of Mood," in M.S. Clark ed.,
     Prosocial Behavior: Review of Personality and Social Psychology, vol. 12 (Thousand Oaks,
     CA: Sage Publications, Inc., 1991) 215-37.

8   Emmons and McCullough, "Counting Blessings Versus Burdens," 377-89.

9   Ibid.

10   Children's Defense Fund, "Moments in America For Children,"
     childrensdefense.org.

11   North American Association of State and Provincial Lotteries, "Fiscal Years 2004 and
     2005 Lottery Sales and Profits," Facts, naspl.org.

12   As calculated using gapminder.org. The data used in this calculation was taken from the
     United Nations Development Programme's Human Development Report 2005, which can
     be found at hdr.undp.org/en/content/human-development-report-2005.

Chapter 9

1   C. D. Batson, *The Altruism Question: Toward a Social-Psychological Answer* (Hillsdale, NJ:
     Erlbaum, 1991). J. S. Coke, C. D. Batson, and K. McDavis, "Empathic Mediation of Helping:
     A Two-Stage Model," *Journal of Personality and Social Psychology* 36 (1978): 752-66; J.
     F. Dovidio, J. L. Allen, and D. A. Schroeder, "The Specificity of Empathy-Induced Helping:
     Evidence for Altruistic Motivation," *Journal of Personality and Social Psychology* 59 (1990):
     249-60; N. Eisenberg and P. Miller, "Empathy and Prosocial Behavior." *Psychological
     Bulletin* 101, no. 91 (1987): 119.

2   Gitta Bauer's story, "The Testimony of a Rescuer," The Museum of Tolerance Online Multi-
        media Learning Center, motlc.learningcenter.wiesenthal.org/text/x00/xm0065.html.

3   Samuel P. Oliner and Pearl M. Oliner, *The Altruistic Personality: Rescuers of Jews in Nazi
        Europe* (New York: Free Press, 1988).

4   For further information on the Roots of Empathy program, visit rootsofempathy.org. See
        also Mary Gordon, *Roots of Empathy: Changing the World Child by Child* (Toronto: Thomas
        Allen, 2005).

5   "Diamond Revenues Benefit Local Communities: USAID Peace Diamond Alliance Empow-
        ers Sierra Leone's Mining Industry," USAID, usaid.gov/stories/sierraleone/cs_sierraleone/
        cs_sierraleone_diamond.html.

6   "Child Soldiers to be Disarmed," news.bbc.co.uk/2/hi/africa/764040.stm.

7   The U.S. Department of Health and Human Services, Insure Kids Now!
        insurekidsnow.gov.

8   National Center for Health Statistics, "Obesity Still a Major Problem," press releases,
        April 14, 2006, cdc.gov/nchs/pressroom/06facts/obesity03_04.htm.

9   AVERT, "HIV, AIDS and Children," avert.org/children.htm; Partners in Health, statement by
        UN Special Envoy for HIV/AIDS in Africa Stephen Lewis on World AIDS Day, December 1,
        2005, pih.org/inthenews/WorldAIDSDay2005-StephenLewis.pdf.

Chapter 10

1   See "Happiness Study," *Time*/SRBI, December 13-14, 2004.

2   R.A. Emmons, "Personal Goals, Life Meaning, and Virtue: Wellsprings of a Positive Life,"
        in C.L.M. Keyes and J. Haidt, eds., *Flourishing: Positive Psychology and the Life Well-Lived*
        (Washington DC: American Psychological Association, 2003), 106.

3   Ibid, 105-128; E. Klinger, "The Search for Meaning in Evolutionary Perspective and Its Clin-
        ical Implications," in P.T.P. Wong and P. S. Fry eds., *Handbook of Personal Meaning: Theory,
        Research, and Application* (Mahwah, NJ: Erlbaum, 1998), 27-50.

4   T. Kasser, and R. M. Ryan, "A Dark Side of the American Dream: Correlates of Financial
        Success as a Central Life Aspiration." *Journal of Personality and Social Psychology* 65
        (1993): 410-422; T. Kasser and R. M. Ryan, "Further Examining the American Dream:
        Differential Correlates of Intrinsic and Extrinsic Goals," *Personality and Social Psychology
        Bulletin* 22 (1996): 280-87.

5   R. F. Baumeister, *Meanings of Life* (New York: Guilford, 1991); D. L. Debats, "The Life Re-
        gard Index: Reliability and Validity," *Psychological Reports* 67 (1990): 27-34; D. L. Debats, P.
        Van Der Lubbe, and F.R.A. Wezeman, "On the Psychometric Properties of the Life Regard
        Index (LRI): A Measure of Meaningful Life," *Personality and Individual Differences* 14 (1993):
        337-45; N. Mascaro and D. H. Rosen, "Existential Meaning's Role in the Enhancement of
        Hope and Prevention of Depressive Symptoms." *Journal of Personality* 73 (2005): 985-
        1014; P.T.P. Wong and P. S. Fry, *The Human Quest for Meaning* (Mahwah, NJ: Erlbaum,
        1998); S. Zika, and K. Chamberlain, "On the Relation Between Meaning in Life and Psycho-
        logical Well-Being," *British Journal of Psychology* 83 (1992): 133-45.

6   Baumeister, *Meanings of Life*; D. L. Debats, "The Life Regard Index"; Debats, et al., "Psy-
        chometric Properties of the Life Regard Index; Mascaro and Rosen, "Existential Meaning's
        Role"; Wong and Fry, *Human Quest for Meaning*; Zika and Chamberlain, "On the Relation
        Between Meaning in Life and Psychological Well-Being."

7　Baumeister, *Meanings of Life*; Emmons, "Personal Goals"; M. Seeman, "Alienation and Anomie," in J. P. Robinson and P. R. Shaver eds., *Measures of Personality and Social Psychological Attitudes* (San Diego, CA: Academic Press, 1991), 291-371; G.T. Reker and P. T. P. Wong, "Aging as an Individual Process: Toward a Theory of Personal Meaning," in J. E. Birren and V. L. Bengston, eds., *Emergent Theories of Aging* (New York: Springer, 1988), 214-46; Wong and Fry, *Handbook of Personal Meaning*.

8　M.E.P. Seligman, "Boomer Blues," *Psychology Today*, (October 1988), 50-5.

9　Viktor E. Frankl, *Man's Search for Meaning* (New York: Simon & Schuster, 1963), 86, 122, 57.

10　Experience Corps, aarp.org/experience-corps.

11　M. Latham, "Young Volunteers: The Benefits of Community Service," University of Nevada, 2003, unce.unr.edu/publications/files/cd/2003/fs0323.pdf.

12　A 2004 national survey by the YMCA and Search Institute, search-institute.org.

Chapter 11

1　Modern sociology is largely built around the idea that the division of labor created by the industrial era—in which people split into increasingly segmented, specialized roles in society—explains the transition from "collective conscience" to a less socially cohesive functional interdependence. In short, the connection (or "solidarity") among members of society is no longer based on a sense of communal attachment, but on the increasingly self-interested premise that each person depends on another for a specific task. If the farmer no longer works the land, no one eats. If the carpenter no longer builds, no one has shelter. In *The Division of Labor in Society* (1893), renowned sociologist Émile Durkheim outlined the transition from "mechanical solidarity" that connects a community through a collective conscience to "organic solidarity," connecting community through functional interdependence, brought on by the increasing division of labor in the industrial era. He also argued that the decline of the collective conscience led to the blurring of morality as individuals became less submerged in the community and more assigned to a specific role. "Even those systems with a highly developed organic solidarity still needed a common faith, a common collective conscience, if they were not to disintegrate into a heap of mutually antagonistic and self-seeking individuals." Lewis A. Coser, *Masters of Sociological Thought: Ideas in Historical and Social Context* (New York: Harcourt, 1977), 129–32.

2　Muzafer Sherif et.al, *Intergroup Conflict and Cooperation: The Robbers Cave Experiment* (Norman: Institute of Group Relations, The University of Oklahoma, 1961).

3　Robert B. Cialdini, *Influence: Science and Practice* (New York: HarperCollins, 1993), 171.

4　York University Resources Online, "Classics in the History of Psychology: Intergroup Conflict and Cooperation: The Robbers Cave Experiment," psychclassics.yorku.ca/Sherif/chap7.htm.

5　R. D. Putnam, *Making Democracy Work: Civic Traditions in Modern Italy* (Princeton, NJ: Princeton University Press, 1993), 167.

6　Jan Zalasiewicz, University of Leicester, "Global Warming: A Perspective from Earth History," le.ac.uk/ebulletin-archive/ebulletin/features/2000-2009/2004/12/nparticle-vkt-hgf-t4c.html.

7　United Nations Office for the Coordination of Humanitarian Affairs, "Disaster Reduction and the Human Cost of Disaster," preventionweb.net/files/2744_irindisasterjun2005.pdf.

8 United Nations, "UN Human Development Index," hdr.undp.org/en/content/human-development-report-2005.

9 CNN Online, "Bin Laden, Millionaire with a Dangerous Grudge," cnn.com/2001/US/09/12/binladen.profile/index.html, "Mano River War," globalsecurity.org/military/world/war/mano-river.htm.

10 Grameen Bank, "December 2005 Update," grameen-info.org/bank/GBGlance.htm.

11 Grameen Foundation USA, "Client Profiles: Annette from New York. Overcoming Obstacles," grameenfoundation.org/resource_centre/print_newsletter/fall_2003/borrower_profile_annette_michael.

12 Mark Potok, "The Year in Hate, 2005: A 5% Annual Increase in Hate Groups in 2005 Caps a Remarkable Rise of 33% Over the Five-Year Period that Began in 2000," Southern Poverty Law Center, splcenter.org/intel/intelreport/article.jsp?aid=627.

13 Mary Wiltenburg and Amanda Paulson, "All in the (Mixed-Face) Family: A U.S. Trend," *The Christian Science Monitor*, August 28, 2003, csmonitor.com/2003/0828/p03s01-ussc.html.

14 See ethnologue.com.

Chapter 12

1 J. A. Bargh, et al., "The Automated Will: Nonconscious Activation and Pursuit of Behavioral Goals," *Journal of Personality and Social Psychology* 81 (2001): 1014-27. M.J. Ferguson, and J. A. Bargh, "How Social Perception Can Automatically Influence Behavior," *Trends in Cognitive Sciences* 8 (2004): 33-39.

2 American Lung Association, "Why Do We Need Alternative Fuels?" lungusa.org/site/apps/s/content.asp?c=dvLUK9OOE&b=34706&ct=67110.

3 Energy Star, energystar.gov/kids.

4 David Suzuki Foundation, "The Nature Challenge," davidsuzuki.org/publications/downloads/2003/GreenGuide.pdf.

5 National Wildlife Foundation, "Keeping the Holidays Green," nwf.org/News-and-Magazines/National-Wildlife/Green-Living/Archives/2006/Keeping-the-Holidays-Green.aspx.

6 University of Illinois, "University Increases Its Recycling (1992)," illinimedia.com/di/archives/1992/November/17/recycle.html.

7 "Soft money," as it is popularly known, is given not directly to a candidate's campaign, but to the political party. It is spent on activities, especially "issue advertising," which involves advertisements for a candidate's positions or thinly veiled attacks on the opponent's positions, that obviously benefit the candidate. Since it is not actually received or spent by the candidate's campaign, there are no legal limits.

8 Robert Kennedy, Day of Affirmation Address, University of Capetown, South Africa, June 6, 1966, jfklibrary.org/Research/Research-Aids/Ready-Reference/RFK-Speeches/Day-of-Affirmation-Address-as-delivered.aspx.

9 Volunteer Today, "Recruiting and Recruiting," volunteertoday.com/ARCHIVES2001/July01recrui.html.

10 The Foundation Center, "What Is Cause-Related Marketing?" grantspace.org/tools/knowledge-base/Funding-Resources/Corporations/cause-related-marketing.

11 Mark Mansley and Claros Consulting—Friends of the Earth Online, "Open Disclosure:

Sustainability and the Listing Regime," solutions.3m.com/wps/portal/3M/en_US/global/sustainability/s/performance-indicators/environment/energy-efficiancy.

12   TCC Group, "Rediscovering a Strategic Resource: Your Employees," tccgrp.com/pdfs/per_brief_rediscovering.pdf.

13   Pham-Duy Nguyen, "Microsoft Diet Working for Many in Seattle", Bloomberg News, October 14, 2005, azcentral.com/health/diet/articles/1014microsoft-diet14-ON.html.

14   Social Venture Partnerships Online, "Companies That Match Employee Giving," svpseattle.org/resource_libraries/Fund_Development/Fund_Development.htm#employers.

15   KMPG, "International Survey of Corporate Sustainability Reporting 2002," kpmg.com.au/Portals/0/GlobalsustainSurvey-Oil_Gas02.pdf.

16   United States Senate, "Women in the Senate, Statistics and Lists," senate.gov/artandhistory/history/common/briefing/women_senators.htm.

17   Inter-Parliamentary Union, "One out of Five Parliamentarians Elected in 2005 Is a Woman," press release, February 27, 2006, ipu.org/press-e/gen220.htm.

18   "Women and HIV/AIDS: Confronting the Crisis," a joint report by UNAIDS, UNFPA, UNIFEM, 2004, unfpa.org/sites/default/files/pub-pdf/women_aids.pdf.

Chapter 13

1   This quotation is from "Eyes on the Prize," a 1987 public television series on the civil rights movement, as quoted in E. R. Shipp, "Rosa Parks, 92, Founding Symbol of Civil Rights Movement, Dies", *New York Times*, October 25, 2005, nytimes.com/2005/10/25/national/25parks.html?8dpc=&ei=5070&en=0fa34f940c4b5bb9&ex=1132030800&pagewanted=print.

2   Ibid.

3   The civil rights movement itself was grounded in centuries of turmoil and perseverance from the days of slavery to the pivotal *Brown v. Board of Education* case against school segregation in 1954, to all of the other battles, big and small, that have been waged for this cause over many years.

4   Paul Rogat Loeb, "The Real Rosa Parks," paulloeb.org/articles/rosaparks.htm.

5   Bill Moyer et al., *Doing Democracy: The Map Model for Organizing Social Movements* (Gabriola Island, BC: New Society Publishers, 2001), 2.

6   Bonnie Eisenberg and Mary Ruthsdofter, National Women's History Project, 1988, "Living the Legacy: The Women's Rights Movement, 1848–1988," nwhp.org/resources/womens-rights-movement.

7   American Association of Fundraising Counsel, 2004, aafrc.org, Giving by Source of Contribution chart.

8   Environmental Protection Agency, epa.gov/garbage/recycle.htm#Figures

9   Human Security Centre/University of British Columbia, "The Human Security Report 2005," humansecurityreport.info; "Dramatic Drop in Global Conflicts Since Cold War," cbc.ca/storyview/MSN/world/national/2005/10/18/global-wars051018.html.

ABOUT THE CONTRIBUTORS

LINDSAY AVNER

Lindsay Avner is a national advocate for involving young people in the fight against breast cancer and has trained and mentored student leaders across the United States. Her dream is to see the end of breast cancer. In 2007, Avner founded Bright Pink, a national non-profit organization focused on prevention and early detection of breast and ovarian cancer in young women. More information on her work can be found at **brightpink.org**.

KATHY BUCKLEY

Actress, comedienne, author, and motivational speaker, Kathy Buckley delivers the message that anything can be achieved when the heart and mind work together. She embodies her mission in life, namely, "I love to make people laugh, but I love it even more if I can teach them something at the same time." For more information on Kathy Buckley, visit **kathybuckley.com**.

DR. JOHN GAITHER

Dr. John Gaither is a retired educator who lives in Toronto, Ontario, with his wife, Dorothea, a clinical psychologist in private practice. Since his retirement in 1999 as a high school principal, he has been an enthusiastic volunteer with Free The Children and serves on its Board of Directors. Dr. Gaither has traveled to developing communities on a number of occasions alongside youth volunteers. He is young at heart and highly respected for his work with young people.

RICHARD GERE

Richard Gere is a well-known actor, humanitarian, and philanthropist. For more than 25 years, he has been inspired by His Holiness the Dalai Lama to help relieve suffering around the world. Through his foundation, Gere supports survivors of war and natural disasters, world health relief, and basic human rights. More information on his work is available at **gerefoundation.org**.

DR. JANE GOODALL

Dr. Jane Goodall met the anthropologist Dr. Louis Leakey in 1957 and soon afterwards began to work for him in Africa. Her research, based on extensive field work, is considered a milestone in the study of primatology. Goodall is the author of numerous books, including *In the Shadow of Man and My Life with the Chimpanzees*. In 1995, she was presented with the CBE by Queen Elizabeth. She founded the Jane Goodall Institute in 1977. More information on her work and that of her youth outreach program, Roots and Shoots, is available at **janegoodall.org**.

TIM LEFENS

Tim Lefens, founder and executive director of A.R.T. (Artistic Realization Technologies), lives in Belle Mead, New Jersey. He is author of the book *Flying Colors*, a moving account of overcoming limitations and the power of creative expression. Tim is the recipient of the Pollock-Krasner Award for Painting and the Robert Wood Johnson Foundation Community Health Leadership Award. He continues to share A.R.T.'s significant breakthroughs through training sessions, lecture seminars, and book readings. More information on Tim's work can be found at **artrealization.org**.

HER MAJESTY QUEEN NOOR OF JORDAN

Her Majesty Queen Noor of Jordan is an international humanitarian activist and an outspoken voice on issues of world peace and justice. Since 1978 she has initiated, directed, and sponsored projects and activities in Jordan to address development needs in the areas of education, culture, women and children's welfare, sustainable development, environmental conservation, human rights, and conflict resolution. Queen Noor is founder and chair of the King Hussein Foundation, a nonprofit nongovernmental organization that fosters peace and security through programs promoting cross-cultural understanding and social, economic, and political opportunity in the Muslim and Arab world. Her autobiography, *Leap of Faith: Memoirs of an Unexpected Life*, is an international bestseller published in fifteen languages.

KIM PHUC

Kim Phuc became world famous when she was photographed as a young girl running naked down a highway, her skin on fire from napalm. Her picture became the defining image of the Vietnam War. Kim Phuc founded the Kim Foundation, a nonprofit organization committed to funding programs to heal children in war-torn areas of the world. Phuc is also a UNESCO Goodwill Ambassador. More information on her work is available at **kimfoundation.com**.

KEITH TAYLOR

Keith Taylor is the founder of Modest Needs, which started as a website providing small financial assistance to those in need. Combining donations and $400 a month from his own income, he began to fulfill his lifelong dream of becoming a philanthropist. Now a national nonprofit, Modest Needs empowers members of the general public to make small, emergency grants to low-income workers who are at risk of slipping into poverty. More information on Keith's work is available at **modestneeds.org**.

ARCHBISHOP DESMOND TUTU

Desmond Tutu was the first black Anglican archbishop of Cape Town, South Africa. He rose to worldwide fame in the 1980s for his opposition to apartheid. On October 16, 1984, he was awarded the Nobel Peace Prize. During the 1990s, he headed the Truth and Reconciliation Commission in South Africa. Tutu is the author of numerous books, including *No Future without Forgiveness*, and holds honorary doctorate degrees from dozens of leading universities around the world. He is an honorary member of Free The Children's Board of Directors.

JORDANA WEISS

Jordana Weiss is a young theatre artist living and working in Toronto. She was actively involved in Free The Children from the ages of nine to eighteen, and was able to assist in the construction of a school built in the name of Emma Jordan Johnstone in Llilla, Ecuador. She attended McGill University with a scholarship through the Canadian Millennium Excellence Award Program. Jordana has stage managed and produced shows with Soulpepper Theatre Company, VideoCabaret, and the Luminato Festival.

DR. JONATHAN WHITE

Dr. Jonathan White is professor of Sociology at Bentley University and Director of the Bentley Service-Learning Center. He specializes in globalization, inequality and civic-engagement. Professor White has received numerous teaching and humanitarian awards and serves on several non-profit boards. Dr. White has authored articles in the fields of inequality and globalization. He is co-author of *The Engaged Sociologist; Sociologists in Action*; and *Sociologists in Action on Inequalities* and is currently writing a book on hunger in the United States.

OPRAH WINFREY

Oprah Winfrey has left an indelible mark on the face of television. From her humble beginnings in rural Mississippi, Winfrey's legacy has established her as one of the most important figures in popular culture. Her contributions can be felt beyond the world of television and into areas such as publishing, music, film, philanthropy, education, health and fitness, and social awareness. As supervising producer and host of the *Oprah Winfrey Show* (1986 to 2011), she entertained, enlightened, and empowered millions of viewers around the world.

ABOUT THE AUTHORS

CRAIG KIELBURGER

Craig Kielburger is a social entrepreneur, *New York Times* bestselling author, and captivating speaker, inspiring millions to improve their communities and the world through daily actions. Craig's journey as a child rights activist began at the age of twelve, when he reached for the morning comics and noticed the newspaper's front page. The headline read: "Battled child labor, boy, 12, murdered." Being twelve himself, Craig felt an immediate connection and took the story with him to school. When he asked his class for help to tackle the issue of child labor, eleven students raised their hands to volunteer. Free The Children was born. What began as a group of a dozen kids has grown into an international movement—WE. Inspired by Craig's life mission, Oprah's Angel Network partnered with WE to fund sixty-eight schools. Craig is the youngest-ever graduate from the Kellogg-Schulich Executive MBA program. For his work to advance human rights, Craig has been awarded fifteen honorary doctorates and degrees, and has received the Order of Canada, the Roosevelt Freedom From Fear Medal, the World Children's Prize for the Rights of the Child, and the Muhammad Ali Humanitarian Award.

MARC KIELBURGER

Marc Kielburger is a social entrepreneur, *New York Times* bestselling author, and charismatic speaker, inspiring millions to improve their communities and the world through daily actions and socially conscious life choices. While working as a page in the House of Commons, Marc was invited on a trip to Thailand to volunteer with AIDS patients in the slums of Bangkok. Mobilized by the suffering he witnessed, Marc extended his two-week stay and didn't return home for a year! Motivated to make a difference, Marc completed his post-secondary education in the U.S. and UK and made a choice that changed his life— he moved back home to help his brother found WE. Marc is the recipient of many honors, including the Order of Canada, and was selected by the World Economic Forum as one of 250 Young Global Leaders. He was also inducted into Canada's Walk of Fame for his humanitarian and youth empowerment efforts. Marc graduated magna cum laude from Harvard University with a degree in international relations. He won a coveted Rhodes Scholarship and completed a law degree at Oxford University. He has also received ten honorary doctorates and degrees for his work in the fields of education and human rights.

CRAIG AND MARC

Craig and Marc are cofounders of WE, the world's leading platform for social change, with the mission of "Making Doing Good, Doable." Dedicated to empowering people of all ages to create positive social change locally and globally, WE was founded twenty-five years ago. Launched to free children from slavery, it is now comprised of a family of organizations and programs that operate both domestically and internationally to help change lives.

WE Schools, currently in 20,000+ schools across North America and the United Kingdom, is a series of innovative service-learning and social- and emotional-learning programs that support teachers and empower students with critical skills to thrive in the classroom and today's world. In addition, the WE Well-being program was developed with leading mental health experts to address the need for youth and families to nurture their well-being and the well-being of others, providing free teaching materials, educator training, and classroom resources. These science-based programs have been adapted for families and workplaces. AP with WE Service, a program made possible by an exclusive partnership between the College Board and WE, offers Advanced Placement teachers the opportunity to incorporate service-learning into their existing courses so students can engage with coursework through a local and global context.

WE has always celebrated the volunteer efforts of youth through WE Day, an annual series of global events featuring renowned speakers and performers that celebrates their extraordinary efforts to make a difference. WE also provides innovative digital distance-learning opportunities to reach remote youth and communities around the globe. And WE Villages works with partner communities in nine countries to help them break the cycle of poverty through a proven model of international development. WE's development projects have empowered more than one million beneficiaries to lift themselves out of poverty; more than 2,000 classrooms and schools around the world have been built, providing education for 250,000 students every day. The WE Villages alternative income program has empowered more than 30,000 women entrepreneurs with tools and skills to launch small businesses and boost family income.

Finally, Craig and Marc are advancing a new vision of philanthropy that connects business to a social purpose. Through WE Social Entrepreneurship, they are providing mentorship and programs to help young entrepreneurs start businesses with the purpose of solving social and environmental challenges. Their social enterprise, ME to WE, reaches hundreds of thousands of socially conscious consumers through a diverse network of partnerships with leading retailers. Half of ME to WE's annual net profit is donated to WE Charity, while the other half is reinvested to grow the enterprise and its social mission. Craig and Marc have authored twelve books, including *Me to We: Finding Meaning in a Material World*; *WEconomy: You Can Find Meaning, Make a Living, and Change the World*; and *The World Needs Your Kid: Raising Children Who Care and Contribute*. Their weekly columns are syndicated in countless newspapers across North America. Their work has been featured on *The Oprah Winfrey Show* and *60 Minutes* on three different occasions, as well as in *National Geographic*, *Time*, and *The Economist*. They are recipients of the Order of Canada, the Roosevelt Freedom Medal, and the World Children's Prize for the Rights of the Child.